# ISRAEL, THE WEST BANK AND INTERNATIONAL LAW

# Israel, The West Bank and International Law

Allan Gerson



FRANK CASS

*First published 1978 in Great Britain by*
FRANK CASS AND COMPANY LIMITED
Gainsborough House, Gainsborough Road,
London E11 1RS, England

*and in the United States of America by*
FRANK CASS AND COMPANY LIMITED
c/o Biblio Distribution Centre,
81 Adams Drive, P.O. Box 327, Totowa, N. J. 07511



British Library Cataloguing in Publication Data
Gerson, Allan
Israel, the West Bank and international law.
1. Jordan (Territory under Israeli occupation, 1967–)—
International status
I. Title
341.42 JX4084.J/

ISBN 0-7146-3091-8





**Filmset by A. Brown & Sons Ltd., Hull.**
**Printed in Great Britain by**
**Billing & Sons Limited, Guildford, London and Worcester.**

# SUMMARY OF CONTENTS

# Contents

## CHAPTER II

## THE PALESTINE CONTROVERSY: HISTORICAL AND JURIDICAL BASIS

CHAPTER III

MANAGEMENT: THE LIMITS OF INSTITUTIONAL CHANGE

CHAPTER IV

DISPOSITION: SOVEREIGNTY AND POSTLIMINIUM PROBLEMS

# Acknowledgments

I am grateful to a number of people and institutions for their individual and collective assistance during the preparation of this manuscript, especially to the Yale Law School under whose auspices this work was undertaken as a doctoral dissertation, and to Professor Eugene V. Rostow, who supervised the project. Bringing to bear his vast knowledge of law and diplomacy, he added immeasurably to the progress of this work. I am indebted to Professor Leon S. Lipson for his careful reading and criticism; to Professor Joseph W. Bishop for many insightful case comments; to Professor Myres S. McDougal for direct exposure to his incomparable scholarship; and to Professor Michael V. Reisman for the wit and the learning he brought to our discussions, and for his assistance in countless ways. The manuscript has been revised since its presentation in doctoral form in 1976 to account for new developments. However its basic arguments, like the problems of law and diplomacy which they address, remain largely unchanged.

In the course of research conducted in Israel, the West Bank and Jordan, many interviews, attributable and not, were conducted with government officials, political leaders, journalists and other close observers of Israel-West Bank relations. They exposed me to many facets of the problem which would have gone unseen but for their kindness. I thank them collectively.

My appreciation is extended to the University Consortium for World Order Studies for providing generous fellowship assistance in the 1973-74 academic year; to Mr. Jan Stephan, librarian of the Harvard International Law Library for providing research space and much kind assistance; and to the Harvard International Law Journal for printing Chapter 1 of this work in its summer 1977 issue.

Finally, I thank my wife, Joan, for gracefully persevering through my years of preoccupation.

ALLAN GERSON

Washington, D.C.
December, 1977

# Introduction

For nearly four hundred years, until conquered by Britain in 1917, the regions now known as Israel, the West Bank, Jordan and the Gaza Strip formed part of the Ottoman Empire and were governed as a portion of the Vilayet or Province of Southern Syria. In 1922 Britain accepted responsibility for governing this area, termed Palestine, in accordance with the terms of a mandate entrusted to it by the League of Nations. Its cardinal precept, like that of all mandates, was that self-determination be encouraged. But in Palestine self-determination was to take a different form. A national home was to be established for a dispersed people whose members constituted only a small percentage of the population of the mandated territory.

Almost immediately after the inception of the Palestine Mandate, Britain invoked Article 25 of its provisions "to postpone or withhold" Jewish national rights east of the Jordan River. Its effect was to confine the ambitions of the Zionist movement to Cis-Jordanian Palestine. But there the Arab population opposed the birth of any Jewish state—small or large. A compromise between these competing national interests in the form of partition was suggested several times in the years between the two great wars but never sought to be implemented by Britain. Partition was, however, an idea that could not remain dormant for long. Increasingly, it appeared as the only means for equitably resolving the dispute over Cis-Jordanian Palestine.

At the end of World War II, amidst Zionist claims for immediate statehood, fierce Arab nationalist opposition and a faltering British administration, the United Nations became vested with the responsibility for finding a solution to the worsening situation. Trans-Jordan had already become independent in 1946. What remained at issue was whether a trusteeship for Palestine be implemented, whether Palestine should somehow be partitioned or whether it should be restructured as a bi-national federal state. The United Nations recommended partition: a second Arab Palestinian state was to be created alongside a new Jewish state.

However, the Arab Palestinians and their allies insisted that all of Palestine be under Arab sovereignty. The 1948 war ensued. In its course, the West Bank, which was intended to form the bulk and heart of the new Arab Palestinian state, fell under Jordanian control. The Gaza Strip, with which it was to be linked, fell under Egyptian rule. Then in the 1967 war Israel gained control.

The problems Israel was to face in administering the West Bank were similar to, and yet very different from, those faced in governing the Gaza Strip. The international legal status of both regions was clouded. In both, Israel continued to apply the pre-existing law of Jordan and Egypt. The West Bank, however, became the focal point of demands for Israeli withdrawal and implementation of self-determination.

Unlike the Gaza Strip, a small impoverished area of roughly 600 square miles with 400,000 inhabitants, mostly refugees, the West Bank boasts 2,270 square miles, much of it rich in agricultural resources. Only a small portion of its population of 700,000 are refugees. Most live in the historic towns of Hebron, Nablus, Ramallah and East Jerusalem. Their communal attachments run deep. Even while under the central authority of Amman between 1950 and 1967 strong local leadership flourished. Yet, the ties of West Bankers to Jordan remain firm. Families are interspersed between both banks. The majority of Jordan's population today consists of Palestinians. Jordan is the chief market for West Bank agricultural produce and its link to the larger Arab world.

The West Bank is, however, also a focal point of identification for Jewish nationalists. They view it as the site of their past and, perhaps, future national home. And it is an area of concern to all Israelis worried about national security. The West Bank juts into the center of Israel, leaving at one point not far north of Tel Aviv a narrow margin of less than ten miles between it and the Mediterranean. These ideological and strategic considerations, sometimes acting independently of each other, sometimes acting in concert, complicated and made more difficult Israel's choice of policies relative to the management and disposition of the region.

This study examines and assesses the policies adopted by Israel in over a decade of military government. They are viewed in the context of the Arab-Israeli conflict which gave rise to the occupation and in the light of contemporary international law and politics. Special focus is placed on the interrelationship of various occupation policies and the quest for peace. We trace the effects of the reform of existing social, economic and political institutions in the occupied territories on their ultimate disposition. Chapter I addresses itself to the doctrinal underpinnings for the limitations international law imposes on institutional change and distinguishes different contexts of occupation. Chapter II presents the author's perception of the historical and juridical basis of the Arab-Israeli conflict which forms the necessary backdrop for any assessment of claims regarding Israeli occupational practices. Chapter III then moves from theory to practice and examines the management of the West Bank's three major institutional systems: government, education and property.

Chapter IV explores problems attendant upon the termination of occupation. Given the recent turn of events in Middle East diplomacy occasioned by President Sadat's visit to Israel, there is greater reason to hope that a peace treaty between Israel and its Arab neighbors might finally become a reality. Nevertheless, even in the best of circumstances, the conclusion of peace treaties between former belligerents remains a precarious exercise to be engaged in with the greatest of wariness. It is in this optimistic yet wary spirit that this chapter focuses attention on the problem of protecting the integrity of the peace treaty and the extent to which rights and obligations arising out of occupation measures can be preserved.

In short, this study seeks to achieve a better understanding of the problems inherent in the application of law to the resolution of disputes arising out of military occupation generally, and those associated with the West Bank dilemma in particular. This could lead to a more rational, consistent and principled approach to the problems of war and peace in the Middle East and elsewhere.

Chapter I

# War, Conquered Territory and Military Occupation in the Contemporary International Legal System

The twentieth century has been witness to an unprecedented quest by the international community to save succeeding generations from the scourge of war. Beginning with limitations on the right to wage war in the Hague Convention of 1907,[1] followed by the further limitations and controls of the Covenant of the League of Nations in 1919,[2] and the Kellogg-Briand Pact of 1928,[3] a sustained effort has been made to constrain war by means of an international normative system founded on juridical agreement and based on collective supranational policing arrangements. The establishment of the United Nations and the promulgation of its Charter,[4] and the effort, spanning more than two decades, of United Nations committees to define 'aggression',[5] mark the latest milestones in this movement. It has been to little avail.[6] War remains a fact of international life. Even the advent of nuclear weapons has not provided an adequate deterrent, as some of its proponents have claimed.[7] Conventional warfare, even among the Superpowers, appears to remain an 'acceptable' risk in foreign policy planning.[8]

With the continuing viability of conventional interstate warfare, recurrence of its almost invariable by-products, conquered territory and military occupation, becomes nearly inevitable. Indeed, territorial gain, either as a means to increased security or greater protection of nationals, or simply for imperial expansion, will often prove the chief lure to war. Regardless, however, of any initial territorial ambitions, upon termination of hostilities[9] one state will usually find itself in control of territory formerly under the jurisdiction or control of another. This is a natural consequence of the fact that the effective prosecution of war requires operations upon the territory of an antagonist or its allies.

This chapter addresses itself to the international law framework as it relates to various aspects of conquered territory. It studies the rules for administration of such territory and their effect in furthering a peaceful reconciliation between the belligerents. Particular emphasis is placed on institutional reform by occupying powers and the limitations imposed thereon. Although international law has been incapable of preventing resort to war, it can prove effective in regulating its aftermath, military occupation, especially when it is of the type termed 'belligerent occupation'.

## A. INVASION, BELLIGERENT OCCUPATION, AND POST-SURRENDER OCCUPATION DISTINGUISHED

Occupation of enemy territory can be functionally subdivided into three classes of control: invasion; belligerent occupation; and post-surrender occupation. In the treatment of occupation in international law, the same distinctions are generally, although not always clearly, drawn.[10]

### 1. *Invasion*

Invasion refers to occupation of foreign territory during the course of on-going war, and where effective and continuing control over held areas has not yet been established. The enemy government's administration remains in a state of disorganization, with no new military administrative structure on behalf of the occupying power to replace it. Martial law governs. Few restrictions are imposed by international law on the invader's powers other than avoidance of unnecessary civilian injuries in achieving immediate military objectives.[11]

## 2. *Belligerent Occupation*

By contrast, under belligerent occupation, effective military control over held areas has been achieved, although the enemy has not surrendered and continues to retain control over substantial portions of his territory.[12] Usually fighting will have been brought to a close by means of a cease-fire or armistice—a contractual arrangement which not only results in cessation of all hostilities but which also contains significant political and economic provisions. Although the antagonists during the course of belligerent occupation do not necessarily relinquish their pre-war goals, the dominant characteristic of this period is that attention is shifted to a non-military resolution of differences. The longer the period of adherence to a cease-fire arrangement, or the more detailed the armistice agreement, the more likely that the antagonists will become strongly committed not only to achieving their pre-war objectives by non-military means, but to making genuine peace as well. Signs of commencement of a peace-making process can be found in radical changes of the antagonists' perspectives relative to strategic priorities, ideological goals, or relations with allies. The most important sign, however, will usually be a willingness to negotiate a binding treaty of peace whereby all major outstanding differences between the parties can be resolved and paths laid for assumption of pacific relations. It is because belligerent occupation is usually characterized by a mutual desire on the part of the antagonists to abandon the military pursuit of their goals that international law can prove effective in the regulation of this phase of military control.

Almost invariably, after commencement of belligerent occupation friction will arise relative to the scope of the occupant's legitimate administrative authority over the held areas. Unlike an invader, the belligerent occupant, upon cessation of active hostilities and establishment of effective control, must assume governmental functions. It will want to monitor movement and activities of the population to ensure the security of its forces. Health and sanitation standards will need to be enforced to prevent potential military and civilian casualties. Welfare, educational, commercial, and other systems of social life must continue to function smoothly, if for no other reason than to create stability and to minimize challenges to the occupant's rule.

To accomplish this, the occupant will need an effective civil service apparatus. Rather than attempt to create a wholly new one, he will strive to mitigate manpower costs by establishing a friendly and cooperative local indigenous government, operating as much as possible according to pre-existing procedures. Of course, so far as matters of major policy formulation are concerned, an indigenous occupation regime will be subordinate to the will of the occupying power. In other matters pertaining to municipal administration it may have substantial independence. Depending on the degree of its freedom to act, the indigenous administration may be expected to object strongly to any attempt by the occupying power to reform fundamental laws and institutions. Where such disputes arise international law favors the occupied and requires as one of its cardinal precepts that, in so far as possible, without risking military security or public welfare, the occupant preserve the laws and institutions existing *ante bellum*. This rule is the necessary corollary of the principle that occupied territory not be annexed but remain an issue for negotiation in anticipated peace discussions.

Turning from disputes surrounding the occupant's administrative powers to disputes revolving around the ultimate disposition of the held territory, it can safely be said that, under international law, it is the ousted power who retains sovereignty, albeit in a state of abeyance, over the held territory.[13] Whether it will in fact regain control depends largely on how willing it is to grant concessions to the occupying power in return for all or part of the held territory. In the interim, until a settlement is achieved whereby territory is returned in exchange for promises of a new relationship between the antagonists based on the terms of the peace treaty, the occupying power may retain control over the conquered territories. It may not, however, take actions tending to promote vested interests in favor of indefinite retention. To ensure that this does not occur and that the peace-making process not be thereby thwarted, international law requires a 'freezing' of the *status quo ante bellum*.

3. *Post-Surrender Occupation*

Post-surrender occupation refers, properly used, to continued occupation of territory subsequent to unconditional surrender of the enemy party and its allies. The *de jure* termination of the state of war, traditionally by means of a peace treaty, is not a prerequisite.[14] Post-surrender occupation is a rather recent phenomenon. Historically, conquest of enemy territory would be followed by annexation at the end of the war. The Allied occupation of Germany's Rhineland after World War I provides the first important exception.[15]

The fact that the post-surrender occupant often desires strongly, for ideological reasons, to undertake major reform of its defeated adversary's social, economic, and political institutions, and that, unlike its belligerent occupant counterpart, it is not constrained by the need to refrain from antagonizing its opponent, poses the issue as to what, if any, limits are imposed on the post-surrender occupant's authority to manage and dispose of held territory. International law, mindful of realistic expectations of compliance with any formulated standard, resolves the issue in favor of granting the post-surrender occupant wide administrative latitude. After all, the enemy has been totally, or almost totally, defeated, and has little or no bargaining power to affect the management and ultimate disposition of the occupied territories. Peace has been established, not by contract, more or less, but by fully successful conquest. Indeed, conquest or the total destruction of the enemy government or state will, more often than not, have been the war aim of the post-surrender occupant. Laws and institutions of the defeated state repugnant to the victor's sense of justice or inconsistent with its strategic requirements will be changed with little hesitation. Because reversion of control to the defeated government is not realistically possible, reasons that might otherwise exist for preserving the obnoxious laws and institutions of the ousted power to further settlement possibilities lose all vitality.

This rationale was employed to justify 'denazification' and other Allied programs after World War II, such as the 'decartelization' of German industry and the compulsory surrender of gold, silver, and foreign exchange, which could hardly have been undertaken pursuant to the *status quo ante bellum* standard regulating belligerent occupation. These measures were justified precisely because they were found to have been undertaken in a post-surrender, rather than a belligerent, occupation context. As such they were outside the scope of the law regulating belligerent occupation.[16] Although there has been some doctrinal confusion, especially in the immediate post-war period, in failing to properly distinguish post-surrender from belligerent occupation contexts, this error in analysis has now been widely realized.[17]

## B. THE MANAGEMENT OF OCCUPIED TERRITORY

### 1. *The Hague Convention of 1907 and its Antecedents*

The composite rules of law relative to the scope of authority of the occupying power in managing conquered territory find their first codified expression in treaty form in the 1907 Hague Convention No. IV, Respecting the Laws and Customs of War on Land.[18] This convention, along with the Geneva Convention of 1949,[19] continues to provide the operative law of belligerent occupation. Article 42 of the Hague Regulations states that 'territory is considered occupied [for the purpose of application of the rules of belligerent occupation] when it is placed under the authority of the hostile army'.[20] Thus application of the Hague Convention commences only when the 'invasion' phase subsides into that of 'belligerent occupation'.

Although a multilaterally accepted codification of the law relative to the management of occupied territory first occurred in 1907, the concept of uniform national laws on the subject had gained ascendancy by the mid-nineteenth century.[21] Over a period of time this body of law took on the appearance of customary international law. A movement then arose for codification through multilateral conventions.[22] Although early efforts failed to achieve sufficient adherence, they provided the basis for the 1907 Hague Convention which then drafted the internationally ratified Hague Regulations.[23] The next codification of the law of belligerent occupation took place in 1949 with the adoption of the Geneva Convention relative to the Protection of Civilian Persons in Time of War.[24]

Article 43 is the important 'purpose' provision of the Hague Regulations. It states:

> The authority of the legitimate power having in fact passed into the hands of the occupant, the latter shall take all the measures in his power to restore, and ensure as far as possible public order [*ordre publique*] and safety, while respecting, unless absolutely prevented, the law enforced in the country.[25]

The same policy is expressed in article 47 of the Geneva Convention which provides:

> Protected persons who are in occupied territory shall not be deprived, in any case or in any manner whatsoever, of the benefits of the present conventicn by any change introduced, as the result of the occupation of a territory, into the institutions or government of said territory, nor by any agreement concluded between the authorities of the occupied territories and the occupying power, nor by any annexation by the latter of the whole or part of the occupied territory.[26]

These two provisions deal with the substance of the legal disputes that most often arise regarding the management of territory under belligerent occupation. The occupying power will often attempt to alter existing institutions of government and social life justifying such change either on the ground of 'military necessity' or 'public order' demands. Elements of the occupied population will frequently deny the proffered justification for such change. Or, perhaps more rarely, the occupying power may justify social reform on the grounds of humanitarian considerations, only to be accused in turn of using such alleged motives as a subterfuge to disguise annexationist intentions. It is to these issues that we now direct our attention.

### 2. *Article 43 of the Hague Regulations: The Problem of Preserving an Unjust Order and Defining Permissible Motives for Social Reform*

Legal scholars are in agreement that the occupying power has the right, and indeed the obligation, to restore order and normal economic and social life in the occupied territory.[27] It is when the occupant attempts legislative and institutional change going beyond 'restoration' of order that dispute arises.

All agree that an occupying power does not acquire sovereignty. The provision in Hague Regulation, article 43—'the authority of the legitimate power having actually passed into the hands of the occupant'[28]—is interpreted as meaning that the exercise of sovereignty by the ousted power is suspended and passes *de facto* into the hands of the occupying power.[29] What have defied agreement and continue to be the subject of learned disputation are the meanings of 'military necessity', 'public order and safety', and 'humanitarianism' as the basis for exceptions to the prohibition of institutional change.

Despite the fact that article 43 of the Hague Regulations requires respect for the law previously prevailing in occupied territory unless *'absolutely prevented'*[30] or, according to article 64 of the Geneva Convention, *'essential* to enable the occupying power to fulfill its obligation under the present convention to maintain the orderly government of the territory and to ensure the security of the occupying power,'[31] these limitations have been interpreted liberally rather than literally.[32] Scholars have pointed out that the word 'safety' as used in the English text of article 43 of the Hague Regulations appears as an inadequate rendition of *'vie publique'* employed in the authoritative French text.[33] *'Vie publique,'* it has been claimed, cannot refer simply to physical safety which is embraced in the preceding *'ordre publique'* (public order), but must refer to allowing the life of the occupied country to find continued fulfillment even under the changed conditions resulting from occupation.[34]

Professor Julius Stone suggests that the permissible limits of the occupant's authority to legislate and introduce institutional reform be limited to 'minor' rather than 'fundamental' changes.[35] Serious problems arise, however, in attempting to apply this dichotomy. First, there is of course the difficulty of drawing the distinction between 'minor' and 'fundamental' change. Is, for example, an enlargement of a municipal council to permit wider representation a minor or a fundamental change? And in what circumstances? Secondly, difficulties arise where admittedly 'fundamental' laws and institutions are responsible for violation of internationally recognized standards of human rights. For example, must an occupant retain legislation which restricts voting and university enrollment on the basis of race or sex? Must a judicial system based on absurd privileges and staffed by appointees of a central government, hateful to and hated by the local population, be retained? Or, should the provision of the Hague Regulations that the occupant 'shall take all measures in his power to restore, and ensure, as far as possible, public order and safety, while respecting, unless absolutely prevented, the law enforced in the country' be construed more liberally to permit such ostensibly positive changes?[36]

In seeking answers to these questions, the legislative history of article 43 of the Regulations becomes important, providing a means for ascertaining the policy behind the prohibition. Article 43 was essentially a reproduction of corresponding provisions in the earlier Brussels Code of 1874 and the Oxford Manual of 1880.[37] As in the earlier codes, it was intended to be applied to instances of belligerent occupation, not to surrender—where annexation was held permissible—or to invasion, where effective control had not been established. The Hague Regulations specifically addressed themselves to parties unable to wrest a fully successful military resolution from their conflict. Accordingly, the Regulations placed emphasis on a settlement whereby reversion of control to the ousted power, in whole or in part, would occur. The predominant theme of both the Hague Convention of 1899 and that of 1907 was the provisional character of occupation, wherein the ousted power retains sovereignty, his authority being merely in a state of abeyance.[38] Interference in the ousted power's legislative and institutional system was thus prohihited, for fear of being inimical to the settlement process. Vested interests for the continuance of an occupation might be created. Moreover, fundamental institutional reform might be used to stir indigenous rebellion against the ousted sovereign. To preserve the rights and authority of the ousted sovereign, the Hague Conventions proscribed any activity on the part of the occupant that might tend to undercut it, with changes in existing laws and institutions being the foremost concern.

True, conciliation between the states party to the conflict

might not necessarily be in the best interests of the indigenous occupied population. They might be opposed to returning to the rule of their former sovereign. But the primary interests sought to be protected in the Hague Regulations were those of the ousted power. Thus even revision of fundamentally unjust laws, although prompted by humanitarian motives, was deemed impermissible. The inherent cost of incurring a renewal of hostile relations with the ousted power was thought too high a price for the benefit of possible humanitarian adjustments.

Moreover, 'humanitarian' motives were suspect. The ease with which such an exception to the prohibition of institutional change could serve as a ruse for creation of *faits accomplis* to the occupant's advantage was well known. Claims by occupants that such change as they initiated was humanitarian, dictated by 'the imperative needs of the population,' would, during the course of occupation, be exceedingly difficult to disprove. To prevent this possibility of abuse the Hague Regulations adopted the measure of common law jurisprudence regarding trustees. An occupant, like a trustee, would be severely restricted in his authority, not because certain activities could not be honestly done, but because of the extreme difficulty of proving them to have been dishonest.[39]

As a result, it would seem that if strong indigenous resistance to a former ruler, even a despot, precedes occupation, such movement must, according to the rationale of the Hague Regulations, be frozen. Continuance, unimpeded, of a rebellious movement, even where democratic in nature, could easily be exploited by the occupying power to create a puppet government, which would in turn sever the ties between the invaded population and its ousted sovereign, and place itself squarely in the occupant's camp. It is an opportunity few occupants could be expected to fail to seize. Yet avoidance of this opportunity might not only require retention of unjust laws but suspension of the activities of pre-existing democratic movements.

For many a contemporary thinker this will often be too high a price to pay for preserving an atmosphere conducive to settlement. The view that a population is the patrimony of a monarch has become less popular. At least on the formal aspirational if not normative level, modern international law has accorded increasingly greater deference to the principles of self-determination and fundamental human rights. In light of this trend, it would seem that, ideally, questions of importance relating to management and disposition of occupied territory should turn on the desires of the population, as expressed in some form of supposedly representative action such as a plebiscite.[40] Yet it is commonly recognized that during the course of occupation, political machinery can give a highly misleading expression of popular desire, especially where there are ideological cleavages between the occupying power, the ousted power, and the population. Expressions of 'free will' in such circumstances are highly suspect, and to the extent unfavorable, are almost certain to be derided by the ousted power and his supporters.

To one sympathetic to the wishes of the population and concerned with fundamental human rights, yet mindful of the possibilites of abuse inherent in a broad reading of article 43 of the Hague Regulations, the determination of an occupant's scope of authority remains a perplexing dilemma, and one without an easy solution. In the end the occupying power will have to do what it feels to be justified in the circumstances. International law cannot provide guidelines for specific exigencies, and if a choice between a relatively flat prohibition of institutional change has to be weighed against the infringements a broader rule is likely to condone, then the better choice is the former. Perhaps all that can be said is that an occupant undertaking institutional and legal reform will be acting under the rebuttable presumption of illegality, pending a showing that such reform was either minor in character, necessitated by public order and security needs, or, if fundamental in scope, based on genuine humanitarian considerations.[41]

### 3. *The Equality of Lawful and Unlawful Occupant: Management Sphere*

The Hague Regulations and Geneva Convention provide that an occupant is entitled to take such measures as are necessary to ensure that his forces, installations, equipment, and sources of supply will be free from hostile acts of the population.[42] Moreover, he may in appropriate circumstances requisition private property,[43] confiscate moveable state property,[44] and administer according to the law of usufruct immoveable state property.[45] Crops may be planted, trees cut down, and natural resources such as oil and coal extracted providing prudence is shown in preserving the corpus of the property and providing their use will not result in depletion.[46]

It has, however, been suggested that unlawful occupants—those gaining entry into foreign territory through means of aggressive designs rather than by permissible self-defence measures[47]—be denied the above enumerated rights.[48] In examining the thrust of the arguments favoring the drawing of the distinctions, one is reminded of the exchange between Sir Thomas More and his son-in-law, William Roper, in Robert Bolt's *A Man For All Seasons*. Roper remarks, 'So now you'd give the Devil benefit of law!' to which More replies at the end of a dialogue,'Yes, I'd give the Devil benefit of law, for my own safety's sake.' Despite the ring of injustice equal treatment of lawful and unlawful conduct carries, for purposes of defining the position of international law on this matter, it is correct to say that courts have generally refused to uphold a distinction in managerial rights accorded occupants based on the lawfulness of their resort to war. The rationale for this position was stated by the court in *Aboitiz v. Price:*[49]

> An enemy conqueror is not a very likely person in whom to repose the trust of administering the occupied territories. He is on the ground, however, and has the power to enforce his commands. And dangerous as it may be to recognize any authority in him, it is better to encourage some proper government than none at all. Without some kind of order, the whole social and economic life of the community would be paralyzed. So international law has recognized the right of the occupant to make regulations for the protection of his military interests and the exercise of police powers.[50]

The United States Military Tribunal at Nuernberg likewise applied the obligations of the Hague Regulations in the case of German belligerent occupation during World War II.[51]

As a consequence of the rule of international law validating administrative acts of the occupant, regardless of his aggressive or defensive posture, claims for restitution or reparations for property appropriated or exploited in conformity with the applicable regulations will be without merit.[52] Whether extension of equal rights to lawful and unlawful occupants is also warranted when disposition rather than management of occupied territory is under discussion is the subject of the following section.

## C. THE DISPOSITION OF OCCUPIED TERRITORY

### 1. *The Inequality of the Lawful and Unlawful Occupant*

Disposition of occupied territory may occur through a variety of means. It may be ceded with or without provisions for demilitarization or other security guarantees. Withdrawal may occur and the *status quo ante bellum* be restored. New states may arise through a plebiscite or through less democratic means. Special regimes may be instituted, governed by a statute incorporated in the peace treaty. These would include zones of occupation, where the defeated parties agree to the more or less temporary occupation of portions of its territory, plebiscite regimes, where the belligerents agree to abide by the will of the inhabitants of the particular area as that will is expressed in a plebiscite whose dates and procedures are specified in the peace treaty, or free territories, usually involving a strategically valuable area such as a port, industrial zone, or large city, which becomes a separate entity because the parties cannot come to terms over its sovereignty.[53]

International law provides 'customary' and 'conventional'[54] rules which delineate rights and obligations relative to the ultimate control of the occupied territories. The most important of these is the standard of article 2, paragraph 4 of the United Nations Charter, prohibiting the threat or use of force.[55] As the first fruits of the aggressive conduct that the provision proscribes will most often be the conquest of enemy territory, it has been reasoned, in an attempt to give viability to article 2, paragraph 4, that states unlawfully gaining control over foreign territory be treated differently by the law *vis-à-vis* their right to retain or acquire such territory than states lawfully gaining control. Those supporting such a position seek support in the principle of *ex injuria jus non oritur*. Applying this maxim, international law is deemed to preclude an aggressor-occupant from deriving any right either to international recognition of the lawfulness of his continued occupation or his capacity to acquire sovereignty.[56]

Most scholars have, however, generally viewed the principle of *ex injuria jus non oritur* and its corollary, non-recognition of conquest, as one of limited utility in a world order without effective central sanctioning power.[57]

Moreover, there is some agreement that an aggressor-occupant may acquire title to annexed territory, provided there is an express act of recognition by other states who 'treat as valid the new title or situation, notwithstanding the initial illegality of the act on which it is based.'[58] As Professor James Brierly has succinctly put it, 'The truth is that international law can no more refuse to recognize that a finally successful conquest does change title to territory than municipal law can change a regime brought about by a successful revolution.'[59]

Thus to the extent the *fait accompli* of annexation followed by international recognition has not occurred—in which case international law is powerless to do anything but accept the new reality—the principle of *ex injuria jus non oritur* remains viable insofar as international law denies an aggressor's claim of a right to continue occupation and eventually to acquire title by annexation or cession.[60] The latest manifestations of this proposition are found in the 1969 Vienna Convention on the Law of Treaties, which denies unlawful occupants rights of territorial acquisition via cession in peace treaties,[61] and in Security Council Resolution 242 of 1967 which emphasizes the principle of the 'inadmissibility of the acquisition of territory by force.'[62] It thus becomes pertinent at this point to examine how the classification of lawful occupant is determined. The following section examines the frequently asserted justifications for assumption of the status of lawful entrant and occupant of foreign territory: self-defense, aid to self-determination movements, and humanitarian motivations.

### 2. *Claims to Lawful Entry*

#### a. *Self-Defense*

As an exception to the proscription of the use of force in

international relations appearing in article 2, paragraph 4 of the United Nations Charter, article 51 provides that '[n]othing in the present Charter shall impair the inherent right of individual or collective self-defense if an armed attack occurs against a Member of the United Nations, until the Security Council has taken the measures necessary to maintain international peace and security.'[63] Suggestions have been made that article 51's references to 'armed attack' as a condition precedent to recourse to self-defense be interpreted as requiring that, in effect, the first bomb touch ground before the attacked state may respond.[64] Such an argument is unfounded from the standpoints of textual and contextual interpretation as well as state practice.[65]

Article 51 speaks of the 'inherent' right of self-defense. Reference is thus made to retention of the customary international law of self-defense preceding the adoption of the Charter.[66] Customary international law requires less than an actual armed attack,[67] and has agreed on a requirement of proportionality, limiting the intensity of the response to what is reasonably connected to terminating the hostile stimulus.[68] What is, in fact, necessary and proportional is ultimately determined only by 'that most comprehensive and fundamental test of all law, reasonableness in a particular context.'[69]

Moreover, article 51 was adopted on the presupposition that the Security Council would be able to undertake the 'collective security' function referred to in chapter VII of the Charter.[70] The international community has, however, proven itself incapable of implementing an adequate policing system. Lacking this safeguard article 51 must now be interpreted more broadly than if the envisioned collective security arrangements had materialized.[71]

Finally, given the normal reluctance of states to sustain the first blow in order to gain the dubious advantage of clear legality, states have freely invoked, perhaps to the point of abuse, the self-defense exception in instances where they were the ones to strike first.[72] While one cannot accept with equanimity the trend, as one commentator has put it, to enlarge the self-defense exception of article 51 from one initially not 'much larger than a needle's eye' to a 'loophole through which armies have passed,'[73] neither can one ignore the fact that a strict interpretation of article 51 would certainly lead to a further 'credibility gap' in the Charter's provisions. A right of anticipatory self-defense cannot be totally denied any more in international law than it can be in any domestic legal system.[74]

The 1974 Definition of Aggression adopted by the General Assembly grasps the logic of the above point as it appears to allow some first strikes as being within the self-defense exception.[75] The first strike is to constitute *prima facie* evidence of aggression. Then the context in which it was launched is to be examined. If deemed sufficiently provocative the charge may be rebutted. Little guidance is, however, available as to what situations justify anticipatory defense other than Webster's formula in the *Caroline* case,[76] and the answer, in any particular context, must rest on the special circumstances of the case, with due regard to the principles of exhaustion of peaceful remedies and proportionality of response.

### b. *Self-Determination*

Despite the United Nations Charter's express limitation on the use of force to instances of self-defense, however defined, the thesis has been advanced, especially in recent years, that even where no threat to the security of the intervening state exists, foreign intervention may be justified if for the purpose of aiding self-determination movements.[77] Since the first notable post-World War II claim, in 1948, the proposition that support for self-determination movements, or wars of national liberation, is exempt from the purview of the United Nations Charter's prohibition on the threat or use of force against the territorial integrity or independence of another state, has gained an increasing number of adherents.[78] When, in 1974, consensus was finally reached by the Special Committee on the Definition of Aggression, the claimed right to use force in aid of self-determination struggles was deliberately handled in an ambiguous manner, to pacify the adherents of such a view.[79] However, notwithstanding the infusion of rhetoric and ambiguity, the traditional rule of international law limiting recourse to force to instances of self-defense appears to have prevailed or at least not to have been clearly deposed.

c. *Humanitarian Intervention*

It has been asserted as well that foreign military intervention for humanitarian purposes provides an exception to the prohibitions of article 2, paragraph 4 as the political independence of states which article 2, paragraph 4 seeks to preserve is not immune from actions designed to remedy fundamental human rights deprivations.[80] In response to this claim it is useful to ask which human rights deprivations are so gross as to warrant, under the suggested rule of humanitarian intervention, invasion of foreign territory for the purpose of terminating such practices. Let us begin with the worst possible case, genocide, and examine the international community's attempt to chart permissible normative responses.

The Genocide Convention of 1950[81] deemed the commission of acts aimed at destroying the existence of a people, race, nationality, or religion an international crime, whether committed 'in time of peace or in time of war.'[82] However, invasion to prevent its occurrence was not a specified remedy. Rather, sanctions were confined to those meted out by the 'competent tribunal in the State of the territory in which the act was committed, or by such international penal tribunals as may have jurisdiction with respect to those Contracting Parties which shall have accepted its jurisdiction.'[83]

'International penal tribunals' as discussed in the Genocide Convention have never materialized. Nor has the envisioned United Nations collective policing machinery ever come to fruition. Only one response to genocide provided in the Convention remains susceptible of use—trial by tribunal of the perpetrating state. But this remedy, of course, can only be effective, if at all, upon the defeat of the delinquent state. At that stage, only retribution, not prevention, is possible. It is in this context of a conventional international law which provides no operative measures for combatting genocide that the issue is posed as to whether states, individually or collectively, may, upon the exhaustion of pacific means, invade the territory of the perpetrating state, independently of the United Nations, for the limited purpose of preventing genocidal practices.

This question was posed, examined, and answered by the United Nations Legal Committee, the Sixth Committee, in its 1954 debate on the work of the Special Committee on the Question of Defining Aggression.[84] It response was that foreign military intervention for prevention of genocide would indeed be 'aggression.'[85] Dominating the reluctance to authorize military intervention for even the most pressing humanitarian considerations was the fear that humanitarian grounds had been and could be too easily invoked to mask ignoble motives. The only permissible ground for military intervention to prevent 'the commission of atrocities by a State against its own nationals' was stated to be 'a case of an offense against the peace and security of mankind rather than an act of aggression, and armed intervention in that connection would be justified only if taken in pursuance of a United Nations decision under Chapter VII of the Charter.'[86]

In the intervening years since 1954, claims of a right to humanitarian intervention have increasingly been heard. They have been predominantly influenced, in varying degrees, by the events in the Nigeria-Biafra Civil War of 1971, the Pakistan-Bangladesh War of 1971, and by South Africa's and Rhodesia's racial policies.[87] Writers seeking to justify these claims point to the United Nations Charter's emphasis on the necessity of community promotion and encouragement of universal respect for human rights. On this basis it is extrapolated that the 'cumulative effect' of the Charter's reference to the preservation of fundamental human rights standards has 'created a separate form of action for human rights deprivation.'[88] In particular it is maintained that article 56 of the Charter, which requires member states 'to take joint and separate action in cooperation with the Organization for achievement of the purposes set forth in article 55,' transforms the commitment in article 55 of the Charter to 'promote,' 'respect,' and 'observe' human rights 'into an active obligation for joint and separate action in defense of human rights.'[89]

Such a reading of article 56, insofar as it permits of an individual right of humanitarian intervention, appears however to be inconsistent with the thrust of the United Nations Charter, whose major purpose is, after all, to curtail unilateral resort to force regardless of 'just' motives in all instances save the need for immediate self-defense. A more consistent interpretation would be that the use of force to remedy human rights deprivations is countenanced by the Charter only where a direct threat to world peace is established, pursuant to a United Nations Security Council decision.

An examination of state practice does not indicate any trend to invoke the right of humanitarian intervention in the period from World War II, despite the repeated occurrences of genocidal practices.[90] The meaning of the Third Reich's 'Final Solution' was known to the United States by 1941, but it was not sufficient to entice American entry into World War II. Earlier Nazi practices engendered little more than limited diplomatic protests by the United States.[91]

In 1960 the International Commission of Jurists, in reference to the situation in Tibet, stated in its report to the United Nations Secretary General that '[t]he Committee found that acts of genocide had been committed in Tibet in an attempt to destroy the Tibetans as a religious group, and that such acts are acts of genocide independently of any conventional obligation.'[92] The General Assembly limited its response to mild censure and the Security Council was never convened. The Congo Crisis of 1964 is often cited as an instance of humanitarian intervention.[93] Yet the Belgian-British-American intervention occurred at the request and not against the wishes of the recognized government. Moreover, intervention was had for the rescue of civilian hostages of foreign nationality, not for members of the indigenous population. In the Nigeria-Biafra War of 1971, not a single state claimed a right to humanitarian intervention despite substantial evidence at the time of attempts to exterminate the Ibos.[94] In the Pakistan-Bangladesh War, it would seem more plausible that India intervened to exploit the opportunity to weaken Pakistan and minimize its presence on India's borders than for humanitarian purposes.[95]

The preceding analysis is not intended to suggest, however, that the author views unsympathetically the prospect of unilateral state action, upon exhaustion of peaceful remedies or where any such effort seems doomed from the start, in order to remedy gross human rights deprivations, especially where genocidal practices are at issue. Its aim is to document the fact that the international community, neither by the terms of the United Nations Charter, the diplomatic history surrounding the Genocide Convention controversy, nor by its practice throughout the twentieth century, has ever condoned a right to humanitarian intervention. Girded by mutual distrust, authority has never been lent to the proposition that humanitarian intervention is permissible for fear that ignoble motives for entry might too easily be fabricated under this motif. International law has consistently presumed an invasion for humanitarian motives to be unlawful.

## CONCLUSION

War cannot be constrained by outlawing it when the machinery of international law—the United Nations, the International Court of Justice, international treaties, and disarmament agreements—retains no significant capability of exacting compliance with its dictates, other than when conformity is convenient. Any empirical study of international affairs in this century should remove all lingering doubt. Even the efforts of the most faithful adherents of the outlawry view—the Special Committee on the Question of Defining Aggression—have been exposed as more concerned with masking the absence of consensus by reaching definitions devoid of operational precision than in dealing realistically with international law's crisis of powerlessness.

But if the possibility for mitigating resort to war by defining and refining international legal doctrine remains dim at best, there is nevertheless the strong prospect that international law, if properly clarified, can help bring order out of the chaos that follows in war's wake. In the phase of conquest termed belligerent occupation, an international normative system relative to the management and disposition of the held territory is not only susceptible to easy adherence but often sought after by the antagonists. This is because they seek, in large measure, the peaceful resolution of their differences. A well-mapped-out normative system, mutually agreed upon, lessens tension and generally furthers this end. Unfortunately, here international legal doctrine has slackened behind rather than, as more usual, outpaced demands for its use. Confusion abounds principally as to the limits of institutional change an occupant may legitimately undertake, the distinction, if any, in rights and obligations to be drawn between lawful and unlawful aggressor-occupants, and the means for determining this distinction.

As a means towards clarification, it is important at the outset to carefully distinguish different types of occupational control, and the relevant rules and policies that pertain to each. It must be realized that the lawful-unlawful dichotomy has no application to the management sphere of occupation, but only to the acquisition of held territory, insofar as claims to potential acquisition of title by aggressor-occupants are not recognized. Perhaps most importantly management policies affecting institutional change need to be examined in light of ultimate dispositionary goals. To the extent that reversion of held territory to the former sovereign in the context of a treaty of peace remains the aim, then all institutional reform inimical to that end, whether inspired in the best interests of the population or not, needs to be deemed presumptively invalid. Finally, in discussing the classification of occupants as lawful or not, the traditional test of self-defense remains the only acceptable justification for entry into foreign territory.

Perhaps in no other situation is peace as precariously in the balance as in the administration of held enemy territory. Insofar as the parties genuinely seek to move from war to peace, international law, if sufficiently clear of ambiguity, can prove the best catalyst.

NOTES

1. Limitation of Employment of Force for Recovery of Contract Debts (Hague II), *signed* Oct. 18, 1907, 36 Stat. 2241, T.S. No. 537, *100 Brit. & Foreign St. Papers* 314 (1906-1907).
2. Treaty of Versailles. June 28, 1919, 2 Bevans, *Treaties and Other International Agreements of the United States of America 1776-1949*, at 43 (1969), *112 Brit. & Foreign St. Papers* 1 (1919). Article 11 of the Covenant declared that 'any war or threat of war . . . is . . . a matter of concern to the whole League, and the League shall take any action that may be deemed wise and effectual to safeguard the peace of nations.' Article 12 obligated members of the League to submit 'any dispute likely to lead to a rupture . . . to arbitration or to inquiry by the Council . . . [and] in no case to resort to war until three months after the award by the arbitrators or the report by the Council.' Article 13 obligated

members of the League to carry out in full good faith any such award or decision, and not to resort to war against a member that complies therewith.

3. Kellogg-Briand Peace Pact, *signed* Aug. 27, 1928, 46 Stat. 2343, T. S. No. 796, 94 L.N.T.S. 57. Article 1 thereof provided that '[t]he High Contracting Parties solemnly declare in the names of their respective peoples that they condemn recourse to war for the solution of international controversies, and renounce it as an instrument of national policy in their relations with one another.' Article 2 provided that '[t]he High Contracting Parties agree that the settlement or solution of all disputes or conflicts of whatever nature or of whatever origin they may be, which may arise between them, shall never be sought except by pacific means.' Sixty-four states are party to this treaty. *U.S. Dep't of State. Treaties in Force* 347 (1977).
4. The Charter obligates all members to 'refrain in their international relations from the threat or use of force against the territorial integrity or political independence of any state, or in any other manner inconsistent with the Purposes of the United Nations.' U.N. Charter art. 2, para. 4. Article 51 provides as an exception to the prohibition of force instances of self defense against an 'armed attack.' Article 39 states that: 'The Security Council shall determine the existence of any threat to the peace, breach of the peace, or act of aggression and shall make recommendations, or decide what measures shall be taken in accordance with Articles 41 and 42, to maintain or restore international peace and security.'
5. The Sixth Committee (the Legal Committee) and the Special Committee on the Question of Defining Aggression have been attempting almost since the inception of the U.N. to determine an acceptable definition of aggression. In late 1974, international consensus was reached regarding a definition. Definition of Aggression, 29 U.N. GAOR, Special Committee on the Question of Defining Aggression, U.N. Doc. A/9619 (1974) [hereinafter cited as 1974 Definition of Aggression], adopted in G.A. Res. 3314, 29 U.N. GAOR, Supp. (No. 31) 142, U.N.Doc. A/9631 (1974). *See* I & II B. Ferencz, *Defining International Aggression: The Search for World Peace* (1975); A. V. W. Thomas & A. J. Thomas, *The Concept of Aggression in International Law* (1972); Ferencz, 'Defining Aggression: Where It Stands and Where It's Going', 66 *Am.J.Int'l L.* 491 (1972).
6. In their study comparing the use of force over different periods of international relations, Professors Osgood and Tucker conclude that 'since World War II, local wars—civil, revolutionary, and between the organized armies of states—have been as pervasive and decisive an instrument of international politics as in any modern period.' R. Osgood & R. Tucker, *Force, Order and Justice* 25 (1967). The most significant conventional interstate wars have been the four Arab-Israeli wars (1948, 1956, 1967, 1973) and Korea (1950-1953). Most international wars have been extended internal wars with international

involvement, the most notable of these being the French Indochina (1947-1954), Burma (1948-1954), Philippines (1948-1954), Malaya (1948-1958), Congo (1960-1963), and Cyprus (1974) wars. Controversy continues to rage over the appropriate classification of the Vietnam War (1959-1972). For an interpretation of the Vietnam War as an instance of interstate war, see J. Moore, *Law and the Indochina War* (1972), and review thereof, Rostow, *82 Yale L. J.* 829 (1973). For a view of the Vietnam War as an internal war with interstate involvement, see 1 *The Vietnam War and International Law* (R. Falk ed. 1968). *See* R. Randle, *Geneva 1954: The Settlement of the Indochinese War* (1954). The 1975-1976 Angolan conflict also presents problems in applying the internal-external war dichotomy.

7. For an explicit presentation of the thesis that nuclear weapons have made war obsolete, see W. Mills, *An End to Arms* (1964); W. Mills & J. Real, *The Abolition of War* (1963). For the projected application of this thesis to the Arab-Israeli conflict, see Tucker, 'Israel and the United States: From Dependence to Nuclear Weapons?' 60 *Commentary* 29 (1975). 'What nuclear power can provide is an environment in which these [basic] problems either must remain unresolved or their resolution sought through means other than war,' *Id.* at 42.
8. *See, e.g.* H. Kissinger, *The Necessity for Choice* 57 (1960).
9. Reference is not made here to the termination of what is technically termed a 'state of war,' regarding which considerable dispute abounds in international law literature. II L. Oppenheim, *International Law* 546-47 (H. Lauterpacht ed. 7th ed. 1952) [hereinafter cited as *Lauterpacht-Oppenheim*], represents the traditional approach that armistices or truces are a temporary cessation of hostilities, not to be compared with peace and not even to be called temporary peace, because the conditions of war remain. A second approach, stressing the difference between the traditional armistice and the 'modern' agreement, maintains that an armistice agreement which allows for resumption of military hostilities is repugnant to the United Nations Charter. N. Feinberg, *The Legality of a 'State of War' After the Cessation of Hostilities Under the Charter of the United Nations and the Covenant of the League of Nations* (1961); Gross 'The Geneva Conference on the Law of the Sea and the Right of Innocent Passage Through the Gulf of Aqaba,' *53 Am.J.Int'l L.* 564 (1959); Levie, 'The Nature and Scope of the Armistice Agreement', *50 Am. J. Int'l L.* 880 (1956). Julius Stone is prominent among those who adopt the contractual approach, sometimes termed *status mixtus*, stressing that whether a 'state of war' has been terminated should be determined by the nature of the agreement signed. J. Stone, *Legal Controls of International Conflicts* 641 (1959). *See also* G. Schwarzenberger, *The Frontiers of International Law* 247 (1962). As for the meaning of 'war,' as opposed to 'state of war,' no common definition exists. II *Lauterpacht-Oppenheim, supra* at 202; A. Wright, *A Study of War* 8-13 (1942); Baxter, 'The Definition of War', 16 *Revue Egyptienne de Droit International* 1 (1960). The definitions of 'war' and 'state of war'

can be of great municipal consequence as they will often be determinative of claims arising out of frustration of contract, insurance liability, and Trading with the Enemy Act violations.

10. M. McDougal & F. Feliciano, *Law and Minimum World Public Order* 732-33 (1961); II *Lauterpacht-Oppenheim, supra* note 9, at 432-35.
11. M. Greenspan, *The Modern Law of Land Warfare* 214 (1959); M. McDougal & F. Feliciano, *supra* note 10, at 732-34; A. McNair, *Legal Effect of War* 319-20 (1948); J. Stone, *supra* note 9, at 694.
12. M. McDougal & F. Feliciano, *supra* note 10, at 733-36; J. Stone, *supra* note 9, at 744-51.
13. II *Lauterpacht-Oppenheim, supra* note 9, at 618.
14. On use of the term 'post-surrender occupation,' see G. Von Glahn, *The Occupation of Enemy Territory* 276 (1957). Regarding the peace treaty as the means for terminating a 'state of war,' see A. McNair, *supra* note 11, at 320; *U.S. Judge Advocate General's School, Charlottesville, Va., Civil Affairs Military Government: Cases and Materials* 37 (1955). A traditional alternative mode for terminating war, subjugation *(debellatio)* is the total destruction of an enemy's legal personality through effective annexation. This action has encountered disfavor in more contemporary international law doctrine. M. Greenspan, *supra* note 11, at 600-03; Gerson, 'Trustee-Occupant: The Legal Status of Israel's Presence in the West Bank', *14 Harv. Int'l L. J.* 1, 2 (1973). The peace treaty may often be but the formal stamp of approval of an existing state of affairs. Thus, for example, although the United States has never signed a peace treaty with Germany, due to disagreement with the Soviet Union over the future of Germany, the functional equivalent has been arrived at through unilateral declarations. United States Proclamation on Termination of the State of War with Germany, *25 Dep't State Bull.* 769 (1951), later approved by a joint resolution of Congress on October 19, 1951, H.R.J. Res. 289, 82d Cong., 1st Sess., Pub. L. No. 82-181, 65 Stat. 451 (1951).
15. The Allied Occupation of the Rhineland entailed 'the [first] application of Wilsonian principles to the field of military occupation.' E. Fraenkel, *Military Occupation and the Rule of Law: Occupation Government in the Rhineland 1918-1923,* at 4 (1943). By the terms of the armistice agreements and the subsequent Treaty of Versailles, the Rhineland was to remain an integral part of Germany but to be occupied for a period of fifteen years as a guarantee for Germany's execution of the treaty. The Allied occupations of Germany and Japan after the Second World War provide the most significant subsequent examples of post-surrender occupation. 'Denazification' and 'democratization' rather than mere prevention of rearmament became the Allies' predominant concerns.
16. The subject of the non-applicability of the Hague Regulations, note 18 *infra,* to the situation after the termination of hostilities in Germany is discussed in Letter of Forrest S. Hannaman, Chief of Legal Service Division of the Office of the United States High Commissioner for Germany, to Major Morton S. Jaffe of the Judge Advocate Division of

EUCOM (Jan. 28, 1952), *summarized in* 10 *Digest of International Law* 595 (M. Whiteman ed. 1968). United States v. Alstoetter (Justice Case), *III Trials of War Criminals Before the Nuernberg Military Tribunals* 954, 960 (1947), held that the Hague Regulations did not apply to the occupation of Germany and the surrender of all opposing German and Axis forces on the field. *Accord Grahame* v. *Director of Prosecutions,* (Germany, Brit. Zone of Control, Control Comm'n Crim. App. 1947). 14 Lauterpacht, *Annual Digest and Report of International Law cases* [hereinafter cited as Annual Digest] 228 (1947).

Note that in the American occupation of Japan following World War II, surrender was at least technically not unconditional as it was agreed that decrees changing Japan's constitution and fundamental institutions were to be passed in the name of the Emperor and not the American military government. Accordingly, the American administration was said to be governed by the rules of belligerent occupation under the Hague Regulations. Cobb v. United States, 191 F.2d 604 (9th Cir. 1951), *cert. denied,* 342 U.S. 913 (1952), reached the conclusion that the Hague Regulations applied to the United States occupation of Okinawa. It considered the United States a belligerent occupant even though all hostilities had ceased because no final treaty or proclamation disposing of the territory had been made, *id.* at 610, and even though Japan's sovereignty had definitively ended. *Id.* at 607.

17. For an example of this early confusion, see J. Brierly, *The Law of Military Occupation* (1943). Brierly states that, while the Germans during the course of World War II had no justification for the introduction of racial laws in the territories they occupied, the United States could, upon occupying Germany, change the laws submitting Jews to discriminatory practices, under the 'restoration of public order' exception to prohibitions in the law of belligerent occupation of institutional and legislative change. Yet, as anti-Semitic measures were not inimical to German 'public order,' it is questionable whether the Hague Regulations could properly be invoked to justify their abolition.

For a good bibliographic survey of the debate on this point, see Kunz, 'The Status of Occupied Germany Under International Law: A Legal Dilemma' 3 *W. Pol. Q.* 538 (1950). The contrary view is made most strongly by German writers. see Laun, 'The Legal Status of Germany', *45 Am, J. Int'l L.* 267 (1951). McDougal and Feliciano conclude that 'the constellation of events with which the Allied Powers were confronted in 1945 was quite different from that with respect to which the law of belligerent occupation has traditionally been invoked and applied.' M. McDougal & F. Feliciano, *supra* note 10, at 769 n.95.

18. Laws and Customs of War on Land (Hague IV), *signed* Oct. 18, 1907, 36 Stat.2277, T.S. No. 539. 100 *Brit. & Foreign St. Papers* 338 (1919) [hereinafter cited as the Hague Convention]. The Hague Convention was accompanied by an Annex containing specific regulations [hereinafter cited as the Hague Regulations]. Regarding prior attempts at codification and the legislative history of the convention generally,

see D. Graber, *The Development of the Law of Belligerent Occupation, 1863-1914,* at 93-109 (1949).

19. Geneva Convention Relative to the Protection of Civil Persons in Time of War, Aug. 12, 1949, 6 U.S.T. 3516, T.I.A.S. No. 3365, 75 U.N.T.S. 287 [hereinafter cited as the Geneva Convention].
20. Hague Regulations, *supra* note 18, art. 42.
21. The first recorded code of the law of belligerent occupation was the Lieber Code, a set of regulations drafted by Professor Francis Lieber at the request of President Lincoln in 1863. It covered the entire law with roughly one-third of its provisions stipulating the manner in which Union forces were to govern the occupied Confederate South. The Lieber Code, Apr. 24, 1863, reprinted in I *The Law of War* 158 (L. Friedman ed. 1972). *See* Davis, 'Dr. Francis Lieber's Instructions for the Government of Armies in the Field', *1 Am. J. Int'l L.* 13 (1907). Almost concurrently, the other major world powers began to adopt similar military codes dealing with the problem of occupation. D. Graber, *supra* note 18, at 13-36.
22. In 1874 the first international conference for the purpose of clarifying the laws and customs of war on land was convened at Brussels. The Lieber Code was the basis for its proceedings, which culminated in the drafting of rules and regulations of land warfare. Project of an International Declaration Concerning the Laws and Customs of War, Aug. 28, 1874, reprinted in *The Laws of Armed Conflicts: A Collection of Conventions, Resolutions and Other Documents* 27 (D. Schindler & J. Toman eds. 1973). These rules were, however, never ratified by the major powers. In 1880 the Institute of International Law meeting at Oxford produced a second codification of the rules of land warfare based on the Lieber Code. Text in J. Scott, *Resolutions of the Institute of International Law* 25 (1916). Then, in 1899, a second attempt at a multilateral treaty on the subject was made when an international conference for that purpose was convened at the Hague. International Convention with respect to the Laws and Customs of War on Land, July 29, 1899, 32 Stat. 1803, T.S. No. 403, 91 *Brit. & Foreign St. Papers* 988 (1898-1899). *See* J. Scott, *The Hague Peace Conferences of 1899 and 1907,* at 522-40 (1909). Although this convention was signed and ratified by all powers present in 1899, its provisions remained unrefined and difficult to implement. Its failure led to the 1907 convention.
23. Hague Convention, *supra* note 18; Hague Regulations, *supra* note 18.
24. Geneva Convention, *supra* note 19.
25. Hague Regulations, *supra* note 18, art. 43.
26. Geneva Convention, *supra* note 19, art. 47.
27. II Lauterpacht-Oppenheim, *supra* note 9, at 434, 436-37.
28. Hague Regulations, *supra* note 18, art. 43.
29. *In re G.,* (Cr. Ct. Heraklion, Crete, Greece 1945) 12 Annual Digest 437 (1945); J. Stone, *supra* note 9, at 698; Schwenk, 'Legislative Powers of the Military Occupants under Article 43 Hague Regulations', 54 *Yale L. J.* 393, 393-95 (1945).

30. Hague Regulations, *supra* note 18, art. 43 (emphasis added).
31. Geneva Convention, *supra* note 19, art. 64 (emphasis added).
32. *See* cases cited in *II Lauterpacht-Oppenheim, supra* note 9, at 437 n.4.
33. Schwenk, *supra* note 29, at 398. As an example of application of this liberal criterion, see Jabari v. Karim, File No. 44/67, Dist. Ct. of Ramallah, The West Bank (1968) (in Arabic and Hebrew), where the court reversed a magistrate's ruling that an Israeli military command permitting Israeli lawyers to represent West Bank clients notwithstanding their failure to comply with the Jordanian Chamber of Advocates Law, for the duration of a strike by West Bank lawyers, was violative of article 43 of the Hague Regulations. The court ruled that military command was 'imperative' to uphold law and the orderly operation of the judiciary. This case is discussed in *Hebrew University Institute for Legislative Research and Comparative Law, Law Courts in the Israeli-Held Areas* (1970).
34. McDougal and Feliciano have written:

    The range of authority needed for effective regulation clearly cannot be limited to the mere suppression of physical violence and anarchy, but must bear some reasonable correspondence to the comprehensiveness and complexity of the society and economic processes of a modern community. It is thus difficult to point with much confidence to any of the usual subjects of governmental action as being a priori excluded from the administrative authority conferred upon the occupant.

    M. McDougal & F. Feliciano, *supra* note 10, at 746. Professor Gerhard von Glahn writes:

    It has to be remembered that the secondary aim of any lawful military occupation is the safeguarding of the welfare of the native population and this secondary lawful aim would seem to supply the basis for such new laws as are passed by the occupant for the benefit of the population and are not dictated by his own military necessity and requirements.

    G. von Glahn, *supra* note 14, at 43.
35. 'The most widely approved distinction is that the occupier, in view of his purely provisional position, cannot make permanent changes in regard to *fundamental* institutions, for instance, change a republic into a monarchy.' J. Stone, *supra* note 9, at 695 (emphasis added).
36. For a general discussion of this issue, see Baty. 'The Relation of Invaders to Insurgents' 36 *Yale L. J.* 966 (1927). Justice Cohn of Israel's Supreme Court has suggested that, at the least, article 43 prevents the occupying power from introducing reforms in law and institutions on the basis of welfare or humanitarian considerations if the proposed reform has not been implemented within the occupying state. Christian Society for the Holy Places v. Minister of Defense, 25 (1) *Piskei Din* [*Judgments of the Israel Supreme Court*] 547, 577 (1972) (Cohn, J., dissenting), denied petitioner's request to disallow as violative of article 43 a military order calling upon the petitioner to proceed to arbitration for settlement of a labor dispute on the grounds that such provision was not included in the applicable Jordanian law.

The Court found that the military order's amendment to the Jordanian law was minor, consistent with its legislative intent, and necessitated by public welfare.

37. D. Graber, *supra* note 18, at 1-36. *See* note 22 *supra*.

38. D. Graber, *supra* note 18, at 37-69. See R. Robin, *Des occupations militaires en dehors des occupations de guerre* (1913), extracts translated and reproduced by *Carnegie Endowment for International Peace, Division of International Law* (1942); *U.S. Judge Advocate General's School, Ann Arbor, Mich., Law of Belligerent Occupation* 38-43 (1945).

39. Suggesting the utility of this test, see Baty, *supra* note 36, at 978.

40. Regarding plebiscites generally, see H. Johnson, *Self-Determination Within the Community of Nations (1967);* A. Wambaugh, *A Monograph on Plebiscites* (1920); Reisman & Chen, Who Owns Taiwan: A Search for International Title, *81 Yale L.J.* 599, 660-69 (1972).

41. Special difficulties arise where institutional reform is justified on the basis of promoting self-determination. Whether this right applies to a populace under belligerent occupation remains an unsettled question. Traditionally, international law does not recognize a rebellious government in a civil war context, regardless of its humanitarian designs, until it has reached the stage of insurgency. II Lauterpacht-Oppenheim, *supra* note 9, at 270-78; R. Vincent, *Non-Intervention and International Order* 286-87 (1974). Presumably the same rule would apply to instances of revolt under belligerent occupation. It is submitted, however, that the temporal span of occupation and the nature of evolved relations between the ousted sovereign and its citizens under occupation be treated as permitting, in special circumstances, deviation from the traditional doctrine of non-recognition of rebellion.

42.

> In addition to the prohibition provided by special Conventions, it is especially forbidden—
>
> . . . .
>
> (*g*) To destroy or seize the enemy's property, unless such destruction or seizure be imperatively demanded by the necessities of war. . . .

Hague Regulations, *supra* note 18, art. 23(*g*).

> Any destruction by the Occupying Power of real or personal property belonging individually or collectively to private persons, or to the State, or to other public authorities, or to social or cooperative organizations, is prohibited, except where such destruction is rendered absolutely necessary by military operations.

Geneva Convention, *supra* note 19, art. 53.

43.

> Requisitions in kind and services shall not be demanded from municipalities or inhabitants except for the needs of the army of occupation. They shall be in proportion to the resources of the country, and of such a nature as not to involve the inhabitants in the

obligation of taking part in military operations against their own country. Such requisitions and services shall only be demanded on the authority of the commander in the locality occupied.

Contributions in kind shall as far as possible be paid for in cash; if not, a receipt shall be given and the payment of the amount due shall be made as soon as possible.

Hague Regulations, *supra* note 18, art. 52.

To the fullest extent of the means available to it, the Occupying Power has the duty of ensuring the food and medical supplies of the population; it should, in particular, bring in the necessary foodstuffs, medical stores and other articles if the resources of the occupied territory are inadequate.

The Occupying Power may not requisition foodstuffs, articles or medical supplies available in the occupied territory, except for use by the occupation forces and administration personnel, and then only if requirements of the civilian population have been taken into account. Subject to the provisions of other international Conventions, the Occupying Power shall make arrangements to ensure that fair value is paid for any requisitioned goods.

. . . .

Geneva Convention, *supra* note 19, art. 55.

44.

An army of occupation can only take possession of cash, funds, and realizable securities which are strictly the property of the State, depots of arms, means of transport, stores and supplies, and, generally, all movable property belonging to the State which may be used for military operation.

All appliances, whether on land, at sea, or in the air, adapted for the transmission of news, or for the transport of persons or things, exclusive of cases governed by naval law, depots of arms, and, generally, all kinds of ammunition of war, may be seized, even if they belong to private individuals, but must be restored and compensation fixed when peace is made.

Hague Regulations, *supra* note 18, art. 53.

45.

The occupying state shall be regarded only as administrator and usufructuary of public buildings, real estate, forests, and agricultural estates belonging to the hostile state, and situated in the occupied country. It must safeguard the capital of these properties and administer them in accordance with the rules of usufruct.

*Id.* art. 55.

Commenting on the restrictions imposed by the law of usufruct, McDougal and Feliciano write that 'as a practical matter, the applicable specific provisions are simply that the occupant must not wantonly dissipate or destroy the public resources and may not permanently (*i.e.,* for the indefinite future) alienate them'. M. McDougal & F. Feliciano, *supra* note 10, at 812–13.

46. This rule has been discussed in the context of exploitation of existing

oil fields and exploration for new ones in the Israeli-held Sinai. Cummings, 'Oil Resources in Occupied Arab Territories Under the Law of Belligerent Occupation', *9 J. Int'l L. & Econ.* 533 (1974) (oil resources may not be exploited); and, taking the opposite view, Gerson, 'Offshore Oil Exploration by a Belligerent Occupant: The Gulf of Suez Dispute' *71 Am. J. Int'l L.* 725 (1977).

47. Articles 51 and 52 of the Charter permit individual and collective self-defense measures as an exception to the general proscription in article 2, paragraph 4 against the use or threat of force in interstate relations. U.N. Charter arts. 51–52.

48. Harvard Research in International Law, 'Draft Convention on the Rights and Duties of States in Case of Aggression', reprinted in *33 Am. J. Int'l L. (Supp.)* 819, 828, 886 art. 3 and comments (1939). Seyersted states, 'It can no longer be maintained that the laws of war apply equally in all respects to the aggressors and the defenders. Basically the aggressor should not derive from his illegal act any rights under the customary laws of war'. F. Seyersted, *United Nations Forces in the Law of Peace and War* 224 (1966). Wright, 'The Outlawry of War and the Law of War', *47 Am. J. Int'l L.* 365, 367 (1953), also supports this view.

49. 99 F. Supp. 602 (D. Utah 1951). This was an action for enforcement of a promissory note given by defendant while a prisoner of war of the Japanese army of occupation of the Philippines. The district court held that regulations of the Japanese army of occupation, which specified currency to be used in the Philippines, was a valid regulation of a belligerent occupant and would be recognized by courts of this country. *Id.* at 611–12.

50. *Id.* at 610.

51. United States v. Krauch (I. G. Farben Case); *VIII Trials of War Criminals Before the Nuernberg Military Tribunals* 1081, 1137 (1948). *See also* United States v. List (Hostage Case), *XI Trials of War Criminals Before the Nuernberg Military Tribunals* 1230, 1247 (1948), wherein the Court states 'that International Law makes no distinction between a lawful and unlawful occupant in dealing with the *respective duties of occupant and population* in occupied territory' (emphasis added).

Fraleigh makes the point most dramatically that non-application of the 'defensive' concept is limited to the management sphere:

> The law supposes that Germans and Japanese may be sentenced to death for waging an aggressive war, but that the validity of their actions affecting property in occupied territories is to be determined by the same rules as are applied to actions of a belligerent fighting a defensive war.

Fraleigh, 'The Validity of Acts of Enemy Occupation Authorities Affecting Property Rights,' *35 Cornell L.Q.* 89, 93 (1949).

52. See cases cited in notes 49–51 *supra;* I. Vasarhelyi, *Restitution in International Law* 51–66 (1964); Martin 'Private Property, Rights, and Interest in the Paris Peace Treaties,' *24 Brit. Y.B. Int'l L.* 273, 276–82 (1947).

53. For an excellent study of employment of these means in the termination of occupations from the 17th century to World War II, see R. Randle, *The Origins of Peace* 5–10 (1973).
54. 'Customary' international law is 'based upon the consent of nations extending over a period of time of sufficient duration to cause it to become crystallized into a rule of conduct'. I. G. Hackworth, *Digest of International Law* 1 (1940). 'Conventional' international law has its basis in doctrine and treaties. *See* Virally, 'The Sources of International Law', in *Manual of Public International Law* 128 (M. Sorenson ed. 1968).
55. 'All Members shall refrain in their international relations from the threat or use of force against the territorial integrity or political independence of any state, or in any other manner inconsistent with the Purposes of the United Nations.' U.N. Charter art. 2, para. 4.
56. 'When the act alleged to be creative of a new [territorial] right is in violation of an existing rule of customary or conventional International Law . . . the act in question is tainted with invalidity and is incapable of producing legal results beneficial to the wrongdoer in the form of new title or otherwise.' *Lauterpacht–Oppenheim* 141–2 (8th ed., 1955); *See* Schwebel, 'What Weight to Conquest?', *64 Am. J. Int'l L.* 346 (1970).
57. Thus Professor Kelsen states, 'States are obliged to respect the territorial integrity of other states; but a violation of this obligation does not exclude the change of the legal situation. The principle advocated by some writers—*ex injuria jus non oritur* . . .—does not, or not without important exceptions, apply in international law.' H. Kelsen, *Principles of International Law* 215–16 (1952).
58. I. Lauterpacht–Oppenheim, *supra* note 56, at 142.
59. J. Brierly, *The Law of Nations* 172–73 (1963). In agreement are I. Brownlie, *Principles of Public International Law* 417 (1966); I. D. O'Connell, *International Law* 432 (1970); Lauterpacht, 'The Limits of the Operation of the Law of War', *30 Brit. Y.B.Int'l L.* 206, 239 (1953). *But cf.* earlier expressions of Professor Lauterpacht on this subject in Lauterpacht, 'Rules of Warfare in an Unlawful War', in *Law and Politics in the World Community* (Festschrift für Hans Kelsen 1953). (Professor Lauterpacht's view changed with time).
60. Regarding the development of the *bellum justum* doctrine and its distinction from the present lawful-unlawful dichotomy, see the excellent discussion in A. Levontin, *The Myth of International Security* 15–69 (1958); Graham, 'The 1974 Diplomatic Conference on the Law of War: A Victory for Political Causes and a Return to the "Just War" Concept of the Eleventh Century', *32 Wash. & Lee L. Rev.* 25 (1975); Kunz, 'Bellum Justum and Bellum Legale', *45 Am. J. Int'l L.* 528 (1951). Regarding the perseverance of the 'just war' doctrine in Islam, see Khadduri, 'Islam and the Modern Law of Nations', *50 Am. J. Int'l L.* 358 (1956).
61. Vienna Convention on the Law of Treaties, opened for signature May 23,1969, art. 52, U.N. Doc. A/CONF. 39/27 (1969), reprinted in *63*

*Am. J. Int'l L.* 875 (1969). Regarding further attempts to codify the prohibitions on the use of aggressive force, see the recent Soviet proposal in the United Nations for a World Treaty on the Non-Use of Force, 31 U.N. GAOR, U.N. Doc. A/31/243 (Sept. 28, 1976); and American opposition thereto on the grounds that the present U.N. Charter provisions suffice, *76 Dep't State Bull.* 30–35 (1977).

62. S.C. Res. 242, 22 U.N. SCOR, Resolutions and Decisions of the Security Council 8, U.N. Doc. A/INF/22/Rev. 2 (1967). Dr. Rosalyn Higgins interprets this phrase as being a restatement of the principle of *ex injuria jus non oritur*. Higgins, 'The June War: The United Nations and Legal Background', *3 J. Contemp. History* 253, 271 (1968).

63. U.N. Charter art. 51.

64. See the suggestions by various states that the 'principle of priority' be upheld as an objective criterion leaving no room for any justification of preventive war. 25 U.N. GAOR, Report of the Special Committee on the Question of Defining Aggression, Supp. (No. 19) 10, U.N. Doc. A/8019 (1971).

Henkin states, 'I have found less than plausible any reading of Article 51 which would permit unilateral force as an exception to the prohibitions of Article 2, other than in the one instance clearly expressed: in self-defense "if an armed attack occurs".' Henkin, 'Force, Intervention and Neutrality in International Law', [1963] *Proc. Am. Soc'y Int'l L.* 147, 148.

Kunz argues, 'The "threat of aggression" does not justify self-defense under Art. 51. Now in municipal law self-defense is justified against an actual danger, but it is sufficient that the danger is *imminent*. The "imminent" armed attack does not suffice under Art. 51.' Kunz, 'Individual and Collective Self-Defense in Article 51 of the Charter of the United Nations', *41 Am. J. Int'l L.* 872, 878 (1947). See also H. Kelsen, *supra* note 57, at 797–98.

65. Indeed, insistence on a strict interpretation of 'first bomb' approach has largely lost favor with the international community. This becomes clear upon an examination of the declarations and voting patterns of those states charged with the responsibility of formulating an acceptable definition of aggression. The Soviet position, dating back to 1933, was that the state which first committed an unlawful act should automatically be deemed the aggressor. The West differed. Over the course of the last twenty years, it had taken the position that the intent of the action, the *animus aggressionis,* should be given no lesser consideration than the chronological fact of who dealt the first blow. II B. Ferencz, *supra* note 5, at 32.

66. M. McDougal & F. Feliciano, *supra* note 10, at 234–38, and authorities cited therein. 'Further, in the process of formulating the prohibition of unilateral coercion in Article 2(4), it was made quite clear at San Francisco that the traditional permission of self-defense was not intended to be abridged and attenuated but, on the contrary, to be reserved and maintained.' *Id.* at 235. See D. Bowett, *Self-Defense in International Law* 187–89, 191–92 (1958).

67. Blockade of the coasts of a state, for example, has been held sufficient. The 1974 Definition of Aggression, *supra* note 5, provides in article 3(c) that 'the blockade of the ports or coasts of a State by the armed forces of another State' constitutes aggression. Since the Resolution on the Definition of Aggression states that it should not 'be construed as in any way enlarging or diminishing the scope of the Charter', G. A. Res. 3314, *supra* note 5, art. 6, it should be understood as interpreting here the 'inherent' right of self-defense provision of article 51 of the Charter.

    In other instances, an adapted version of Daniel Webster's formula in the classic case of the *P. S. Caroline* has been held the test. The *Caroline* was the intended instrument of an armed expedition, organized in the United States, intended to be used in the struggle to wrest Canada from Britain in 1841. Shots having been actually fired into Canada by the expedition, a British force from Canada crossed into the U.S., seized and burned the *Caroline,* and shot two of her crew. Webster provided that there need be shown a 'necessity of self-defense, instant, overwhelming—leaving no choice of means and no moment for deliberation.' Furthermore, 'the act, justified by the necessity of self-defense, must be limited by that necessity and kept clearly within it.' Letter of Daniel Webster to H. Fox (Apr. 24, 1874), *29 Brit. & Foreign St. Papers* 1129, 1138 (1841). See Correspondence between Great Britain and The United States, respecting the Arrest and Imprisonment of Mr. McLeod, for the Destruction of the Steamboat *Caroline,* 29 *Brit. & Foreign St. Papers* 1126 (1841). Webster's choice of words was probably influenced by the circumstances of the particular case. In using the phrase 'no moment for deliberation', Webster may have been thinking that reference to the United States Government's knowledge of the *Caroline's* purpose and objection thereto might have prevented the necessity for the violation of American territory. As interpreted by scholars and statesmen, the 'instant' branch of the principle of self-defense has been deemed rhetorical and replaced by the necessity of exhaustion of remedies. D. Bowett, *supra* note 66; Brownlie, 'The Use of Force in Self-Defense', *37 Brit. Y.B. Int'l L.* 183 (1961).

68. D. Bowett, *supra* note 66; Brownlie, *supra* note 67; McDougal, 'The Soviet-Cuban Quarantine and Self-Defense', *57 Am. J. Int'l L.* 597 (1963); Wright, 'The Cuban Quarantine', *57 Am. J. Int'l L.* 546 (1963).
69. M. McDougal & F. Feliciano, *supra* note 10, at 218.
70. *U.N. Charter* arts. 39–51.
71. Thompson, 'Collective Security Reexamined', in *From Collective Security to Preventive Diplomacy* 285 (J. Larus ed. 1965).
72. Invocations of 'self-defense' by states prior to actual armed attack include India's entry into the Bangladesh-Pakistan War in 1972, the United States 'quarantine' of Cuba during the 1962 missile crisis, the British-French-Israeli action in the Sinai in 1956, Pakistan's entry into Kashmir in 1948, and the Egyptian attack on Israel in 1973. Regarding Egypt's justification for entry into the 1973 war, see Shihata,

'Destination Embargo of Arab Oil: Its Legality Under International Law', *68 Am. J. Int'l L.* 591, 607 (1974). *But see* Rostow, 'The Illegality of the Arab Attack on Israel in 1973', *69 Am. J. Int'l L.* 272 (1975). Although it has been suggested that the Israeli action in 1973 provides an example of a willingness to sustain an initial attack for purposes of public image, the real explanation for Israeli inaction seems to be that the Israeli government simply did not believe that the probability of an Egyptian attack was very great. C. Herzog, *The War of Atonement* 52–54 (1975).

73. Hoffman, 'International Law and the Control of Force', in *The Relevance of International Law* 21, 29 (K. Deutsch & S. Hoffman eds. 1968).

74. As one author has observed:

Even internal law recognizes that acts committed in self defense to avert an illegitimate attack which has 'commenced' or is 'impending' are legitimate. In this situation it would evidently be impossible to expect that the party attacked should wait and try to obtain his rights by asserting them before the courts. The same must be all the more valid in International Law where there is no organized administration of justice to turn to.

A. Ross, *A Textbook of International Law 244* (1947). A generation ago, Elihu Root described an appropriate context for measuring claims to self-defense:

It is well understood that the exercise of the right of self-protection may and frequently does extend in its effect beyond the limits of the territorial jurisdiction of the state exercising it. The strongest example probably would be the mobilization of an army by another Power immediately across the frontier. Every act done by the other Power may be within its own territory. Yet the country threatened by the state of facts is justified in protecting itself by immediate war. . . . [T]hat is to say, [there is a] right of every sovereign state to protect itself by preventing a condition of affairs in which it will be too late to protect itself.

Root, 'The Real Monroe Doctrine', *8 Am. J. Int'l L.* 427, 432 (1914), quoted in A Chayes, *The Cuban Missile Crisis* 124–25 (1974).

75. Article 2 of the 1974 Definition of Aggression, *supra* note 5, entitled 'Evidentiary Value of the First Strike and Other Circumstances', states that:

The first use of armed force by a State in contravention of the Charter shall constitute *prima-facie* evidence of an act of aggression although the Security Council may, in conformity with the Charter, conclude that a determination that an act of aggression has been committed would not be justified in light of other relevant circumstances including the fact that the acts concerned or consequences are not of sufficient gravity.

The first salient point to be noted in the above article is that, despite the headnote's reference to 'Evidentiary Value of the First Strike', the text thereof addresses itself to 'the first use of armed force by a State *in contravention* of the Charter' (emphasis added). It thus appears to sanction some first strikes as within the Charter.

Secondly, the meaning of 'prima facie' was left far from clear. Some states took the position that it created a presumption of aggression, rebuttable only by a Security Council finding to the contrary. To others, it simply gave rise to a suspicion that there might be aggression which, for confirmation, would require a Security Council finding to that effect. II B. Ferencz, *supra* note 5, at 33.

Likewise, the term 'other relevant circumstances' was left to individual interpretation. Those who favored consideration of *animus aggressionis* insisted that it was included. Those who had been opposed to considerations of intent continued to insist on its irrelevance. *Id.*

76. Letter of Daniel Webster to H. Fox, *supra* note 67.

77. The Soviet Union is the forerunner and leading proponent of this view. Ginsburgs, '"Wars of National Liberation" and the Modern Law of Nations—The Soviet Thesis' *29 Law & Contemp. Prob.* 910–42 (1964). Contrast Soviet views on justifiable intervention in support of 'national liberation movements' with views on justifiable intervention for preserving 'socialist internationalism' in the case of Hungary (1956) and Czechoslovakia (1968). P. Bergmann, *Self-Determination: The Case of Czechoslovakia 1968–1969* (1972). For a general discussion, see U. Umozurike, *Self-Determination in International Law* 192–203 (1972); 'Political Rights in the Developing Countries', [1966] *Proc. Am. Soc'y Int'l L.* 141, 149–50 (panel discussion).

78. The first claim in the post-World War II era to a right of foreign intervention on behalf of self-determination was made by the Arab states invading Palestine in 1948. The League of Arab States formally justified its armed intervention as being based on defense of the inhabitants' right of self-determination to establish a unitary government based on majority rule. Cablegram from the League of Arab States to the U.N. Secretary General (May 15, 1948), 3 U.N. SCOR, Supp. (May 1948) 83, U.N. Doc. S/745 (1948). Similar cablegrams were sent by Egypt, 3 U.N. SCOR (292d mtg.) 2, U.N. Doc. S/743 (1948); and Transjordan, 3 U.N. SCOR, Supp. (May 1948) 90, U.N. Doc. S/748 (1948). The Security Council rejected the claim, deeming the Arab action a violation of Charter obligations. 3 U.N. SCOR (302d mtg.) 41–42, U.N. Doc. S/p.v. 302 (1948).

During the course of the 1966 deliberations of the U.N. Special Committee on Principles of International Law concerning Friendly Relations and Co-operation among States, a proposal affirming the principle of self-determination was only narrowly defeated. It would have established that 'peoples who are deprived of their legitimate rights of self-determination and complete freedom are entitled to exercise their inherent right of self-defense, by virtue of which they may receive assistance from other States.' 21 U.N. GAOR, Special Committee on Principles of International Law Concerning Friendly Relations and Co-operation Among States, U.N. Doc. A/AC. 125/L. 31 (1966).

79. Article 7 of the 1974 Definition of Aggression, *supra* note 5, states:

Nothing in this definition, and in particular article 3, could in any way prejudice the right to self-determination, freedom and independence, as derived from the Charter, of peoples forcibly deprived of that right and referred to in the Declaration on Principles of International Law Concerning Friendly Relations and Co-operation among States in accordance with the Charter of the United Nations, particularly peoples under colonialist and racist regimes or other forms of alien domination nor the right of these peoples to struggle to that end and to seek and receive support, in accordance with the principles of the Charter and in conformity with the above mentioned Declaration.

Article 7 is, if anything, replete with undefined terms—'peoples', 'alien domination', 'colonial and racist regimes', the right 'to seek and receive support'. Indeed 'support' is never defined to include military assistance and, moreover, such support must be in conformity with the principles of the Charter which presumably deny military intervention in such circumstances. It is possible to characterize this provision as part of the 'unmistakeable trend appearing from various recent U.N. instruments to use language so ambiguous that it remain[s] possible to argue that force could lawfully be used to achieve objectives which, in the party using force, [appear] to have won U.N. approval.' II B. Ferencz, *supra* note 5, at 48, *See* Stone, 'Hopes and Loopholes in the 1974 Definition of Aggression', *71 Am. J. Int'l L.* 225 (1977).

80. For general discussion favorable to humanitarian intervention, see Lillich, 'Forcible Self-Help by States to Protect Human Rights',*53 Iowa L. Rev.* 325 (1967); Lillich, 'Forcible Self-Help Under International Law', *22 Naval War C. Rev.* 53 (1970); McDougal & Reisman,' 'Responses', *3 Int'l Law.* 438 (1969). Opposing the existence of a right of humanitarian intervention, see Franck & Rodley, 'After Bangladesh: The Law of Humanitarian Intervention by Military Force', *67 Am. J. Int'l L.* 275 (1973).

81. Convention on the Prevention and Punishment of the Crime of Genocide, adopted by the General Assembly of the United Nations, Dec. 9, 1948, *78 U.N.T.S.* 277 [hereinafter cited as Genocide Convention].

82. Article 1 of the Genocide Convention, *supra* note 81, states: 'The Contracting Parties confirm that genocide, whether committed in time of peace or in time of war, is a crime under international law which they undertake to prevent and punish.'

83. Genocide Convention, *supra* note 81, art. 6. The additional relevant provisions merely states that the Contracting Parties should enact legislation for the punishment of genocide, *id.* art. 5; that offenders should indeed be punished, *id.* art. 4; and that, as was undoubtedly beyond dispute, any Contracting Party could call upon a competent organ of the United Nations to take such action as it might consider appropriate, *id.* art. 9. Despite the innocuous nature of its provisions, the United States has nevertheless refused to accede to the Convention

for the fear of interference in America's internal politics. Finch, 'The Genocide Convention', *43 Am. J. Int'l L.* 732 (1949); Kunz, 'United Nations Convention on Genocide', *43 Am. J. Int'l L.* 738 (1949); McDougal & Arens, 'The Genocide Convention and the Constitution', *3 Vand. L. Rev.* 683 (1950). Regarding the 1974 Senate debate on ratification of the Genocide Convention, excerpts may be found in *Investigation into Certain Past Instances of Genocide and Exploration of Policy Options for the Future: Hearings Before the Subcomm. on Future Foreign Policy Research and Development of the House Comm. on International Relations,* 94th Cong., 2d Sess. 139 (1976).

84. 9 U.N. GAOR, Sixth Committee (404th–20th, 433–34th mtgs.) 37–124, 175–78, U.N. Docs. A/C.6/SR. 404–20, 433–34 (1954). The representative from Greece stated that he favored a formula which would specify cases in which the use of armed force, for a purpose other than self-defense or in pursuance of a decision of a competent organ of the United Nations, might *fail* to constitute aggression. By way of example, he mentioned the hypothetical case of two states, one of which had in its territory an ethnic minority composed of *nationals of the other*. If State A began to exterminate that minority, and State B, *after* appealing in vain to the competent organs of the United Nations, decided to use force against State A, would State B be an *aggressor* or not? U.N. GAOR, Sixth Committee (409th mtg.) 65, U.N. Doc. A/C.6/SR. 409 (1954).

85. The statement of the Israeli representative reflected the prevailing views.

It seems advisable to refrain from any action that might be construed as authorizing military intervention in favour of a co-national minority. Humanitarian grounds had frequently been invoked to justify intervention, although the true motives had been very different . . . . Since the Second World War, moreover, the problem of minorities had been greatly reduced. Consequently, neither the realities of modern life, nor the accepted concepts of legal and illegal use of force, nor the teachings of history, could justify the use of force in such a hypothesis.

9 U.N. GAOR, Sixth Committee (412th mtg.) 83, U.N. Doc. A/C.6/SR. 412 (1954).

86. Statement of the Chinese representative, 9 U.N. GAOR, Sixth Committee (417th mtg.) 110, U.N. Doc. A/C.6/SR. 417 (1954). The Panamanian representative also summarized the Sixth Committee deliberations on this point.

[Some representatives] had tried to imagine cases, apart from those arising under the Charter, in which the use of armed force would not constitute *aggression*. The representative of Greece had spoken of the hypothetical case of armed intervention by a State to halt the extermination by another State of part of the former's population on racial, religious or other grounds. Such intervention would certainly conflict with the principles of the Charter. In such a case, the provisions of the Convention on the Prevention and Punishment of the Crime of Genocide would apply or else the competent organ should be asked to apply enforcement measures.

Statement of Panamanian representative, 9 U.N. GAOR, Sixth Committee (418th mtg.) 113–14, U.N. Doc. A/C.6/SR. 418 (1954) (emphasis added).

87. In the 1968 Proclamation of Tehran which was subsequently adopted by the International Conference on Human Rights, the text provides that as the 'policy of "apartheid", condemned as a crime against humanity, continues seriously to disturb international peace and security . . . [i]t is therefore *imperative* for the international community to use *every possible means to eradicate* this evil. The *struggle* against apartheid is recognized as legitimate' (emphasis added). Text in International Conference on Human Rights, Final Act, U.N. Doc. A/CONF.32/41. 'Every means' and 'struggle' appear to encompass OAU African Liberation.

88. McDougal & Reisman, *supra* note 80, at 444.

89. *Id.*

90. One learned author concludes that 'state practice justifies the conclusion that no genuine case of humanitarian intervention has occurred, with the possible exception of the occupation of Syria in 1860 and 1861.' I. Brownlie, *supra* note 59, at 340. Lillich disagrees. Lillich, 'Forcible Self-Help Under International Law', *supra* note 80. Relatively few of the instances Lillich cites appear to stand up to careful scrutiny. Claydon, 'Humanitarian Intervention and International Law', *1 Queen's Intra. L.J.* 36 (1969); Franck & Rodley, *supra* note 80, at 279–83.

91. H. Feingold, *The Politics of Rescue: The Roosevelt Administration and the Holocaust, 1938–1945* (1970), documents the view of the United States government prior to its entry into the war that Germany's Jewish policies were an internal matter and, later, that any effort at rescue or destruction through aerial bombardment of concentration camp facilities would be an unwarranted dissipation of energies from the overall war effort.

92. *International Commission of Jurists, Tibet and the Chinese People's Republic* 3 (1970).

93. Lillich 'Forcible Self-Help Under International Law', *supra* note 80, at 62; Weisberg, 'The Congo Crisis 1964: A Case Study in Humanitarian Intervention', *12 Va. J. Int'l L.* 261 (1972).

94. The African states overwhelmingly supported Nigeria and rejected humanitarian operations from relief organizations as well as from the individual states and United Nations agencies. *4 and 5 Africa Res. Bull.* (1968).

95. India had not sought military intervention as soon as the mass slaughter of Bengalis became known. It was only nine months later, when Pakistan committed alleged 'aggression' against India, that India asserted its right to intervene. This 'aggression' was alleged to be of a two-fold nature: 'civil', insofar as India was forced to strain its

resources to care for 10 million people who came to India as refugees; and 'armed', insofar as the Pakistani air force attacked India's cities and military airfields. Statement by the Representative of India, 26 U.N. GAOR (2003d mtg.) 13–17, U.N. Doc. A/p.v. 2003 (1971). The great majority of the General Assembly was unconvinced by India's reasoning and passed a resolution calling for an immediate ceasefire and Indian withdrawal from West Pakistan. G.A. Res. 2793, 26 U.N. GAOR, Supp. (No. 29) 3, U.N. Doc. A/8429 (1971). India refused to pay the resolution any heed. By December 15, India was able to obtain the surrender of all West Pakistani forces in Bangladesh.

The members of the United Nations, then, leaned toward 'a fresh concern for a political settlement' subsequent to the *fait accompli, viz.* the surrender of West Pakistan's army and the grant of recognition by many states of Bangladesh's status as an independent state. Yet the United Nations condemned India's intervention into Bangladesh, even insofar as it contained a humanitarian aspect.

Chapter II

# The Palestine Controversy: Historical and Juridical Basis

The problems of scholarship and diplomacy raised by the present international debate on territorial rights in the Middle East conflict are not new. The question of the admissibility of territorial acquisition by force, now appearing so current, was the subject of intense diplomatic examination during the course of and in the aftermath of the first Arab-Israeli war. Then as now, the issue posed was whether Israeli withdrawal from newly conquered territory need be immediate or, alternatively, reserved for execution within the framework of a peace treaty. Then too, the debate revolved around the legitimate basis of claims for territorial retention or reversion.

A sense of historical continuity regarding these issues seems to have been largely lost. Historical perspective regarding the regional and major power interests in the conflict appears to have suffered the same fate. They are examined as if immutable in their present state, with little recall of their record of flux. In this setting, resolution of conflict in conformity with international law becomes impossible; the requisite elements of identification and analysis of issues and interests are missing or treated superficially. The discussion that follows attempts to remedy this defect. Drawing largely on primary material and some of the better secondary sources, it traces the present dilemmas of the West Bank controversy to basic issues left unresolved by the Palestine Mandate and the 1948-1949 War.

## A. 1917-1949: THE BASIS OF THE TERRITORIAL DISPUTE

### 1. *The Mandate System*

Upon the defeat of Turkey on October 30, 1918, nine-tenths of her imperial holdings in the Middle East, from the Nile to the Euphrates and from the Mediterranean to Baghdad, fell under British control. The remaining portion fell to the French. The problem that now faced Britain was how to retain control of this vast region, which it had always coveted,[1] while making good the pledges made in the course of acquiring it and remaining true to the new principles of non-annexation and self-determination of peoples introduced by President Wilson into the Paris Peace Conference.[2]

In 1915, in an exchange of letters between Sherif Husain of Hejaz and Sir Henry McMahon, British High Commissioner at Cairo, a pledge of British support for Arab independence in the regions of contemporary Syria and Iraq was made in exchange for Arab military assistance against Turkey.[3] In 1916, during the course of hostilities, an Anglo-French accord, the Sykes-Picot Agreement, had provided for a post-war settlement whereby France would get Cilicia (Syria and Lebanon), Britain, southern Mesopotamia (Iraq), while Palestine was, essentially, to be internationalized.[4] Eighteen months later the Balfour Declaration was issued by Foreign Secretary A. J. Balfour stating:

> His Majesty's Government views with favour the establishment in Palestine of a national home for the Jewish people, and will use their best endeavours to facilitate the achievement of this object, it being clearly understood that nothing shall be done which may prejudice the civil and religious rights of the non-Jewish community in Palestine, or the rights and political status enjoyed by the Jews in any other country.[5]

Passage of the Balfour Declaration angered the Arabs. They maintained that the Declaration's terms were inconsistent with those of the McMahon-Husain understanding. Based on the fact that the pledge to Husain omitted explicit reference to Palestine, it has been claimed that Palestine was not excluded from the area in which the British promised to help the Arabs gain independence. This is untrue. The British government and all of the officials connected with the negotiations have repeatedly declared that their intention was that '(t)he whole of Palestine west of the Jordan (be) excluded from Sir Henry McMahon's pledge.'[6]

Britain's principal motivation for controlling Palestine was to achieve a 'strategical buffer' for Egypt and the Suez Canal.[7] This imperial ambition was to become continually more difficult to reconcile with the new mandate system that evolved. The League of Nations Covenant provided that:

> To these colonies and territories which as a consequence of the late war have ceased to be under the sovereignty of the states which formerly governed them and which are inhabited by peoples not yet able to stand by themselves under the strenuous conditions of the modern world, there should be applied the principle that the well-being and development of such peoples form a sacred trust of civilization. . .[8]

Mandates were divided into three classes—A. B. and C. 'C' Mandates, such as South West Africa (Namibia) were to be administered under the law of the Mandatory Power as integral parts of its territory, subject to certain safeguards in the interests of the indigenous population.[9] 'B' Mandates were created for territory in Central Africa and covered territories 'at such a stage of civilization that the Mandatory must be responsible for the administration of the territory, subject to certain conditions.'[10] By contrast, Syria, The Lebanon, Mesopotamia (Iraq) and Palestine were designated 'A' Mandates and, as such, recognized as 'communities that have reached a stage of development where their existence as independent nations can be provisionally recognized, subject to the rendering of administrative advice and assistance by a Mandatory until such time as they are able to stand alone.'[12] The right of these regions to sovereignty was recognized, but deferred and placed in the trust of the Mandatory Power,[13] subject to the ultimate control of the League of Nations,[14] until responsible self government could be established.[15]

Thus, when on April 25, 1920 the League of Nations conferred the Class A Mandate for Palestine on Britain,[16] Britain undertook an international legal obligation, despite any contrary designs it may have harbored, to fulfill the terms of the Palestine Mandate whereby sovereignty, now held in abeyance, would vest in the beneficiary people or peoples of the Mandate upon its termination and the achievement of independence.

## 2. *The Special Problem of the Palestine Mandate*

The Palestine Mandate represented a special problem because two 'peoples'—the indigenous Arab population and the Jewish people throughout the world—vied for the designation as the beneficiary people entitled to exercise sovereignty upon the Mandate's end. Jews constituted only 12 per cent of Palestine's population at the time of the Mandate's inception.[17] Yet the Mandate for Palestine, by virtue of its incorporation of the Balfour Declaration calling for the establishment of a national home for the Jewish people in Palestine, gave priority to the national aspirations of a non-inhabitant people over those of an indigenous populace. In this respect the Palestine Mandate was *'sui generis'* among mandated territories.[18]

Some writers have suggested the illegality of the Palestine Mandate's incorporation of the Balfour Declaration on the grounds that by the terms of the Covenant the 'sacred trust of civilization' was to be exercised solely for the inhabitant people of mandated territories.[19] This argument is pointless. The fact that the Palestine Mandate was *'sui generis'* in the Mandate System in no way detracts from its legality. As Judge Moore, in his opinion in the Permanent Court of International Justice in the *Mavrommatis Case* put it, the embodiment of the Balfour Declaration in the Palestine Mandate was 'an (international) legislative act of the Council.'[20]

The question remains, however, as to whether the Jews were intended to be the exclusive beneficiary people under the terms of the Palestine Mandate. In an attempt to explain the issue Britain issued the Churchill White Paper on June 3, 1922.[21] It provided that Palestine was not to be reconstituted as 'the' Jewish national home but rather that the Balfour Declaration envisaged only the establishment 'in' Palestine of 'a' national home for the Jewish people.[22] The Zionist Executive was required to approve the Churchill interpretation of the Balfour Declaration as a condition precedent to British assumption of the Palestine Mandate. Dr. Chaim Weizmann, Chairman of the Zionist Executive, acceded to this request.[23] The Council of the League of Nations then approved on July 24, 1922 the British Mandate over Palestine which included in its terms the duty of fulfilling the Balfour Declaration, as officially interpreted by the Churchill White Paper.

The Palestine Mandate included the whole of historic Palestine east and west of the Jordan River. Article 25 of the Mandate provided, however, that the Mandatory was authorized, upon the consent of the Council of the League of Nations, 'to postpone or withhold' existing provisions and to make special administrative provisions under the Mandate 'within the territories lying between the Jordan and the eastern boundary of Palestine.'[24] On September 16, 1922, nearly two months after the League's approval of the Palestine Mandate, the League Council gave its assent to a British proposal to suspend application of Jewish national rights under the Palestine Mandate to the area of Trans-Jordan. Commenting upon British motivation for this act, the *Palestine Royal Commission Report* stated:

> The field in which the Jewish National Home was to be established was understood, at the time of the Balfour Declaration, to be the whole of historic Palestine and the Zionists were seriously disappointed when Trans-Jordan was cut away from the field under Article 25. This was done . . . in obedience to the McMahon Pledge which was antecedent to the Balfour Declaration.[25]

Although the Churchill White Paper of 1922, published about three months prior to the League's assent to suspend application of the Jewish National Home provisions to Trans-Jordan, made no express mention of this impending event, it contained language foreshadowing the move. In its reference to the McMahon pledge as excluding 'the whole of Palestine west of the Jordan,' it left the clear implication that Palestine east of the Jordan was included in the pledge. Moreover, in stating that the 'terms of the Balfour Declaration (as incorporated into the Mandate) . . . *do not contemplate that Palestine as a whole* should be converted into Palestine but that such a Home should be founded *in* Palestine' (emphasis added), the impression was left that Cis-Jordan would be the area for creation of the Jewish National Home. When the Zionist Executive acquiesced to the terms of the Churchill White Paper as the blueprint for the form of political organization for the British Mandate over Palestine, they did so already cognizant that the Jewish National Home provisions would be limited to Cis- Jordan.[26]

During the early years of the Mandate, the Zionist Executive therefore devoted its efforts to increasing immigration and to laying the foundations for a future Jewish state encompassing Cis-Jordanian Palestine. From the beginning the indigenous Arab population opposed any application of the Balfour Declaration to any part of Palestine. In their view such action violated the espoused Arab rights to independence and self-determination in all of Palestine.[27] Attempts at Arab-Zionist rapprochement soon proved abortive as Arab leaders escalated the intensity of their demands and made it clear that they deemed them unnegotiable.

By 1937, the British Royal Commission to study the future of Palestine was able to report, unequivocally, that it would be impossible to obtain Arab acquiescence to minority status or even agreement to a bi-national state in Cis-Jordanian Palestine—or simply 'Palestine' as it became popularly called.[28]

The Commission concluded that:

> An irrepressible conflict has arisen between two national communities within the narrow bounds of one small country . . . There is no common ground between them. They differ in religion and in language. Their cultural and social life, their ways of thought and conduct. . . . In the Arab picture the Jews could only occupy the place they occupied in Arab Egypt or Arab Spain. The Arabs would be as much outside the Jewish picture as the Canaanites in the old land of Israel. The National Home, as we have said before, cannot be half-national. In these circumstances to maintain that Palestinian citizenship has any moral meaning is a mischievous pretense. Neither Arab nor Jew has any sense of service to a single State.[29]

It became clear that conversion of Palestine into either a Jewish or bi-national state in attempt to fulfill the Mandate's National Home provisions could not possibly be peacefully achieved and that, at best, it would require continual warfare between the Zionists and the Arabs of both Palestine and the surrounding states.[30] Accordingly the Royal Commission concluded that 'a scheme of partition (of Palestine into separate spheres of Jewish and Arab sovereignty) represented the best and most hopeful solution of the deadlock.'[31] The Royal Commission's partition plan contemplated the creation of only a very small Jewish state which would include the sub-districts of Acre, Safed, Tiberias, Nazareth, Haifa, and the City of Tel Aviv, and a sliver of territory south of Jaffa. The rest of Palestine, except for new Jerusalem and a corridor to it from the coast, would be Arab controlled—not as a new independent Palestine state but rather as the western sector of an expanded Trans-Jordan, now constituting a unitary Arab Palestine.

The Jewish leadership reacted to the Royal Commission's partition proposal with mixed feelings. Although it failed to accept the suggested scheme of partition, it empowered its Executive to enter into negotiation with Britain for further study aimed at implementation of partition.[32] The Arabs totally rejected the idea of partition and manifested their uncompromising disapproval in an outburst of sporadic demonstrations and violence in 1937 and 1938.[33] Britain, influenced by the intensity of Arab opposition to partition, withdrew its support.[34]

The subsequent holocaust which befell European Jewry in World War II crystallized Jewish demands for an immediate termination of the Mandate and establishment of a Jewish state.[35] Britain, in attempting to deal with these demands sought American cooperation and in October, 1945 instituted the Anglo-American Commission of Inquiry to: (1) 'examine political, economic and social conditions in Palestine as they bear upon the problem of Jewish immigration and (2) the position of the Jews in those countries of Europe where they have been the victims of Nazi and Fascist persecution.' The Committee, on April 30, 1946, reached its conclusions. Partition was rejected as impractical and a bi-national state was urged instead. But the report was stillborn. Britain rejected it as unmindful of British interests. The United States disapproved it as not sufficiently meeting Zionist demands. And all parties concerned scorned bi-nationalism as an ideal which had not a glimmer of a hope of succeeding.[36]

Finally, on February 14, 1947, Britain, apparently convinced that the Mandate was unworkable, concerned over the prospect of continuing to govern Palestine in light of escalating terrorism from both Jewish and Arab quarters and troubled by the world community's protest over British mismanagement of the Mandate, announced her desire to terminate her role as Mandatory and to refer the question of Palestine's future to the United Nations. On April 2, 1947, Britain requested a special session of the U.N. General Assembly to convene for the purpose of making recommendations under Article 10 of the Charter, concerning the future government of Palestine.[37] On November 29, 1947, the General Assembly voted in favor of the Palestine Partition Plan, as recommended by the United Nations Special Committee on Palestine (UNSCOP).[38] UNSCOP'S minority proposal, known as the 'Federal State Plan', was rejected. Partition was to take effect by the 1st of August, 1948 upon evacuation of Britain's armed forces from Palestine. The Jewish Agency accepted the Partition Resolution as the 'ultimate minimum acceptable.'[39] The Palestinian Arab representatives and those of the Arab States rejected it, unanimously declaring instead that they did not consider themselves bound by the resolution and that they reserved 'the full right to act freely in whatever way (they) deem fit, in accordance with the principles of right and justice.'[40]

### 3. *The 1947 General Assembly Partition Resolution*

Partition was the best and indeed only option available to the General Assembly in its attempts to provide the means whereby Arab and Jewish national interests in Palestine could be reconciled without bloodshed and without the need for continued international supervision of the Mandate. In the deliberations undertaken by the General Assembly in its quest to reconcile these conflicting interests, the United Nations

General Assembly assumed the functions relative to supervision of mandated territories which had previously been performed by the League of Nations.[41] In this capacity, the General Assembly's action in voting for partition may have been legally binding and not merely recommendatory, as General Assembly resolutions normally are.

Initially, at least, the Zionist position backed mainly by the Soviet Union was that the Partition Resolution had a legally binding effect;[42] the Arab posture was that it did not.[43]

In its 1971 Namibia opinion, *Legal Consequences for States of the Continued Presence of South Africa in Namibia Notwithstanding Security Council Resolution 276 (1970)*, the International Court of Justice had an opportunity to reexamine the question of whether the General Assembly has competence to adopt binding resolutions when acting in its capacity as successor to the League in reference to mandated territory. Addressing itself to the scope and legal effect of General Assembly Resolution 2145 (XXI) (1966) declaring that South Africa's mandate over South-West Africa having been terminated ('South Africa has no other right to administer the territory'), the International Court of Justice pronounced:

> This is not a finding on facts, but the formulation of a legal situation. For it would not be correct to assume that, because the General Assembly is in principle vested with recommendatory powers, it is disbarred from adopting, in specific cases within the framework of its competence, resolutions which make determinations or have operative design.[44]

The decision is, however, hardly a model of clarity in resolving the issue of whether the General Assembly resolutions affecting mandated territory can be legally binding. Most of the concurring opinions of the Justices took the position that General Assembly resolutions had binding effect in such circumstances.[45] The official decision, however, favored the view that General Assembly Resolution 2145 and others of a similar nature obtain binding legal effect only on receiving the endorsement of the Security Council.

Whatever conclusion one may reach as to the merits of the recommendatory or obligatory debate surrounding the 1947 Partition Resolution, it is clear that the majority of the then assembled states believed that the Resolution could have legally binding as well as practical effect only after a Security Council decision to implement the Partition Resolution. Indeed, the Resolution itself called upon the Security Council to implement its terms. But this was a commitment which the world community proved reluctant to undertake. Thus, although after the Resolution's passage the Secretary General called upon the Security Council to consider giving instructions to the Palestine Commission 'with a view of implementing the (Partition) Resolution of the General Assembly,'[46] the Security Council, nevertheless, refused to take any action to enforce the Partition Resolution. Trygve Lie, then Secretary General, was later to write that the deliberations of the Security Council over enforcement of the Partition Plan symbolized to him 'the most disheartening head-in-the-sand moments of the Chamberlain appeasement era.'[47] The explanation of the Security Council's inaction probably lies in the fact that, as Professor J. C. Hurewitz has put it, the then unfolding international events made '(t)he Palestine issue in the Fall of 1947 (and 1948) an Arab-Zionist contest within an Anglo-American controversy about to be drawn into the Soviet-American cold war.'[48] In the absence of any meaningful commitment by the major powers to enforcement of partition of Palestine, and in the face of a pan-Arab commitment to the creation of a unitary state in Palestine, war became inevitable.

## B. WAR OVER PALESTINE, 1948–1949

### 1. *Arab Intervention into Palestine, 1948: U.N. Security Council Inaction*

Upon passage of the U.N. Partition Resolution in November, 1947, the Palestinian Arabs, encouraged, trained and armed by the Arab states, commenced an escalating campaign of guerilla activities aimed at frustrating partition.[49] Starting in January, 1948, there began a steadily growing incursion into Palestine of armed Arab irregulars from neighboring states.[50] As the major Western powers at the United Nations vacillated, the Arab states drew the conclusion that an escalating violence in the region might lead to either withdrawal of the Partition Resolution or the refusal by the Security Council to enforce it in the event of joint Arab military intervention into Palestine. These assumptions proved to be well founded.

Reacting to the Arab threat to forcefully oppose implementation of the partition, the Chairman of the United Nations Palestine Commission urged the Security Council, more than three months prior to the announced date of termination of the Palestine Mandate on May 15, 1948, to consider organizing the international security force recommended in the Partition Resolution, for the purpose of implementing its terms. [51] Collective Security Council action to enforce partition was, however, an unpalatable prospect to both the United States and Britain. Instead, they sought means to abandon the Partition Proposal or to effectively frustrate its implementation. Although the American delegate, Mr. Austin, stated his agreement with the Palestine Commission conclusion that it 'cannot fulfill its functions under the General Assembly Resolution (implementation of Partition) unless armed forces are provided to the Committee by the Security Council,'[52] he nevertheless recommended that the Security Council do no more than establish a committee to look into questions of possible threats to peace.[53] Three weeks later, on March 19, 1948, the American turnabout was complete: Mr. Austin proposed to the Security Council that Palestine be placed under United Nations trusteeship and that the Palestine Committee suspend its efforts at implementation of the Partition Plan.[54] The Soviet Union vetoed the American proposal which, had it been approved, might have indefinitely suspended the recommendations of the U.N. Partition Plan.

Britain's determination to forestall implementation of partition exceeded even that of the United States. Moreover, being in control of Palestine, Britain had the direct capacity to do so. Until two weeks prior to termination of the Mandate, Britain severely hindered the United Nations Palestine Commission in its task of delineating the Partition frontier, in establishing provisional Councils of Government, in allowing a free port to be instituted in the area proposed in the Jewish state, and in consulting with parties to the conflict.[55]

Moreover, Britain continued during the period between the Resolution and the Mandate's end to freely ship armaments to Trans-Jordan, Egypt, and Iraq, knowing full well their intended purpose. Even subsequent to the Security Council's prohibition in June, 1948, of all arms shipments to the Middle East, 'the British were still continuing to supply arms to the Arabs, and the British officers who had joined the Arab forces as instructors were also taking an active part in the war.'[56] In regard to the possibility of collective Security Council action, Britain stated unequivocally that it would not 'undertake, either individually, or collectively in association with others, to impose that decision by force.'[57]

Thus when Egypt, Lebanon, Syria, Trans-Jordan and Iraq finally sent their regular forces into Palestine for the declared purpose of frustrating implementation of partition through obliteration of the newly proclaimed and recognized state of Israel,[58] no one in the international community was taken by surprise. Since passage of the Partition Resolution in November 1947 the Arab states had made clear their intent to intervene. The retreat of the United States and Britain from their initial commitment to the plan only fortified their resolve. Realizing that collective Security Council action to prevent the forceful frustration of partition had become most improbable, the Arab states inferred that armed intervention could be achieved with impunity and, perhaps, even with the blessings of Britain which had been actively obstructing all efforts at orderly and gradual transition of power. Indeed, Britain's role ranged from that of deciding to simply withdraw authority and to let the antagonists fight it out, to fomenting further the existing explosive situation. Whether Britain's actions reflected premeditated policy or were the result of blunder remains a mystery.[59]

America's stance, though not as pernicious as Britain's, helped to fan the flames of war. In addition to retreating from support for partition, the United States made no meaningful attempt to dissuade the Arab states from undertaking their threatened invasion. American oil interests and many members of the military establishment viewed with disfavor the possibility of any American intervention in Palestine on behalf of a new Jewish state. They appear responsible for having influenced America to adopt its 'hands-off position'.[60] American support for Israel, it was felt, would estrange the Arab world from the west. Military strategists feared that the Palestinian Jewish population would be the underdog in an Arab-Jewish clash and that, accordingly, support for Zionism would mean continued Israeli military dependence on the United States in an increasingly more powerful Arab world.[61] Rising cold-war tensions also had their effect. Since the Partition Resolution's adoption, American-Soviet relations had rapidly deteriorated. Soviet support of Communist parties in Italy and France, and intervention in support of Communists in the Greek civil war and the destruction of popular rule in central Europe were the main bones of contention. Enforcement action by the Security Council was feared by the United States as a potential means of increasing Soviet involvement in the Middle East.

Yet, had the United States affirmed its commitment to the General Assembly Partition Resolution by manifesting its will to employ Security Council enforcement measures, the Arab states might well have been dissuaded from intervening militarily. Instead, the American abetting of the British flight from responsibility helped create the vacuum of international authority which led directly to the outbreak of war. If containment of Soviet ambitions in the region was the aim of American foreign policy, war was not the answer. Its inevitable wake of turmoil and instability could provide little confidence for containment of Soviet ambitions.

### 2. *Termination Attempts: From Resolution by Imposition Toward Resolution by Negotiation*

The first ceasefire of the 1948 War, commencing on June 11, 1948, was arranged through the efforts of the U.N. Mediator pursuant to the United Nations Security Council Resolution of May 29, 1948.[62] By the terms of that resolution the cease-fire was to last four weeks. The United Nations Mediator, Count Bernadotte, then undertook discussions with representatives of both belligerents separately, at Cairo and Jerusalem. No accommodation between the two sides was reached because, as Count Bernadotte described it:

> the parties were in no mood for compromise . . . . While the Arabs retained their former stand against partition of any kind, the Jews were equally adamant in their attitude as regards an independent Jewish state, in accordance with Assembly Resolution 181 (II) of Nov. 1947, and toward unrestricted immigration.[63]

On July 15, 1948, the United Nations Security Council passed Resolution No. 54 determining that Arab refusal to abide by requests for prolongation of the first ceasefire created a situation which constituted a threat to the peace under Article 39 of the Charter.[64] Unlike the earlier Security Council resolution setting a four-week limit, subject to extension of the truce, the resolution of July 15th stated in Paragraph 8 that the ceasefire should endure 'until a peaceful adjustment of the future situation in Palestine is reached.'[65]

a. *The Bernadotte Proposals*

A second ceasefire based on the above Resolution No. 54 came into effect on July 18, 1948. By this time the Jewish forces had established themselves in almost all of northern Galilee. The central plains towns of Lydda and Ramle fell to them. They had however been unable to reverse their losses in the Negev, where their settlements remained isolated, and in Jerusalem, where the Arab Legion controlled the eastern Arab sector. Nevertheless, the tide had turned in their favor.

Count Bernadotte again attempted to achieve a compromise solution but failed.[66] It was impossible to attain any agreement which might serve as a basis for resolution of the outstanding issues. The requisite mutual commitment to abandoning a military solution in favor of a political one was simply absent. The state of war continued unabated.[67] The Arab states were unwilling to recognize the existence of their opponent as a juridical entity, regardless of its territorial compass, and were committed to the use of any means to implement their resolve. Attempts by Israel to seek a peaceful settlement through mediation or direct negotiation[68] were consistently met by the Arab response that they would never recognize the existence of the State of Israel, either *de facto* or *de jure*.[69]

In this context, on October 15, 1948, Count Bernadotte

suggested to the United Nations that an Arab-Israeli peace settlement would require a radical departure from the Partition Plan Resolution.[70] According to his scheme, Trans-Jordan was to be allotted nearly all of Palestine exclusive of Western Galilee, including parts which, by the terms of the Partition Plan, were to be under Jewish control. This meant that all territory in Palestine then under Arab control—and this included major portions of the Negev, the southern part of Palestine—would be merged with Trans-Jordan. An independent Palestinian state, contrary to the terms of the Partition Resolution, would not be established. The new enlarged Trans-Jordanian state and Israel would then come to terms over a peace treaty.[71]

The Mediator's plan was rejected by Israel as even a basis for discussion. Israel would not agree under any conditions to forego any part of the Negev.[72] Moreover, Israel stated that she would prefer to see the establishment of an independent Palestinian state in non-Jewish Palestine rather than see that territory be attached to the Kingdom of Trans-Jordan.[73] The Arab states,[74] and the Palestinians,[75] unanimously rejected the Bernadotte Plan in its entirety. They demanded, in its stead, formation of a unitary Palestinian state governed on the basis of majority rule.[76]

Britain, as could be expected, favoured Bernadotte's proposal[77] and sought to secure its acceptance by the United Nations.[78] By adding the West Bank and the Gaza Strip to the territory of Trans-Jordan, Britain stood to gain great strategic advantages. Control would be regained of the former British bases in the Gaza Strip. Trans-Jordan, already under British control, would increase its strength in the Middle East.[79]

The United States lent its support briefly to Britain's position[80] and then reverted to support of the Partition Resolution.[81] The Soviet Union strongly opposed the Bernadotte proposals from the start. Mr. Gromyko, the Soviet delegate, expressed his belief that they had been shaped by Britain to implement her imperial ambitions in the Middle East through the enlarged vassal state of Trans-Jordan.[82] The final draft resolution adopted by the First Committee made no mention of the drastic departure from the Partition Plan which Bernadotte had recommended.[83]

b. *The Bunche Mediation*

The discussions in the United Nations of the Bernadotte proposals must be viewed in the light of events then transpiring in Palestine. The growing realization that a political settlement would not emerge from the ceasefire of July 18 led to an escalation by both sides of sporadic military clashes.[84] Jewish terrorists, incensed at the Bernadotte proposals, assassinated the Count. Shortly thereafter, on October 15, 1948, an Israeli convoy carrying food to isolated settlements in the Negev was attacked. Israel responded by unleashing a well-prepared concentrated offensive in the north and south of Palestine. The military action was, in the view of the new United Nations Mediator, Ralph Bunche, 'on a scale which (as) could only be undertaken after considerable preparation and could scarcely be explained as simple retaliatory action for an attack on a convoy.'[85] Israeli leaders had undoubtedly earlier come to the conclusion that, despite inclusion of the Negev in territory to be allotted the Jewish state by the terms of the Partition Plan, only the use of force in violation of the ceasefire would secure the region.

On October 22, 1948, the Arab states and Israel agreed to a third ceasefire[86] pursuant to an earlier call by the Security Council on October 19.[87] That call was in the form of adoption, with certain amendments, of the conclusion which the United Nations Mediator, Ralph Bunche, had earlier submitted to the Security Council regarding the situation in the Negev area.[88] Regarding the issue of shifts in territorial control as a consequence of the fighting, the Security Council's position was as follows:

> After the ceasefire, the following might well be considered as the basis for further negotiations looking toward insurance that similar outbreaks will not again occur and that the truce will be fully observed in this area
>
> (a) Withdrawal of both parties from the positions not occupied at the time of the outbreak;
> (b) Acceptance by both parties of the conditions set forth in the Central Truce Supervision Board Decision No. 12 affecting convoys;
> (c) Agreement by both parties to undertake negotiations

> through United Nations intermediaries or directly as regards outstanding problems and the permanent stationing of United Nations observers throughout the area.[89]

The territorial shifts which resulted from Israel's counter-offensive were major. In seven days Israel destroyed most of the Egyptian army in the south, took control of the whole of Galilee in the north, and penetrated two to six miles inside of Lebanon.[90]

The Security Council now had to consider whether in implementing the third ceasefire it would continue to rely on its prior endorsement of the United Nations Mediator's position that the terms of withdrawal were to be an issue for negotiation between the parties, or whether to adopt a different stance—one that would require an immediate withdrawal to the pre-October 14 lines. The Acting United Nations Mediator, Ralph Bunche, had since his report of October 18, regarding the terms of the ceasefire, taken an equivocal stance on the issue of territorial conquest. In an attempt at clarifying his position, he made the following statement before the Security Council on October 29, 1948:

> (I)n dealing with cases of advance made as a result of local fighting under the truce, the basic principle upon which we have to operate is that there shall be no advance, or else it entails a military advantage; this does not mean, however, that in every case there must be a rigid restoration of the fighting lines as they existed prior to the incident. This would only mean that a situation would be recreated in which the incident—or one of a similar kind—would soon be repeated.[91]

Mr. Bunche's concrete recommendation was that the Truce Supervision staff under his control be vested with discretion to fix new lines between the antagonists in such a manner as to minimize the potential resumption of fighting.

Great Britain and China then sponsored a resolution calling for Israel and the Arab states to immediately withdraw from territories gained as a result of the fighting to pre-ceasefire lines.[92] Subsequent to such withdrawal the parties were to negotiate, either directly or indirectly, 'permanent truce lines and such neutral or demilitarized zones as may appear advantageous.' If no agreement were possible, the draft resolution authorized the United Nations Mediator to fix such permanent lines.[93]

The Israel Government strongly objected to the resolution arguing that by 'isolating the current episode from a host of others in which military advantage is now being enjoyed'[94] (the initial Arab entry into Palestine in violation of United Nations resolutions and subsequent Arab refusal to accede to ceasefire attempts) the United Nations was engaging in the selective application of the law. Israel's juridical right to be in the Negev was asserted to exist by virtue of the 1947 Partition Plan. Egyptian interference with the terms of the previous truce relative to freedom of transport was cited as justification for Israel's violation of the truce and entry into the Negev. Outstanding issues between the parties, Israel further asserted, required final resolution through negotiation; the United Nations Mediator had no authority by the terms of the Charter to fix final demarcation lines.[95]

The only champion of Israel's position in the Security Council was the U.S.S.R. and the Ukrainian Soviet Republic. Mr. Taransenko, the Ukrainian delegate, opposed the British-Chinese draft and submitted a different draft resolution more akin to that of the October 19 Security Council resolution, placing emphasis on resolution of the issue of conquered territory through negotiations. The draft called 'upon the two parties to begin negotiations, either directly or indirectly through the intermediary of a United Nations Representative, on the basis of the aforementioned resolution, with a view to the peaceful settlement of unresolved questions.'[96]

The Soviet pressure in the Security Council in support of a negotiated solution to the conquered territory issue was, however, unavailing. The Security Council adopted (with abstentions by the U.S.S.R.) on November 4, 1948, Resolution 61 calling upon the concerned Governments:

> 1. To withdraw those of their forces which have advanced beyond the positions held on October 14, the Acting Mediator being authorized to establish provisional lines beyond which no movement of troops shall take place;
> 2. To establish, through negotiations conducted directly between the parties, or, failing that, through the intermediaries in the service of the United Nations,

> permanent truce lines and such neutral or demilitarized zones as may appear advantageous, in order to ensure henceforth the full observance of the truce in that area. Failing an agreement, the permanent lines and neutral zones shall be established by decree of the Acting Mediator.[97]

Security Council Resolution 61 was, however, to be short-lived in terms of the support it was to receive from the international community. A dramatic shift in emphasis was to take place during the next few sessions of the Security Council. The concept of immediate withdrawal from conquered territories to be followed with the fixing of 'permanent truce lines' either through negotiations or directly by the U.N. Mediator faded. In its place the new formula of no withdrawal until successful conclusion of a final peace settlement won approval. This shift was to be of great significance as it determined the final pattern of the terms for a settlement of the Arab-Israeli conflict upon which the international community was to find agreement and indeed laid the basis for Security Council Resolution 242 of November 22, 1967.

The United Nations Mediator, Ralph Bunche, played an influential role in this change of outlook. Mr. Bunche suggested to the Security Council that it adopt a new draft resolution which would call for establishment of a negotiated armistice as a means of effecting the difficult transition from a tenuous truce, regarded by each party as a mere interruption of the hostilities, to a permanent condition of peace as the indispensable condition for an eventual settlement of all the political issues. No mention of conditions precedent to initiation of armistice negotiations was made.[98] In the ensuing discussion in the Security Council regarding the Bunche draft resolution, Britain, the sponsor of the previous November 4 resolution, calling for withdrawal, stated, somewhat apologetically, that it had 'submitted that draft resolution rather hastily.'[99] Moreover, Britain added, approvingly, that 'the Acting Mediator goes further and wider afield, and seeks to establish an armistice all along the line, as it were, leading to a definite cessation of hostilities and the establishment of a state of peace.'[100]

Canada, supported by France and Belgium, then submitted

a draft resolution[101] to the Security Council, refining and amplifying the terms of Mr. Bunche's suggested draft resolution. The text of that draft stated in its operative paragraphs that the Security Council:

> 1. *Decides* that, in order to eliminate the threat to the peace in Palestine and to facilitate the transition from the present truce to permanent peace in Palestine, an armistice shall be established in all sectors of Palestine;
> 2. *Calls upon* the parties directly involved in the conflict in Palestine, as a further provisional measure under Article 40 of the Charter, to seek agreement forthwith, by negotiations conducted either directly or through the Acting Mediator, with a view to the immediate establishment of the armistice, including:
>
>    (a) The delineation of permanent armistice demarcation lines beyond which the armed forces of the respective parties shall not move;
>
>    (b) Such withdrawal and reduction of their armed forces as will ensure the maintenance of the armistice during the transition to permanent peace in Palestine.

Mr. Bunche endorsed the draft resolution stating:

> It is essential to move out of the framework of the existing truce, which is universally regarded in Palestine, as merely an interruption of hostilities, to a new framework which will signal at least the beginning of an end of hostilities in Palestine. It has seemed to us (the United Nations Truce Supervision Commission) that, to accomplish this, a call from the Security Council—a firm call—for an armistice, might be the most effective vehicle. We appreciate, of course, that there is no magic in the word 'armistice' as opposed to the word 'truce.' What is important is the objective which will be defined for the armistice in any resolution which may be adopted as against the terms of the existing truce, which calls only for a permanent ceasefire.[102]

The Soviet delegate, Mr. J. Malik, had only one objection to the Canadian draft. The wording of the resolution should be changed, he suggested, to read that the goal of the proposed negotiations between the parties be the conclusion of 'formal peace' rather than 'armistice.' His remarks on the importance of his proposed change in casting the psychological mood of the parties toward negotiation merit repetition:

> Philologists might find that these terms (peace and armistice) differed in some respects, but as we know the author of the proposal has himself admitted, that neither from the legal nor from the technical point of view is there any particular difference between the two terms. . . . We have been told about progressive stages in the development of a truce; we have been told of the psychological effect upon the Governments concerned of the transition from one kind of truce to another. But, however hard we may try to find and prove any difference between the present truce and the kind we are being offered here, there is, in fact, no real difference between them. Measures of this kind do not constitute a step forward on the road from a truce to peace; they would mean merely marking time. The psychological state of the parties would be hardly altered. The relations between them would still be determined by a state of truce and not of peace.[103]

France and the United States both took the lead, however, in opposing the proposed Soviet amendment. Mr. Parodi, the French delegate, defended 'armistice' as being distinguishable from 'truce' on the grounds that the former 'indicates a desire to establish a more stable set of affairs than has resulted from the truce.'[104] The American delegate, Mr. Jessup, stated that while 'the U.S.S.R. has suggested an even bolder course, namely, that we should move at once into the state of final peace, for our part, we do not feel that it is practicable to move immediately into that state, and we do think that the intermediate state of armistice is a feasible and necessary step on the way toward the final goal.'[105]

Israel, somewhat surprisingly, did not strongly rally behind the Soviet proposed amendment. 'The central purpose, which we applaud,' stated Mr. Eban, as representative of the Provisional Government of Israel, 'is the termination of the truce and the initiation of a new phase—call it what you will—looking toward a peace settlement.'[106] 'It would be valuable if the Security Council would declare that the object of any projected negotiation between the parties is to secure swift, if not immediate, transition from these provisional measures to a state of permanent peace.'[107]

Mr. El-Khouri, the Syrian delegate, stated that '(a)n armistice cannot be imposed upon parties, it must be accepted by both sides when they find that it is according to their interest.'[108] Furthermore, both the Syrian and Egyptian delegations stated that they would reject any resolution which compelled them to recognize under any conditions the existence of a Jewish state in Palestine.[109]

The Canadian sponsored resolution was adopted by the Security Council as Res. No. 62 on November 16, 1948.[110] It was to serve as the juridical basis for all of the subsequent Armistice Agreements that were to take place in 1949 between Israel and the Arab states which were to formally bring the active hostilities of what is commonly designated as the first Arab-Israeli war to a close. These agreements were, in turn, to serve as the sole juridical basis for a settlement of the overall Arab-Israeli conflict—at least until 1967.

The third ceasefire period lasted until December 22, 1948. At that time Israel again launched an offensive in the Negev. Her objective was to oust the Egyptians from that region, and gain control of the port of Eilat, the southernmost portion of Palestine and its access to the Red Sea. Israel again defended its attack on the grounds that this territory was within the geographical confines assigned to the proposed Jewish state by the Partition Plan and as such was merely engaging in the defense of its territory.[111] Moreover, Israel justified its action as a legitimate means of applying pressure on Egypt and other states to come to terms with the existence of Israel and to force acquiescence in Security Council Resolution 62.[112] Toward this end, Israel's attack was not confined to Palestinian territory, but extended across the Egyptian border in Sinai.[113]

Pursuant to Security Council Resolution 66[114], a fourth and final ceasefire came into effect on January 7, 1949. Resolution 66 called for the parties to cease hostilities and to comply with Resolution 61 of November 4, 1948 and Resolution 62 of November 16, 1948. Those two resolutions took, however, diametrically opposed stands on the issue of conquered territory. Whereas Resolution 61 required withdrawal to the pre-second ceasefire lines, Resolution 62 treated withdrawal as but one issue that would have to be negotiated directly between the parties in the proposed armistice discussions. Israel and its then supporters at the United Nations, the U.S.S.R. and Ukrainian S.S.R., pointed out the inherent contradiction contained in Resolution 66's joint reference to Resolutions 61 and 62. Moreover, they took the position that only negotiations without preconditions, as embodied in Resolution 62, would be conducive to peace. Again, Britain's motives were cast under suspicion by the Soviet delegate. Britain, the sponsor of Resolution 66, was accused of being primarily interested in strengthening Trans-Jordan by implementing Israeli withdrawal to be followed by Jordanian assumption of control of areas presently under Israeli occupation.[115]

Israel responded to Resolution 66 with disregard as its forces continued to consolidate its positions in the Negev and to proceed to cross the international Egyptian-Palestine frontier and push into northern Sinai.[116] Only an Anglo-American ultimatum threatening intervention halted the Israeli offensive.[117]

By January 9, earlier Egyptian victories in Palestine had been reversed. Egypt retained control only over the five square mile grid known as the Gaza Strip. The other Arab belligerent states had, in the course of the fighting that followed violation of the third ceasefire, chosen not to intervene on Egypt's behalf. Disheartened by its losses and the defection of its allies, Egypt decided to disengage itself from the Palestine imbroglio and agreed to commence armistice negotiations.[118]

On February 24, 1949 the Israeli-Egypt Armistice Agreement was signed.[119] Soon thereafter, the remaining major Arab belligerent states followed suit and executed similar agreements.[120]

## C. ATTEMPTS AT PEACE-MAKING 1949–1954

### 1. *The 1949 Armistice Arguments*

Each of the four armistice agreements stipulated that it was undertaken pursuant to the directives of Security Council Resolution 62. As such, they delineated permanent demarcation lines, provided for withdrawal and reduction of armed forces and made clear that armistice was only an intermediary stage between ceasefire and an ultimate peace settlement wherein all the outstanding issues between the protagonists would be ultimately resolved.[121] They clearly provided that the armistice agreements should not be regarded as more than a military settlement. The terms of the agreements were, each armistice expressly stipulated, dictated exclusively by military rather than political considerations. The rights, claims and positions of the parties were not to be prejudiced in any way by the terms of the agreements. Thus, although provision was made for a mixed armistice commission to supervise the demarcation lines, no mention was made as to how the final frontier might be established. And, while refugees and other civilians were forbidden to cross demarcation lines, the question of refugee repatriation was never raised. These were political issues to be settled in the envisioned subsequent peace negotiations.

The 1949 Armistice Agreements between Israel and Egypt, Lebanon, Trans-Jordan and Syria were markedly different from most preceding instances of armistice in international affairs. The armistices of the pre-United Nations period—the Armistice of 1918[122] terminating World War I, the Shanghai Armistice Arrangement of 1932[123] ending the Sino-Japanese conflict over Manchukuo, the Peace Protocol of 1935[124] between Bolivia and Paraguay ending their dispute over the San Chaco region—and the series of armistices upon the conclusion of World War II,[125] were all characterized by capitulation with the victor imposing his terms upon the vanquished.[126] In the post-Charter world, the two armistice agreements preceding those entered into by Israel and the Arab states—between India and Pakistan[127] and between the Netherlands and Indonesia[128]—set a different pattern. In those two instances neither side had suffered a decisive defeat. The major impetus for conclusion of the armistice agreements came not only from the war, but also from the United Nations. The Security Council had, in its calls for a ceasefire, detailed the terms of a proposed armistice. The Arab-Israeli Armistice Agreement followed this trend. The Arab and Jewish Nationalist movements neither suffered total defeat nor gained full victory. The Zionists did secure control of all the territory of Palestine allotted them in the Partition Plan, as well as substantial additional portions. But the ambition to 'liberate' all of 'Eretz Israel' (historic Palestine) had not come to fruition. Trans-Jordan had wrested control of the West Bank. Only half of Jerusalem was under Jewish dominion with access thereto from the populous plain region of Israel limited to a narrow corridor. Egypt gained the Gaza Strip. Syria and Lebanon neither won nor lost any territory.

As in the prior India-Pakistan and Netherlands-Indonesia armistice agreements, so too in the Arab-Israeli armistice, the United Nations Security Council was responsible for facilitating negotiations aimed at settlement. Here, however, the Security Council saw fit to go beyond calls for mediation to propose, on its own, the terms of the armistice. It justified its action on the grounds that, unlike prior situations, the Arab-Israeli armistice negotiations were undertaken pursuant to a determination by the Security Council under Art. 39 of the Charter, 'that the situation in Palestine constitutes a threat to the peace,' hence broadening Security Council supervisory powers.

## 2. *The United Nations Palestine Conciliation Commission*

Soon after the close of the first armistice agreement, a new United Nations organ, the Palestine Conciliation Commission (PCC), was formed to aid the transition from armistice to peace, just as it was the task of the U.N. Mediators, Bernadotte and Bunche, to facilitate transition from ceasefire to armistice.[129] Based in Jerusalem, the PCC's earliest efforts were expended in visiting the neighboring Arab countries to gain first-hand information on the perspectives on peace. By April, 1949, the PCC was able to score a major success when it arranged for Arab and Israeli delegations to meet in Lausanne for the purpose of beginning negotiations of final peace settlements.[130]

On May 12, 1949, Israel and the attending Arab states at Lausanne signed a protocol constituting the basis of the PCC's work. It provided that the 1947 Partition Plan be the starting point for discussions of territorial and related issues.[131] Israel, however, soon committed itself to the position that the 1949 demarcation lines were immutable save for minor border rectifications.[132] The Arab states, on the other hand, claimed on behalf of the Palestinian Arabs not only the territories allotted to them by the U.N. Partition Plan but also the Negev and Eastern Galilee. The PCC deemed both demands excessive.[133] Complicating its attempt to resolve the territorial issue was the question of refugee repatriation (to where and in what numbers), over which agreement proved even less susceptible of achievement.

After two unsuccessful attempts at Lausanne the talks resumed in New York on October 13, 1949 and then in Geneva on January 16, 1950. Arab-Israeli differences proved insurmountable. At this time Arab attention turned increasingly inward. Jordan was racked by a crisis of succession following King Abdullah's assassination in 1951. Egypt was the scene of a successful coup d'etat in 1952 by a group of army officers headed by Mohammed Naguib. Syria too was racked by internal disorder and a coup d'etat. As a result, internal stability became the predominant concern.

The key to countering the mounting internal disorder and political tension became denunciation of Israel, an apparently cost-free rallying point. Infiltration of armed bands across frontiers escalated as did, in return, the severity of Israeli retaliatory operations. The stage for the 1956 crisis was set.

## D. THE SINAI CAMPAIGN, 1956

### 1. *Prelude* (the Lavon Affair, Czech-Egypt Arms Agreement, 'Fedayeen,' Failure of the Eden Proposal, Closing the Straits of Tiran)

1954 marked the 'turning point' in worsening Arab-Israeli relations. On July 27, 1954 Prime Minister Nasser, on behalf of the Egyptian government, successfully concluded the Anglo-Egyptian agreement for the evacuation of all British military forces from the Suez Canal Zone within twenty months. The expulsion of Britain had long been the standard goal of every political party in Egypt and Nasser, who had assumed power just three months earlier, emerged from the event as the undisputed leader of Egypt. Israel, however, which viewed the presence of British forces in the Canal Zone as a vital buffer against Egypt, saw cause for concern.

Moshe Sharrett, then Prime Minister of Israel, favored a more moderate policy in Arab relations than did his predecessor, Ben Gurion. For Ben Gurion, the prospect of movement toward Arab unity, progress and efficiency which Nasser represented was seen as threatening to Israel. Prior to his departure from government, he advocated a tougher line toward Egypt. This the majority of the cabinet rejected causing him to resign in protest, but not before appointing Moshe Dayan as Chief of Staff and Pinhas Lavon as Minister of Defense—two men publicly noted for their distrust of each other. When it became known that an Egyptian-British accord regarding British evacuation from Suez would be imminent, one, two or all of these men—the real figures remain unidentified—set into motion a plan to sabotage the coming accord.

In July of 1954, bombs exploded in Cairo's cinemas and post offices and later in the American Embassy and information offices. Egyptian authorities discovered that the group responsible was an Israeli intelligence network which had orders to plant bombs in American and British offices throughout Egypt, thereby creating tension between Egypt and Britain and the United States. The tension was intended to enable members of the British Parliament to rally against the agreements for evacuation of the Suez bases. It was also designed to disprove the thesis that the Egyptian regime was a stable and solid base for Western policy and thereby make Israel more attractive as the West's only stable ally in the region. The embarrassment caused the Sharrett government by the 'Lavon Affair' helped bring Ben Gurion back to power as Defense Minister on February 17, 1955.

Ben Gurion immediately gave notice that continued terrorist infiltration would be answered with massive Israeli retaliation. On February 28, Ben Gurion launched such a raid on the Gaza Strip, destroying the Egyptian headquarters there and killing 38 Egyptian soldiers and wounding 31. It was the largest military action taken since the Armistice Agreement of 1949. Its effect was to upset the entire equilibrium of the Middle East as it then existed. No unusual acts of infiltration from Gaza, other than what had become the pattern for years, preceded the attack.[134]

Instead of discouraging further incursions and encouraging peace talks, the attack weakened the position of the Arab moderates. In the meantime, for reasons largely independent of the deterioration of relations with Israel and more as a consequence of a political decision 'to "break up" the Western "arms monopoly" and, consequently, "to do away with" the Western "spheres of influence",' Nasser turned to the Communist bloc for weapons.[135]

In August of 1955, shortly after the first arrival of Czech arms, and perhaps inspired by a new confidence in his military capacity, Nasser pronounced his fateful decision to organize a para-military unit of commandoes—'fedayeen.' In response to their continued infiltrations Israel, in September, invaded and occupied the El Auja triangle, a demilitarized zone under the 1949 Armistice situated in the northern tip of the Sinai Peninsula and controlling all the key roads that led southward.

Alarmed by this further deterioration of Egyptian-Israeli relations and by growing Soviet influence in Egypt, British Prime Minister Eden proposed at a speech made at Guildhall on November 9, 1955 to personally mediate a settlement, on the basis of the 1947 Partition Plan.[136] London, like Washington, was of the opinion that Nasser did not desire war with Israel and as both feared the consequences of growing Soviet involvement in the Middle East, they were ready to push for Israeli territorial concessions.

Nasser accepted the offer. So, too, did the other Arab states and organizations with whom he had consulted in advance. Nasser publicly suggested that the U.N. should mediate and that the terms of Eden offered 'a very good basis' for negotiation.[137] Israel rejected the proposals and disavowed the possibility of territorial concessions beyond the 1949 Armistice lines.[138]

Why did Nasser take this step of publicly agreeing to peace talks with Israel—especially at a time when Arab-Israeli tension had been steadily increasing ever since Ben Gurion's reascendence to power and the Gaza raid?

Several possible explanations can be offered. One is that Nasser was afraid of an Israeli attack on Egypt,[139] and wanted to prevent or postpone its occurrence by giving the impression of willingness to negotiate. Another is that he really wanted peace with Israel and that the Eden initiative offered a chance at an eventual peace settlement palatable to the Arab states.

Eden's initiative, however, quickly collapsed. Washington's response after initial endorsement, became lukewarm.[140] In the House of Commons, M.Ps sympathetic to Israel attacked Eden's suggestion that Israel should concede territory.[141] Moreover, continued Egyptian anti-Western subversive activity in North Africa and the Arab peninsula complicated any possible compromise and led to the further deterioration of relations.[142]

On September 10, 1955, Egypt announced that all ships seeking to enter the Straits of Tiran must first obtain Egyptian permits,[143] thus blockading Israeli shipping and that of Israel-bound cargo aboard neutral ships from going through the Straits to the newly developed Israeli port of Eilat on the Red Sea. This Egyptian action was in direct violation of the Security Council Resolution of September 1, 1951, declaring that 'neither party can reasonably assert that it is actually a belligerent or requires to exercise the right of visit, search and seizure for any legitimate purpose of self-defense.'[144]

In response, Moshe Dayan, Defense Minister, and Prime Minister Ben Gurion urged Israel's Cabinet to approve military action to open the Gulf of Aqaba to Israeli shipping. Most of the Cabinet advised against acting at the time, but they agreed to act when conditions proved more favorable.[145]

2. *The Suez Expedition*

The Suez expedition of 1956 was undertaken jointly by Britain, France and Israel pursuant to a secret treaty signed at Sevres on October 23, 1956. The avowed Israeli motive for participation was to:

> a. render ineffective the Egyptian preparation for an offensive, by destroying the bases created for this purpose; b. eradicate the Fedayeen springboards in the Gaza Strip and on the eastern border of Sinai; (and) c. to open the Gulf of Eilat to the free movement of Israeli shipping by liquidating the Egyptian blocking position in that region.[146]

The real motivations were more complex and revolved around a willingness to exploit a favorable international situation and the immediate community of strategic interests that had developed between Israel and Britain and France to Israel's military advantage.[147]

From the strategic viewpoint, the Suez Line was more defensible than the 1949 Armistice lines. It was a waterway, and one which could not be crossed without alarming the interests of the outside world. Egyptian air bases would, as a result, be one hundred and fifty miles further away from urban Israel. A military presence on the Canal might also have been seen by Israel as a means of access to the Canal for shipping purposes after years of Egyptian blockade.

The primary military objective of the Israeli campaign was the capture of the Egyptian port of Sharm el-Sheikh which commanded the Straits of Tiran—the access route to the port of Eilat. The aim of the British action in occupying the Canal Zone was to reverse Nasser's nationalization of the Suez Canal Company. France, in addition, was motivated by Nasser's refusal to stop helping the Algerian revolution. Thus by toppling the Nasser government the insult to their national pride might be obviated and the Egyptian movement toward the Soviet bloc halted. The plan was for Israel to invade Sinai and for Britain and France to then issue a joint ultimatum for an Egyptian-Israeli withdrawal of forces as a pretext for permitting Anglo-French military units to intervene and occupy the canal area, ostensibly to protect it from the ravages of war.[148]

### 3. *Termination and International Expectations*

Upon learning of the Sinai invasion, the United States took the initiative in calling for a meeting of the Security Council where it introduced a resolution[149] condemning the Israeli action and calling for 'immediate withdrawal' behind the armistice lines. Britain and France vetoed the resolution.

On November 1 the United States introduced a resolution to the same effect in the General Assembly where it was overwhelmingly approved.[150]

A ceasefire was then arranged and the U.N. Emergency Force (UNEF) brought in to replace withdrawing British and French units. Israel refused however to comply with resolutions for an immediate withdrawal,[151] until her major conditions were met. These were the stationing of UNEF forces in the Gaza Strip and at Sharm el-Sheikh and the guarantee of freedom of navigation through the Straits of Tiran with the understanding that

> interference, by armed force, with ships of Israeli flag exercising free and innocent passage in the Gulf of Aqaba and the Straits of Tiran, will be regarded by Israel as an attack entitling it to exercise its inherent right of self-defense under Article 51 of the Charter and to take all such measures as are necessary to ensure free and innocent passage of its ships in the Gulf and in the Straits.[152]

Israel's display of superior military strength enabled her to gain her main objective—cessation of 'fedayeen' raids and freedom of movement in the Straits of Tiran. It did not succeed in abating Arab hostility which continued to smoulder until erupting again in 1967.

## E. THE 1967 WAR AND THE SUBSEQUENT FRAMEWORK FOR SETTLEMENT

### 1. *Prelude: The Spiral of Miscalculations*

For ten years following the Suez Crisis an uneasy calm of 'no war—no peace' settled over the Middle East. The cycle of Egyptian based raids and Israeli reprisals that preceded the war abated. Raids from Syria in the North and Jordan in the West began to occur more frequently. Nevertheless, offense and retaliation remained limited in scope and roughly balanced. In the spring of 1967, a hardly foreseeable cycle of belligerent actions, threats and grave miscalculations by all immediate parties to the conflict, by the Soviet Union and by the Secretary-General of the United Nations led to the conflagration. The story has been documented by many sources[153] and requires little retelling here except in so far as it touches upon the juridical question of the justifiability of Israel's response. This is pertinent to a determination of the lawfulness of Israel's entry into the West Bank in 1967.

### 2. *The Lawfulness of Israel's Entry into the West Bank*

Jordan claims Israel unlawfully entered the West Bank during the 1967 War in violation of article 2(4) of the U.N. Charter forbidding recourse to 'the threat or use of force against the territorial integrity or political independence of any state, or in any other manner inconsistent with the purposes of the United Nations.'[154]

Jordan does not deny initiation of hostilities along the Jordanian-Israeli frontier (and in Jerusalem in particular) on June 5, 1967,[155] but contends her recourse to force was permissible under Article 51's exception of 'collective self-defense if an armed attack occurs against a Member of the United Nations.' Israel's attack on Egyptian airfields in the earlier part of June 5, 1967 is alleged to have constituted an 'armed attack' under Article 51 and thus justified an attack by Jordan—an ally of Egypt—against Israel as a collective self-defense measure.[156]

The legal question that therefore arises is whether Israel's action in firing 'the first shot'[157] of the 1967 War against Jordan's ally, Egypt, earlier on the morning of June 5, was an act of aggression or justifiable self-defense. Phrased differently, were Egyptian actions prior to the 1967 War sufficiently provocative to be deemed an 'armed attack' against Israel, permitting, in return, resort to military measures for self-defense under Article 51 of the Charter?

It has been suggested that the 'cumulative effect' of Egyptian provocations—the closing of the straits of Tiran and passage through the Gulf of Aqaba; the ejection of the United Nations Emergency Force and the resulting immediate deployment of strong contingents of Egyptian forces along the frontier; the signing by Egypt of joint defense pacts with other states and subsequent mobilization on all frontiers and the 'sabre-rattling' war fever generated in the streets in Cairo—was to create a situation whereby Israel would by inaction risk sustaining an imminent and potentially overwhelming strike, and that, accordingly, the series of Egyptian actions must be deemed an 'armed attack.'[158]

This argument is founded on the supposition that the Israeli authorities had good cause to believe Egypt was about to strike and that Israel's only alternative to being attacked was to attack first. This may or may not be true.[159] In any event, it is not fully certain that fear of an imminent Egyptian attack prompted the Israeli issuance of battle orders. However, such a determination is not necessary to justify a finding of Israeli self-defense.

Israel's Foreign Minister, Abba Eban, in his speech before the General Assembly on June 19, 1967 made the following justification of Israel's conduct:

> Never in history have blockade and peace existed side by side. From May 24 onward, the question of who started the war or who fired the first shot became momentously irrelevant. . . . From the moment at which the blockade was imposed, active hostilities had commenced and Israel owed Egypt nothing of her charter rights.[160]

Israel's right of innocent passage through the Straits of Tiran was guaranteed by international law.[161] Closure of the Straits, in itself, may or may not have been sufficient justification for initiating a general war under the terms of the Charter. True, Article 51's reference to the 'inherent' right of self-defense encompasses pre-Charter international law. And true, the American-British-French-Israeli-Egyptian agreements of 1957[162] acknowledged Israel's rights of response to a renewal of blockade. But in the instant case it was not only closure of an international waterway that occurred, but also the issuance of credible threats of 'all out' war[163] against the target state, should it attempt to secure its right of free passage by either a forceful opening or reprisals. In such a situation where closure is coupled with the threat of war, it is submitted that international law allows the blockaded state, upon exhaustion of peaceful avenues for redress, to resort to war.

Between the time of the closure of the Straits and the initiation of the war, Israel attempted unsuccessfully to enlist both the aid of the United Nations and the support of the maritime powers in reestablishing Israeli access to shipping in the Straits.[164] Recourse to self-help, it could have been objectively concluded, was Israel's only viable option for opening the Straits. Yet any 'self-help' measures carried the threat of an immediate, full-scale, and potentially overwhelming Arab response.

H. Haykal, editor of Cairo's *Al Ahram* and Egypt's reputed unofficial spokesman, clearly expressed these views in an article entitled 'An Armed Clash with Israel is Inevitable—Why?'[165] Writing in the May 26, 1967 edition of *Al Ahram* he stated: 'It is in the light of the compelling psychological factor that the needs of security, or survival itself, make [Israel's] acceptance of the challenge of war inevitable.'[166] After detailing the actions by Egypt prior to the outbreak of the War—'. . . the march of events during the 10 great days which changed the situation and the balance of the Middle East. . . . One calculated and effective move followed another'[167]—Haykal went on to state:

> The next move is up to Israel. Israel has to reply now. It has to deal a blow. We have to be ready for it, as I said, to minimize its effect as much as possible. Then it will be our turn to deal the second blow, which we will deliver with the utmost effectiveness.[168]

The threat to Israeli shipping and access to the East had escalated to the threat of a full-scale Arab attack. Viewed in the context of Israel's military and economic position, maintenance of the status quo was equivalent to slow strangulation. Her 10-mile waist now exposed to a westward Jordanian attack under Egyptian control or to an Egyptian drive of less than 25 miles from the Gaza Strip, Israel had to maintain full mobilization. A continued high level of mobilization, with 80 per cent of the military personnel composed of reservists, meant the closing of most businesses and shops, the operation of factories at greatly reduced levels, and unharvested crops. Yet with the potential, and perhaps 'imminent,' danger of a surprise Arab attack, mobilization could not be stepped down. If Israel was not to succumb to the Egyptian blockade of the Straits of Tiran—a step which carried no assurance of a peaceful outcome once the escalation of threats had taken place—then the decision for war had to be made.

The international community in its formal consideration of 'aggression' in the 1967 War has in fact favored Israel's action as a legitimate and proper exercise of its rights of self-defense. Attempts, mainly by the Soviet Union, to deem Israel's response as 'aggression' failed in both the General Assembly[169] and Security Council of the United Nations—organs which have not exhibited hesitancy in censuring Israel on other occasions. In the Security Council the Soviet Union was alone among the permanent members in voting in favor of similar resolutions.[170]

3. *Termination and International Expectations: Security Council Resolution 242*

Subsequent to the cease-fire arrangement of June 11, 1967, the U.N. General Assembly convened almost continually in an attempt to formulate a framework for an overall comprehensive settlement of the conflict. The procedural basis for these sessions was the General Assembly Uniting for Peace Resolution of November 3, 1950,[171] authorizing emergency special sessions of the Assembly within twenty-four hours of a request when the Security Council fails, due to a lack of unanimity among its permanent members, 'to exercise its primary responsibility for the maintenance of international peace and security in any case where there appears to be a threat to the peace, breach of the peace, or act of aggression.'[172]

The Emergency General Assembly of 1967 failed, however, to reach consensus on a formula for Israeli withdrawal based on an unequivocal Arab declaration of peace.[173] By mid-October the effort to reach an acceptable formula shifted again to the Security Council. This time the Security Council was successful and the very important Security Council Resolution 242 of November 22, 1967[174] was the product of its labors. Like earlier Security Council Resolution 62, which called for an end to the 1948/49 War, Security Council Resolution 242 did not require an immediate Israeli withdrawal from conquered territories.[175] Rather, as did Security Council Resolution 62, it made the future of the territories an issue for negotiation in the context of peace treaty deliberations. Thus, Paragraph 1 of the Security Council Resolution 242 provided that peace was to be accomplished through an exchange based on:

(i) Withdrawal of Israeli armed forces from territories occupied in the recent conflict;
(ii) Termination of all claims or states of belligerency and respect for and acknowledgement of the sovereignty,

> territorial integrity and political independence of every state in the area and their right to live in peace within secure and recognized boundaries free from threats or acts of force.

In this respect, Security Council Resolution 242 further pursued the policy established by the Security Council in 1949 that the necessary means for termination of the Arab-Israeli conflict was a freely negotiated peace treaty. This is the meaning of the principle stated in the preamble to the Resolution regarding the 'need to work for a just and lasting peace in which every state in the area can live in security.' There is little room for argument on this point.

Where disagreement arises is on the issue of withdrawal of Israeli forces. Are they, as the Arab side contends, required to be withdrawn prior to the conclusion of a peace treaty and, if so, is such withdrawal to be total or may it be partial? Proponents of the Arab case contend that the preamble of Security Council Resolution 242—'emphasizing the inadmissibility of the acquisition of territory by war'—must be interpreted as meaning that an immediate Israeli withdrawal is required. In the words of Prof. Quincy Wright, this phrase 'required that Israel gain no political advantage, in respect to the establishment of a boundary with its Arab neighbors. . . . Israel would certainly be at an advantage if it negotiated independently with each of its neighbors while it occupied the disputed territories.'[176]

Prof. Wright has, however, made an error in blurring the notion of territorial acquisition, which the Resolution refers to, with that of territorial occupation, to which the Resolution makes no reference.[177] A lawful entrant has a right of occupation—which may, of course, be voluntarily relinquished for reasons of political expediency—pending conclusion of a peace treaty or its functional equivalent. Any other rule would impose no sanction on aggressive behavior and thus defeat the basic quest of international law, or any law, in distinguishing lawful from unlawful behavior.[178] A rule or policy requiring lawful entrants to relinquish gains in bargaining power gained in reacting against unlawful behavior would condone aggression and penalize defensive action.

But if Israel, as a lawful entrant, may continue occupation until conclusion of a peace treaty, may it also utilize its new found bargaining advantage to exact territorial concessions? The answer requires a careful look at Security Council Resolution 242. That resolution unanimously called for 'withdrawal from territories' rather than 'withdrawal from all *the* territories.' Its choice of words was deliberate and the product of much debate. They signify that withdrawal is required from some but not all of the territories.[179] Final boundaries are to be negotiated in peace treaty proceedings. This is what was required by the 1949 Armistice Agreement[180] and this is what Security Council Resolution 242 now seeks to bring to fruition.[181] The extent of territorial concessions that may be negotiated or bargained for is, however, very limited. Security Council Resolution 242 restricts such claims, as do the 1949 Armistice Agreements to territorial adjustments mandated by 'security considerations.'[182]

Applying these principles of accommodation to the West Bank controversy, Israel was, by virtue of Security Council Resolution 242, to yield to Jordan, as the successor government to Trans-Jordan with whom she had signed the 1949 Armistice Agreements, the West Bank, save for minor mutually agreed territorial adjustments for Jerusalem.[183] In exchange, Israel was to receive formal termination of belligerency and recognition of sovereignty, all in the context of a treaty of peace. Yet, given the unsettled legal question of Jordan's status in the West Bank between 1949 and 1967, dispute arose regarding the mutual obligations and rights of Jordan and Israel vis-a-vis the West Bank.

### F. POST-1967: JORDANIAN, ISRAELI AND INDIGENOUS PALESTINIAN RIGHTS TO SOVEREIGN CONTROL OF THE WEST BANK

Since 1923, when the League of Nations permitted Britain as the Mandatory Power to 'postpone or withhold' application of Jewish rights to Trans-Jordan, Trans-Jordan had continued to be governed as part of the Palestine Mandate. On April 18, 1946, Britain secured the approval of the Council of the League for its action, taken one month earlier, in granting independence to Trans-Jordan.[184] On May 25, 1946 Trans-Jordan formally declared its independence and its transformation into the Hashemite Kingdom of the Jordan under King Abdullah I. Thus, when Jordanian troops crossed into Palestine in 1948 for the purpose of thwarting, in conjunction with other members of the Arab League, the existence of the newly proclaimed independent Jewish state in Palestine, Jordan was, at the time, crossing an international frontier.

This entry into Palestine clearly violated Article 2(4) of the United Nations Charter prohibiting members 'from the threat or use of force against the territorial integrity or political independence of any state.' Nevertheless, it would be unwarranted to assume, as have many commentators,[185] that the unlawfulness of Jordan's entry into Palestine precluded her from any acquisition of title to areas not controlled by the Jewish state. Jordan, at least ostensibly,[186] entered Arab Palestine on behalf of and as an ally of Palestinian Arab people in their rejection of partition. Thus, it would seem that, although Trans-Jordan could not acquire title in the Israeli sector of Palestine, nothing precluded her succession to rights of the Palestinian Arabs, in so far as they were voluntarily ceded.

On September 20, 1948, an independent West Bank Palestinian Government was established by proclamation under the leadership of the Mufti el Hussaini of Jerusalem.[187] On October 1, that Government came to an abrupt end when Jordan's King Abdullah obtained, at the Jericho Conference, a vote of acclamation from five thousand West Bank notables as the sovereign of Arab Palestine. The voluntary nature of the West Bank Arabs' desire to merge with Jordan, as expressed at the 1948 Jericho Conference is, however, subject to serious doubt. Jordan viewed the decision at the Conference to integrate the West Bank into Jordan as an expression of 'the majority of the people of Palestine to unite the two sister countries'.[188]

It is questionable, however, whether the decision to merge expressed at the Jericho Conference represented, in fact, the will of the West Bank rather than having been the product of coercion.[189] Moreover, it is especially doubtful that that decision, no matter how interpreted, indicated an intent to transfer sovereign rights wholly and irrevocably. This becomes clear on examination of the contemporaneous political context. On December 14, 1948, the day after Jordan's Parliament confirmed the Jericho decision, the Arab League sent a resolution to King Abdullah reminding him of the policy adopted by the League on April 12, 1948. That policy was as follows:

> The Arab armies shall enter Palestine to rescue it. His Majesty (King Farouk, representing the League) would like to make it clearly understood that such measures should be looked upon as temporary and devoid of any character of the occupation or partition of Palestine, and that after completion of its liberation, that country would be handed over to its owners to rule in the way they like.[190]

Although, with the exception of England and Pakistan, international recognition has not been subsequently accorded to the 1950 annexation of the West Bank by the Hashemite Kingdom of Jordan, tacit *de facto* recognition of the act evolved among all parties to the conflict, and the international community in general. Between 1948 and 1967 Jordan administered the West Bank peacefully, without interruption and without protest, as an integral part of its kingdom. Indeed there was international consensus that the future of the West Bank was an internal matter for Jordan to decide. Israel's rights to the region were governed by the Armistice Agreement it had signed with Jordan establishing *de facto* international boundaries, the exact parameters of which were to be delineated in a peace treaty, which would allow for minor territorial adjustments[191] mutually agreed upon.

### 1. *Jordan as Ousted Trustee-Occupant*

Given the historical context of Jordan's assumption of control in the West Bank, its legal status there prior to 1967 may be termed something less than that of legitimate sovereign and something more than that of a belligerent-occupant. Belligerent occupancy can occur only where the occupying power is at war with the government of the territories it occupies.[192] But Jordan's entry into the West Bank in 1948 occurred with the consent, if not at the request, of the indigenous Arab population, who, by virtue of the Partition Resolution and general international consensus, had the right to assert sovereignty over the area of Palestine not accorded to the Jewish state. Yet, if the West Bank Palestinians invited Jordanian intervention, it is doubtful that they ever formally ceded their rights to control of the region, either by virtue of the 1948 Jericho Convention or through their subsequent participation in the 1950 general elections for a joint Parliament. What seems most probable is that the intent was to cede sovereignty temporarily to Jordan until such time as the indigenous population might find it opportune to reassert control. In the interim, Jordan's legal status in the West Bank might, as this author has suggested in a previous article, best be termed that of a 'trustee-occupant'.[193] As such 'it would (unlike a belligerent occupant) not be barred from implementing any changes in the existing laws or institutions provided such amendments were in the best interests of the inhabitants.'[194] Jordan, after all, assumed custodianship of the West Bank, according to the terms of incorporation, until such time as the 'Palestinian problem' might be solved. Whatever the exact meaning of that phrase, it certainly connoted more than refugee settlement or repatriation and was interpreted instead as restoration of Arab Palestinian sovereignty; perhaps, as was often hinted, through the 'liberation of all of Palestine'.[195]

Assuming, then, Jordan's status in its term of control over the West Bank to be that of trustee-occupant, its responsibility in administering that trust is subject to serious question. Until such time as Arab Palestinian sovereignty might be restored, Jordan was to promote the development of Palestinian self-rule in the West Bank. At the least, it was not to hinder its development. Jordan, however, pursued the opposite course. Its ruling Hashemite Bedouin elite channelled economic development to the East Bank at the expense of the West Bank. The centers of industry, commerce and higher learning were likewise established almost entirely in Amman's immediate environment.[196]

Institutionalization of a Palestinian identity was feared as a threat to Jordan's quest for permanent control of the West Bank. While bemoaning the loss of territories in the Palestine Mandate, Jordan simultaneously suppressed Palestinianism as part of a calculated policy aimed at retaining control over its majority Palestinian population. The Palestine Liberation Organization, formed in 1964, was permitted to operate as a propaganda tool against Israel, but its activities were kept under control once attempts at inspiring a separate Palestinian identity took concrete form.[197]

## 2. *Israel as Lawful Belligerent-Occupant*

Given Jordan's legal status in the West Bank between 1948 and 1967 as that of a trustee-occupant, and given the estrangement between the West Bank and Amman which has since occurred, it becomes especially difficult to adequately characterize Israel's present legal status in the region. If one considers, as we do, that Israel gained control of the West Bank in the lawful exercise of self-defense, one might assume that Israel's status can only be that of a lawful belligerent-occupant. There are, however, other possibilities.

It has been advanced that Israel's rights in the area surpass those of a lawful belligerent-occupant and encompass title to the region.[198] This school of thought views Jordan as an unlawful occupant, having entered the West Bank in violation of Article 2(4) of the Charter. When Jordan's sovereign rights in the West Bank are then compared with those of Israel, a lawful occupant, Israel's are deemed superior. What is, however, ignored by this view is the question of indigenous Arab Palestinian rights to the West Bank. Moreover, it overlooks the fact that Jordan's entry into Palestine in 1948, while an act of aggression against Israel, was not aggression against the indigenous Arab West Bank population. And Israel, between 1949, when it signed Armistice Agreements with Jordan, and 1967, when it conquered the West Bank, never challenged the lawfulness of Jordan's control of the West Bank. Its practice in those years was to call for a peace treaty providing for minor mutual border rectifications along the 1949 lines. These facts negate any claim that Israel's rights to sovereignty over the West Bank are superior to those of either Jordan or the indigenous population.

Jordan's trust relationship with the West Bank is, however, no longer purely Jordan's internal concern. Indeed Jordan has abandoned its claims to sovereignty, at least formally, and calls for self-determination. In this context, can Israel still be deemed to be a lawful belligerent-occupant, who, as such, assumes an obligation to manage the held territory in a manner conducive to its reversion to the previous sovereign or, in this case, previous trustee-occupant?

Elsewhere, in an earlier publication, 'Trustee-Occupant: The Legal Status of Israel's Presence in the West Bank'[199] the author suggested that Israel should replace Jordan as trustee-occupant for the indigenous Palestinian Arabs. As such, Israel should be held responsible for fostering the political and economic self-determination of the region, unburdened by the traditional restraints imposed by the law of belligerent occupation against alteration of the *status quo ante*. A U.N.-administered plebiscite would be held after a number of years of Israeli trusteeship. In the interim Israel would foster achievement of that goal by aiding the West Bank to reach a stage of economic and political viability whereby the choice of independent status would become a meaningful option in an impending referendum.

Further reflection in the interim years has only led to repeated confirmation of the author's thesis, first presented in winter, 1973, that Israel's appropriate legal status is that of a trustee-occupant. Not because Israel is well suited for this task or that it has any natural competence to ensure that self-determination in the West Bank is furthered. The situation of an occupying power changing its colors to that of a trustee is admittedly paradoxical and not without grave danger for the peacemaking process. Earlier we warned against a rule permitting an indigenous rebellion against a former sovereign to run its course.[200] Such a situation could be too easily exploited by an occupying power intent on permanently consolidating control. Puppet regimes seeking separation from their former ruler for reasons unrelated to the will of the majority of the occupied population can often be established without difficulty.

Nevertheless there is an inherent contradiction in preserving Jordan's laws and institutions over a considerable temporal span when Jordan's status is that of an ousted trustee-occupant, rather than an ousted sovereign. There is, to be sure, the danger of abuse of authority should Israel assume trustee-occupant status. Yet, in the absence of any movement toward peace between Jordan and Israel in the course of over ten years, continued maintenance of the *status quo ante* results in the countervailing danger of unnecessarily stifling any momentum toward self-determination. This, after all, is Jordan's responsibility should reversion occur and this has become the espoused goal of the Arab confrontation states as well. Whether the danger of annexationist intentions acting under the guise of benevolence outweighs the danger of inertia, can only be determined on a case to case basis, wherein due account is taken of the occupier's perspective and the likelihood of reconciliation between the belligerents. Based on such an investigation the author concluded that Israel's own legitimate interests as well as those of all parties concerned would be best served were it to shed the mantle of belligerent occupant and take up instead that of trustee-occupant.

Whatever the merits of the author's suggestion that Israel assume, voluntarily or by agreement, the role of trustee-occupant, it is obvious that this has not occurred. While leaving 'open' the question of the Geneva Convention's *de jure* applicability, Israel has stated that its administration will be governed, *de facto,* by its provisions. Implicitly, therefore, Israel has agreed that the standard by which its occupational conduct is to be governed is that of a lawful belligerent-occupant. And this has been the standard by which the international community and the Arab states have chosen to assess Israel's conduct. Accordingly, the forthcoming chapter judges Israel's management of the West Bank in light of the standard of belligerent-occupancy rather than the suggested concept of trustee-occupancy. It is assumed that Jordan is entitled to reversion of control over the West Bank. Thus management policies affecting the region's basic institutional structures are assessed in light of the Hague Regulations and the Geneva Convention as well as in light of their effect on the ousted power's reversionary interest.

NOTES

1. *See* the masterful study by B. Tuchman, *Bible and Sword: England and Palestine from the Bronze Age to Balfour* (1956), advancing the thesis that Britain's conquest of Palestine from the Turks in 1918 represented

the culmination of a steady British thrust for control of the region tracing its origins to ancient Anglo-Saxon fable.

2. See I. R. Baker, *Woodrow Wilson and The World Settlement* 55 ff. (1922); I. D. Miller, *The Drafting of the Covenant* 41 ff. (1928). H. Notter, *The Origins of the Foreign Policy of Woodrow Wilson* 651–2 (1937). See also Pomerance, 'The United States and Self-Determination: Perspectives on the Wilsonian Conception', 70 *Am. J. Int'l L.* 1 (1976).
3. Great Britain, *Correspondence,* CMD No. 5957 (1939); reproduced in W. Laqueur (ed.) *The Israel-Arab Reader* at 15 (1970) (hereinafter cited as *Laqueur).* See on the McMahon – Husain understanding the analysis in the excellent work by the Esco Foundation for Palestine, Inc., I *Palestine: A Study of Jewish, Arab and British Policies* 63–70 (1947). See E. Kedourie, *In the Anglo-Arab Labyrinth: The McMahon-Husain Correspondence and Its Interpretations 1914–39,* (1976).
4. *Laqueur* at 12.
5. *Id.,* at 17.
6. Statement by Winston Churchill in Churchill White Paper of 1922 *Id.,* at 48. *See also* statement by Sir Gilbert Clayton, Chief Secretary of the Palestine Government, in *House of Lords Offic. Report,* July 20, 1937, col. 629; statement by Mr. Ormsby-Gore, Secretary of State for the Colonies, in *House of Commons Offic. Report,* July 21, 1937, cols. 2249/50; and, especially, letter to *The Times,* July 23, 1937, reprinted in Esco, *supra* note 3 at 184–187.

   > 'I feel it my duty to state, and I do so definitely and emphatically, that it was not intended by me in giving this pledge to King Husain to include Palestine in the area in which Arab independence was promised.
   >
   > I had also every reason to believe at the time that the fact that Palestine was not included in my pledge was well understood by King Husain.'

   Moreover, the British Government subsequently claimed the Sykes-Picot Treaty to be inoperative because of the disappearance of the Russian regime that had been a party to it. The provisions of the Sykes-Picot accord had been incorporated into a corollary agreement with Russia which purported to recognize Russia's postwar claim to Constantinople. See G. Lenczowski, *The Middle East in World Affairs* 72 (1962); C. Sykes, *Cross Roads to Israel* 37 (1965).
7. See Lord Curzon's speech to the British Cabinet, in favor of Britain's assumption of the role of Mandatory Power for Palestine, Lloyd George, II *Memoirs of the Peace Conference* 739–43 (1939).
8. *League of Nations Covenant,* Art 22, para. 1.
9. *Id.,* Art 22, para. 5.
10. *Id.,* Art. 22, para. 5.
11. Omitted.
12. *Id.,* Art. 22, para. 4.
13. In its 1950 *Advisory Opinion on the International Status of South-West*

*Africa,* the International Court rejected South Africa's contention that the Mandatory Power of the lowest class of Mandates—'C' Mandates—could acquire sovereignty thereover. *See* 1950 *I.C.J.* 128–32.

14. Control by the League of Nations over the mandatory was exercised in three ways: (1) the Council of the League of Nations could define and interpret the terms of the mandate; (2) the Permanent Mandate Commission was empowered to receive annual reports from the Mandatory Power; and (3) the inhabitants were empowered with the right to petition the League. Thus, for example, the exclusion of Trans-Jordan from the application of Jewish rights under the Palestine Mandate could not be effected solely through Britain's 'sovereign' power but required League approval. Note also that in the Palestine Mandate, the Mandatory's own Law, Art. 81 of the *Palestine Order in Council,* gave any considerable section of the population a general right of appeal through the High Commissioner and the Secretary of State to the League of Nations of any action of the Mandatory it thought inconsistent with the terms of the mandate. H. Lauterpacht concluded that the 'cumulative effect of the limitations' placed on the rights of the Mandatory Power justify the inference that the League retained 'ultimate responsibility,' *Private Law Sources and Analogy of International Law* 194–6 (1927).

15. '(Sovereignty) is in abeyance; if and when the inhabitants of the territory obtain recognition as an independent state, as has already happened in some Mandates, sovereignty will revive and vest in the new State.' Lord McNair, International Status of South-West Africa Case 1950 I.C.J. at 50. *The ICJ Advisory Opinion on Legal Consequences for States of the Continued Presence of South Africa in Namibia (South West Africa) notwithstanding Security Council Resolution* 276 (1971) *I.C.J.* affirms Lord McNair's analysis: 'It is self-evident that the "trust" had to be exercised for the benefits of the peoples concerned, who were admitted to have interests of their own and to possess a potentiality for independent existence on the attainment of a certain stage of development.' at 28–9. *See also* Separate Opinion of Ammoun, J., at 69, who states that 'Stoyanovsky . . . . took a more accurate view (of the nature of sovereignty in mandated territory) when he upheld the notion of sovereignty residing in a people deprived of its exercise by domination or tutelage.' *See* generally regarding the question of sovereignty in the Mandatory system, H. Hall, *Mandates, Dependencies and Trusteeships* 429 ff. (1948); Q. Wright, *Mandates Under the League of Nations,* 726 ff. (1930); R. Chowdhuri, *International Mandates and Trusteeship Systems* 229–36 (1955); I Lauterpacht-Oppenheim 222 n. 5 (8th ed. 1955); R. Margalith, *The International Mandates* 145–200 (1930); Leeper, 'Sovereignty over the Mandated and Trust Territories', 49 *Mich. L. Rev.* 1119 (1951); Sayre, 'Legal Problems Arising from the United Nations Trusteeship System', 42 *Am. J. Int'l. L.* 268–72 (1948); J. Stoyanovsky, *La Theorie Generale Des Mandats Internationaux* 83

ff. (1925); Pic, 'Le régime des mandats d'après le Traité de Versailles', 30 *Revue generale de droit international public* 321 (1923).

16. Formal confirmation of Great Britain as Mandatory Power for Palestine did not occur until July 22, 1922. The Mandate was not to commence formal operation until September 29th of that year. The formal peace treaty with Turkey ceding sovereignty over Palestine did not occur until July 23, 1923 when Turkey and the Principal Allied Powers signed the treaty of Lausanne. British Treaty Series, No. 16 (1923). Reprinted in 18 *Am. J. Intl. L. Supp.* 1–115 (1924). Turkey's continued foreign and domestic upheavals were responsible for the delay. *See,* generally, regarding the British Mandate I *League of Nations, The Mandate System, Origin—Principles—Application* 23–4 (1945; Royal Inst. of Int'l Aff., *Great Britain and Palestine* 12–17 (1946); J. Stoyanovsky, *The Mandate of Palestine* (1928).
17. See *Palestine Royal Commission Report,* CMD, No. 5479 at 92 (1937).
18. Many of the terms of the Palestine Mandate addressed themselves specifically to means of fulfilling the pledge of a Jewish national home.

    Article 2 of the Palestine Mandate imposed on the Mandatory the positive duty of fulfilling the terms of the Balfour Declaration by requiring Britain to 'secure the establishment of a Jewish national home' by placing Palestine under appropriate political, economic, and administrative conditions while 'safeguarding the civil and religious rights of all the inhabitants of Palestine.' Article 1 extended the Mandatory's role in Palestine beyond the rendering of 'administrative advice and assistance' common in class A mandates to the actual administration and legislation characteristic of class B mandates. Article 4 required the Mandatory to seek the advice of the Jewish Agency, 'recognized as a public body for the purpose of advising and cooperating with the Administration of Palestine in such economic, social and other matters as may affect the Jewish national home and the interests of the Jewish population in Palestine.' Article 6 imposed the duty to 'facilitate Jewish immigration under suitable conditions' and to encourage land settlement. Article 7 required the Mandatory to 'facilitate the acquisition of Palestine citizenship by Jews who take up their permanent residence in Palestine.' Article 22 made Hebrew, as well as Arabic and English, an official language.
19. Mallison, 'The Zionist-Israel Juridical Claims to Constitute "the Jewish People" Nationality Entity and to Confer Membership in it: Appraisal in Public International Law', 32 *Geo. Wash. L. Rev.* 983, 1030 (1964); H. Cattan, *Palestine and International Law* (1976).
20. Permanent Court of International Justice, Series A, No. 2, The *Mavrommatis Palestine Concessions* 69 (1924). Note also that the U.S. Congress on June 30, 1922 adopted a resolution essentially identical to the Balfour Declaration, 42 Stat. 1012 (1922), and on Dec. 3, 1924 entered into a covenant with Britain confirming complete American acceptance of all the Mandate's provisions. 44 Stat. 2184 (1924).
21. Reproduced in *Laqueur* at 27.
22. 'The terms of the Declaration referred to do not contemplate that

Palestine as a whole should be converted into a Jewish National Home, but that such a Home should be founded in Palestine . . . (W)hen it is asked what is meant by the development of the Jewish National Home in Palestine, it may be answered that it is not the imposition of a Jewish Nationality upon the inhabitants of Palestine as a whole but the further development of the existing Jewish community with the assistance of Jews in other parts of the world in order that it may become a centre in which the Jewish people as a whole may take, on grounds of religion and race, an interest and pride.' *Id.*

23. C. Weizmann, *Trial and Error* 290 (1949). *See also* reference to Jewish Agency's acceptance of this interpretation in Prime Minister MacDonald's letter addressed to Dr. Chaim Weizmann, February 13, 1931, reproduced in *Laqueur* at 34.
24. Article 25 was inserted into the terms of the Mandate in 1921 at the insistence of Winston Churchill, who had just recently replaced Lord Curzon as the Colonial Secretary. At the Cairo Conference of March, 1921, designed to discuss British commitments in Iraq and Palestine (including Trans-Jordan), Churchill, in an attempt to reach a settlement with the leaders of Arab nationalism, elevated Faisal (later King Faisal I) to be the ruler of Iraq and acknowledged his older brother, Abdullah, as the ruler of the Trans-Jordan territory where he had established himself. The administration of Palestine was to remain under one High Commissioner but provisions of the Mandate relating to the establishment of a Jewish national home would be limited to Cis-Jordan. See Sykes, *supra* note 6, at 50–58.
25. *Royal Commission Report,* Ch. II, para. 42(3). *See* regarding the McMahon letter, *supra* note 6 and accompanying text.
26. *See* regarding Zionist reaction to limiting the Jewish National Home provisions of the Mandate to Cis-Jordanian Palestine, P. Riebenfeld, *Israel, Jordan and Palestine* (1974) (unpublished paper serving as the basis for 'The Integrity of Palestine: Jews and Arabs—Israel and Jordan', *Midstream* August-Sept. 1975) who states the Jewish leadership was interested in 'conciliation' and thus 'an agreed policy which allowed for unhindered Zionist development of western Palestine was the next best thing.' at 14, 15.

Christopher Sykes writes:

> In later years Zionist propaganda referred to the transaction as a 'serious whittling down of the Balfour Declaration,' as the cause of a 'rankling sense of disappointment,' and as a betrayal (I. Cohen, *The Zionist Movement,* 1945). It was sarcastically noted that the British Government had been a remarkably long time in discovering that Palestine stopped short at Jordan. It could be said back that the Jews had been a remarkably long time in registering a claim that would certainly have been resisted from the beginning. There is little Israelite history to be recalled east of Jordan, and the National Home was a monument to History.
>
> But if the later Zionist propaganda about Transjordan was contrived, the feeling and anxiety which it expressed were real. The

> chances of a permanent Arab-Zionist reconciliation were always extremely slight, but they were inevitably brighter when and if Zionism had some room to manoeuvre. Gradually it became clear that the separation of Transjordan from Palestine removed this freedom from Zionism and confined it to close limits.

*Supra* note 6 at 57–8.

27. *See* R. Gabbay's excellent work, *A Political Study of the Arab-Jewish Conflict* (1959) at 30.
28. Riebenfeld writes that the origin of the practice of designating Cis-Jordanian Palestine simply as Palestine was due more to erroneous popular usage and improvident Zionist acquiescence than to accurate characterization.

> The suspension of Zionist colonization in Transjordan did not bring about its separation from Palestine but. . . . because of Zionist development and the constant clashes between Arab and Jewish claims, accompanied by enquiry commissions, worldwide publicity and parliamentary debates, public interest and controversy remained focused on Cis-Jordan.
>
> It was natural, from 1922 on, for the habit to grow of referring to Palestine only as that part of the mandate area associated with the Jewish National Home. The Zionists themselves, with the exception of Jabotinsky and his followers, thought they were displaying moderation in tactfully omitting from their maps of Palestine and from their land and immigration policy the Transjordanian parts of the country. *Supra* note 26, *Midstream* at 13–14.

29. *Royal Commission Report,* Cmd. 5479 in *Laqueur* at 57.
30. J. Marlowe, *The Seat of Pilate: An Account of the Palestine Mandate,* 138–48 (1959). For an analysis depicting the existence of a strong Palestinian nationalism in 1937 favoring the termination of the Mandate and the establishment of an independent Palestinian government, *see Royal Commission Report* 130–36 (1937). The independent Arab states, too, began at this time to press for either the termination of the Mandate or the creation of an independent Palestinian state. Gabbay, *supra* note 27 at 35–8.
31. Statement of Policy (Cmd. 5513) July 7, 1937 by his Majesty's Government accepting the conclusions and recommendations of the Royal Commission Report. *See* Appendices for map of 1937 Partition Plan.
32. The question of the acceptability of partition in any form was debated at length at the Twentieth Zionist Congress held at Zurich in 1937 where the following resolution was adopted as definitive of the Jewish leadership's stance on the issue:

    1. The 20th Zionist Congress solemnly reaffirms the historic connection of the Jewish people with Palestine and its inalienable right to its homeland.

    2. The Congress takes note of the findings of the Palestine Royal Commission with regard to the following fundamental matters: first,

that the primary purpose of the Mandate, as expressed in its preamble and in its articles, is to promote the establishment of the Jewish National Home; secondly, that the field in which the Jewish National Home was to be established was understood, at the time of the Balfour Declaration, to be the whole of historic Palestine, including Trans-Jordan; thirdly, that inherent in the Balfour Declaration was the possibility of the evolution of Palestine into a Jewish State; fourthly, that Jewish settlement in Palestine has conferred substantial benefits on the Arab population and has been to the economic advantage of the Arabs as a whole.

3. The Congress rejects the assertion of the Palestine Royal Commission that the Mandate has proved unworkable, and demands its fulfilment. The Congress directs the Executive to resist any infringement of the rights of the Jewish people internationally guaranteed by the Balfour Declaration and the Mandate.

The Congress rejects the conclusion of the Royal Commission that the national aspirations of the Jewish people and of the Arabs of Palestine are irreconcilable. The main obstacle to co-operation and mutual understanding between the two peoples has been the general uncertainty which, as stated in the Report of the Royal Commission, has prevailed in regard to the ultimate intentions of the Mandatory Government, and the vacillating attitude of the Palestine Administration; these have engendered a lack of confidence in the determination and the ability of the Government to implement the Mandate. The Congress reaffirms on this occasion the declarations of previous Congresses expressing the readiness of the Jewish people to reach a peaceful settlement with the Arabs of Palestine, based on the free development of both peoples and the mutual recognition of their respective rights.

6. The Congress declares that the scheme of partition put forward by the Royal Commission is unacceptable.

7. The Congress empowers the Executive to enter into negotiations with a view to ascertaining the precise terms of His Majesty's Government for the proposed establishment of a Jewish State.

8. In such negotiations the Executive shall not commit either itself or the Zionist Organization, but in the event of the emergence of a definite scheme for the establishment of a Jewish State, such scheme shall be brought before a newly elected Congress for decision. *See* text of above resolutions and comments in *Palestine Partition Commission Report,* Cmd. 5854 (1938) at 18–19.

33. *Id.* at 17–18.
34. *See* Marlowe, *supra* note 30 at 145.
35. *See* Sykes, *supra* note 6 at 291, 276–326.
36. *Id.* at 300–308.
37. *See* however, Jon and David Kimche's account of British motivations in *Both Sides of the Hill* (1960), concluding that no matter how hard the British espoused the policy of withdrawal, they had in mind that 'the Jews or the Arabs or both would ask the British to stay on and save the country from chaos.'

38. G. A. Res. 181 II, U.N. GAOR 131–50 (1947). *See* Appendix for text and map. The Jewish state was to include Eastern Galilee, The Coastal Plain (from a point south of Acre to one north of Ashdod in the Gaza sub-district) and the Negev which was defined so as to exclude some 500,000 acres in the vicinity of Beersheba. The Arab state was to include Central and Western Galilee, the central hilly part of Palestine and the Gaza Strip along the Mediterranean. Jerusalem was to be an international enclave and to include the new and old cities, the area around them and the town of Bethlehem.
39. UNGAOR, 2nd Special Session, Vol. II, 175–176 (1947).
40. Statement by the representative of Saudi Arabia, UNGAOR 1947, II Ad Hoc Committee at 1425. See also similar statements made by the representatives of Iraq, *Id.* at 1426–1427; Syria, *Id.* at 1427; Yemen, *Id.*
41. *See* regarding the General Assembly's role as successor to the League of Nations in regard to mandated territory as a consequence of the operation of Article 80 of the Charter preserving the rights of parties under the mandate system, *Advisory Opinion on the International Status of South-West Africa* 1950 *I.C.J.* 128, 130, and an affirmation of the principle in the *Namibia Opinion* 171, *I.C.J.* 70.
42. About three weeks prior to termination of the Mandate, the U.S. withdrew its support for partition and suggested trusteeship instead, see discussion in *infra* pp. 50–52. In response, Mr. Shertok, representative of the Jewish Agency to the United Nations remarked: (Rapporteur's comments)

    > With reference to the status of Assembly resolutions in international law, (Shertok) admitted that any which touched the national sovereignty of the Members of the United Nations were mere recommendations and not binding. However, the Palestine resolution was essentially different for it concerned the future of a territory subject to an international trust. Only the United Nations as a whole was competent to determine the future of the territory and its decision, therefore, had a binding force. U.N. Doc. A/c.1/SR 127 at 7 (April 27, 1947).

    The American delegate, Mr. Jessup, chose not to respond to the argument but to continue to press for trusteeship. *Id.* at 14–17. The Soviet delegate, Mr. Gromyko, stated there could not be 'any legal justification for considering alternative proposals until the partition resolution had been revoked.' *Id.* at 17.
43. The five Arab states had asked the General Assembly to declare the independence of a unitary Arab state upon the Mandate's termination. They further took the position that the only organs qualified to make a legally binding determination of respective Arab-Jewish rights in Palestine were the International Court of Justice and the General Assembly, upon prior approval by the International Court of Justice of its competence. Subcomm. 2 of the Ad Hoc Comm. on the Palestinian Question proposed that eight questions dealing with interpretations of the various rights of Jews and Arabs in Palestine, as well as the competence of the United Nations to decide on Palestine's

future, be submitted to the International Court of Justice. The proposal was defeated in the General Assembly, 2 U.N. GAOR, Ad Hoc Comm. on the Palestinian Question. Annex 25 at 300–01 (1947). *See* generally, regarding the legal effect of the U.N. Partition Resolution, T. Khang, *Law, Politics and the Security Council* 77–80 (1904); Akzin, 'The United Nations and Palestine', 1948 *Jewish Y.B. Int'l L.* 871; Eagleton, 'Palestine and the Constitutional Law of the United Nations, 42 *Am. J. Int'l. L.* 397 (1948); Elaraby, 'Some Legal Implications of the 1947 Partition Resolution and the 1949 Armistice Agreements', 33 *L. & Contemp. Prob.* 97 (1968); Halderman, 'Some International Constitutional Aspects of the Palestine Case', 33 *L. & Contemp. Prob.* 79 (1968). See also H. Cattan, *Palestine, the Arabs and Israel, The Search for Justice* 261–9 (1969), and rebuttal in F. Feinberg, *On an Arab Jurist's Approach to Zionism and the State of Israel* 25–28 (1971); J. Castaneda, *Legal Effects of United Nations Resolutions* 131–35 (1969); and O. Asamoah, *The Legal Significance of the Declarations of the General Assembly of the United Nations* 68–75 (1966).

44. 1971 *I.C.J.* at 49–50.
45. Although not precise in their formulations, the following judges, issuing separate opinions, favored the view that the General Assembly resolution alone had binding effect: Kahn, 1971 *I.C.J.* at 61; Petrin, *Id.* at 131; Onyeama, *Id.* at 146–147. Judge Dillard draws the distinction between U.N. General Assembly action under Article 10 of the Charter and instances of breach of the Mandate, when it might possess binding power, *Id.* at 163–166. Judge Fitzmaurice, in a strong dissenting opinion reaches the conclusion that 'the Assembly has no power to terminate any kind of administration over any kind of territory' *Id.* at 283, and implies that the Court's opinion made a finding to the contrary. *See,* Dugard, 'Namibia (South-West Africa): The Court's Opinion, South Africa's Response, and Prospects for the Future' 11 *Col. J. Transnat'l L.* 14, 29 (1972); Lissitzyn, 'International Law and the Advisory Opinion on Namibia' *Id.* at 50, 59–63.
46. 10 U.N. SCOR, 263d meeting (1947). In a letter dated December 2, 1947, the Secretary-General requested the Security Council to draw its attention to the Partition Plan, particularly to paras. (a), (b), and (c) of the operative part of that resolution. In para. (a) the General Assembly requested the Security Council to 'take the necessary measures as provided for in the Plan for its implementation;' in para. (b) to consider 'whether the situation in Palestine constitutes a threat to the peace' and, if so, 'to supplement the authorization of the General Assembly by taking measures under arts 39 and 41 of the Charter to empower the United Nations Commission, as provided in this resolution, to exercise in Palestine the functions which were assigned to it by this resolution'; and in para. (c) that '(t)he Security Council determine as a threat to the peace. . . in accordance with Article 39 of the Charter, any attempt to alter by force the settlement envisaged by this resolution.'

During the Security Council debate on the implementation of the Plan, Mr. Austin, the American representative, emphasized that the Council was not empowered to enforce a political settlement of any kind and, therefore, that any action which it took must be solely for maintaining international peace and not for enforcing Partition. Dr. T. F. Tsiang, the Chinese representative, subsequently stated that the 'distinction between enforcement of partition by force and the maintenance of peace by force—while legally valid and important—seemed 'unreal' in the present situation' 4 UN Bull, 211 (1948).

47. Trygve Lie, *In the Cause of Peace, Seven Years with the United Nations,* 175 (1954).
48. Quoted in Sykes, *supra*, note 6 at 337. This issue is explored in further depth in *infra*, sect. B.
49. See, for extensive documentation, Gabbay, *supra* note 27 at 55–69.
50. See U.N.P.C. (United Nations Palestine Commission) 1st Spec. report, S/676, Feb. 16, 1948, paras. 8 & 9. See also accusations by Jewish Agency for Palestine that the Mandatory Government was doing nothing to prevent such infiltrations, S/721 at 10–14.
51. UNSCOR, 3rd yr. 253d meeting, Feb. 24, 1948 at 263. See also U.N. Doc. S/663 and U.N. Doc. S/676. Resolution 181 (II) had provided, inter alia, that:
    (a) The Security Council take the necessary measures as provided for in the plan for its implementation;
    (b) The Security Council consider, if circumstances during the transitional period require such consideration, whether the situation in Palestine constitutes a threat to the peace. If it decides that such a threat exists, and in order to maintain international peace and security, the Security Council should supplement the authorization of the General Assembly by taking measures, under Articles 39 and 41 of the Charter, to empower the United Nations Palestine Commission, as provided in this resolution, to exercise in Palestine the functions which are assigned to it by this resolution;
    (c) The Security Council determine as a threat to the peace, breach of the peace or act of aggression, in accordance with Article 39 of the Charter, any attempt to alter by force the settlement envisioned by this resolution.
52. UNSCOR, *Id.*, at 268,
53. *Ibid.* See regarding the Security Council's constitutional power to implement the Partition Plan, Asamoah, *supra*, note 43.
54. UNSCOR, 3rd yr. 270th meeting, 141–3 and 271st meeting 157–68. See also U.S. Draft Resolution S.705 of March 30, 1948.
55. UNPC *1st Monthly Report to the Security Council,* S/663, 1/29/48 at 7–11.
56. See the memoirs of Count Bernadotte, the then U.N. Mediator, in *To Jerusalem,* 6–7 (1950). See also Schultz in 'Conspiracy Against Partition,' *Nation,* Jan 31, 1948, at 119–20.
57. Statement by Mr. Creech Jones, United Kingdom delegate quoting

from address by his Foreign Minister, Mr. Bevin, at UNSCOR, 3d yr. 253d meeting, February 24, 1948, at 272.

58. See U.N. Doc. S/743 of 15 May 1948, cable to the Secretary General from Minister of Foreign Affairs of Egypt, and U.N. Doc. S/748 of 17 May 1948, cable from King Abdullah of Trans-Jordan. For official statement by the Arab League justifying intervention into Palestine, see U.N. Doc. S/745 of May, 1948, cable from the Secretary of the League of Arab States to the Secretary General of the United Nations, informing him 'of the intervention of the Arab States in Palestine ... out of the anxiousness to check the further deterioration of prevailing conditions and to prevent the spread of disorder and lawlessness into the neighboring Arab lands, and in order to fill the vacuum created by termination of the Mandate and the failure to replace it by any legally constituted authority.'

59. Christopher Sykes offers three different explanations—Zionist, Arab and his own—for British policy in the last days of the Mandate:

> Zionist apologists, with good reason, see British policy as clearly motivated by a wish to soothe Arab exasperation at Unscop and indeed at the whole past thirty years of Zionist increase under British protection; they see Britain as helping the Arabs to thwart the rise of a Jewish State and to keep the National Home small and manageable, in the interests of the British Empire and its oil supplies. Arab apologists, also not without reason, see British policy motivated by a wish to keep on good terms with international Jewry and for that reason anxious to prevent the Arabs gaining more than a token area of their despoiled heritage: to oppose Unscop, but not so much as to exasperate dangerously the Jewish lobbies in England and America.
>
> [In Sykes' opinion the most likely answer lies in the fact that letting the parties fight it out was a deliberate decision]
>
> It should be remembered that when these things happened the war had ended only two years before and men were living in its aftermath during which brutal deeds on a large scale were daily items of news. Men had supped full with horrors. 'Radical solutions,' no matter what suffering they entailed, were often admired by people who had not seen what such euphemisms hide.
>
> Sykes, *supra* note 6 at 346–7

60. See S. Welles, *We Need Not Fail* 63–71, 72–8 (1949); U.S. Cong. Armed Services Committee Hearings (80th Cong. 2nd Series, 1948); F. Manuel, *The Realities of American-Palestinian Relations,* (1949). See also, generally on American policy on Palestine as having become 'almost as complicated and self-contradictory as that of the erratic Mandatory,' Sykes, *supra* note 6 at 358, 357–62.

61. See Welles, *Id.*, at 72–8.

62. U.N. Doc. S/801. Reproduced in Appendix.

63. U.N. Doc. S/865 July 5, 1948.

64. U.N. Doc. S/902, reproduced in Appendix. Israel may have been following a 'calculated risk policy' in its attempt to prolong the first

ceasefire. Although Israel fared badly in the first round of fighting, it had in the interim ceasefire period received new shipments of arms from abroad. It is probable that the Israel Government actually longed for the termination of the truce as an opportunity to resume fighting and thus consolidate and enlarge its territory. Tactical considerations may have dictated acceptance of the U.N. appeal for truce prolongation in the expectation that the other side would reject or try to evade the appeal and thus bear the onus of defying the U.N. See Gabbay, *supra* note 27 at 143.

65. Also compare S.C. Res of 7/15/48 with that of 5/29/48, *supra* note 62. The later resolution states that the failure of any of the parties to comply with a ceasefire may result in U.N. enforcement action under Ch. VII of the Charter. The earlier resolution limited itself to an 'appeal' to the parties to refrain from resumption of hostilites.
66. Bernadotte, *supra* note 56 at 130.
67. Regarding different definitions of a 'state of war'—all of which however agree that a minimum requirement for its termination is a 'de facto' agreement between the antagonists regarding terms for defusing the conflict—see, McNair & Watts, *The Legal Effects of War*, 6 (1966) and the extensive documentation in note 6 thereof and *supra* note I, 9.
68. See appeal of the Israel observer at the Security Council, Mr. Eban, during the 350th meeting, August 18, 1948.

> We have asked for peace talks with Arab representatives. No positive response has yet come from any quarter. . . It is obvious therefore that we are not yet in a state of armistice, which is a phase of peace but rather in a state of truce, which is a phase of war . . . it is obvious that there is only one hope for a radical solution (other than resumption of war) and that is the immediate instigation of peace talks with the issue of refugee resettlement high on the Agenda.

See UNSCOR, 350th meeting pp. 12, 14; U.N. Doc. A/648 at 12–14. Regarding attempts of Israeli leaders to contact their counterpart through the officers of the United Nations Mediator, See Bernadotte, *supra* note 56 at 229.

69. See, for example, U.N. Doc. S/967, August 13, 1948: 'The Arab states have never accorded *de facto* or *de jure* recognition to the so-called State of Israel created by Zionist terrorist bands and are therefore unable to accept the claim of this so-called 'state' to represent in discussion or negotiation any part of Palestine whatever.' It is important to note the extent of the territory in Palestine occupied by the Arab states during the course of the 2nd truce. Egypt was in control of almost all of the Negev—$\frac{2}{3}$ of the territory allotted Israel by the Partition Plan. Syria and Trans-Jordan controlled much of Western Galilee. Trans-Jordan was also in control of all of Judea and Samaria (the West Bank). The only contacts between Israeli and Arab leaders with a view toward territorial compromise were meetings between King Abdullah of Trans-Jordan and Israeli officials that reportedly took place at that time.

70. U.N. Mediator Report, U.N. Doc. A/648, presented to 1st General (Political) Committee on their opening of discussions on the Palestine Question UNGAOR, 3rd Session, Pt. 1, 1st Comm. 161st meeting, October 15, p. 165; U.N. Doc. S/863.
71. *Id.*
72. See statement by Mr. Shertok, Israel's Foreign Minister at the 1st Comm. UNGAOR, 3d session, pp. 640–47.
73. *Id.*
74. UNGAOR, 3d Session, Part 1, 1st Committee, pp. 647–53 (Speech of the Rep. of the Higher Committee); 653–5, 664–71 (Rep. of Syria); 655–60 (Egypt); 660–4 (Iraq); 687–9 (Yemen).
75. *Id.*, at 647–704, 746–51 Arab Higher Committee, the Palestinian Arab organ.
76. See, for example, the statement by Mr. Cattan, Representative of the Arab Higher Committee:

    It had been claimed that the Partition solution had the merit of being based on political realities. But the only natural permanent immutable political reality which must be taken into account is the opposition of the Arabs to a Jewish State in Palestine, *Id.,* at 749.
77. See statements of the British representative, Mr. McNeil, to the 1st Committee urging abandonment of the Partition Plan, UNGAOR, 3d Session, Part I, 1st Comm. pp. 675–676.
78. See British draft resolution calling for establishment of a Security Council Committee, charged with the strict duty of implementing Count Bernadotte's proposals. U.N. Doc. A/C 1/394.
79. See Schultz, 'Who Wrote the Bernadotte Plan?' *Nation* Oct. 23, 1948 at 453. Schultz suggests that Count Bernadotte was influenced by Britain in preparing his proposals. This accusation was made by the Soviet delegation throughout the 1948 Security Council debates. Whatever Bernadotte's motivation, it seems likely that Bernadotte took into consideration British support of his proposals.
80. See statement by Gen. Marshall, The American Secretary of State, endorsing the Bernadotte Proposals, *New York Times*, September 22, 1948, p. 1.
81. See statement by Mr. Jessup, the American delegate to the United Nations, UNGAOR, 3d Sess., Part 1, 1st Comm. 680–683. President Truman's reaffirmation of support of the Partition Plan may have been influenced by his desire to gain the Jewish vote in the closely contested elections of 1948, see *New York Times,* October 25, 1948, pp. 29–30, *Nation,* October 30, 1948, p. 477. A definitive account of Truman's motives is yet to be written.
82. See discussions at the 329th, 330th and 331st meetings of the Security Council, third year.
83. UNGAOR, 3d Sess., Part 1; 1st Comm. 184 meeting, 935–96.
84. See statement of the United Nations Mediator, in his report to the General Assembly that:

    It would be dangerous complacency to take for granted that with no settlement in sight the truce can be maintained indefinitely. . .

The strain on both sides in maintaining the truce under the prevailing conditions in Palestine is undoubtedly very great.

U.N. Doc. A/684, p. 4. See also the Mediator's Report in U.N. Doc. S/955 of 8/7/48. Regarding escalation of ceasefire violations, see U.N. Doc. S/961 of August 12, 1948. See also daily reports on the situation in the *New York Times*, August 16–20, 1948.

85. U.N. Doc. S/1042, Report of October 18, 1948 of the Acting United Nations Mediator to the Secretary General concerning the situation in the Negev. See also U.N. Doc. S/1041, Egyptian allegation of October 16, concerning violation of the truce by Jewish forces; U.N. Doc. S/1043, letter of October 18, 1948, from the Provisional Government of Israel concerning an alleged breach of truce by Egyptian forces.
86. U.N. Doc. S/1058.
87. U.N. Doc. S/1044.
88. U.N. Doc. S/1042.
89. U.N. Doc. S/1044, Sect. 18.
90. See U.N. Doc. S/1055 of 10/25/48 regarding the situation in the North and U.N. Doc. S/1071 of 11/5/48 regarding the situation in the Negev. See also E. O'Ballance, *The Arab-Israeli War of 1948*, 180–6, 190–1, (1956).
91. UNSCOR, Third Session No. 123, October 29, 1948, P. 7.
92. See U.N. Doc. S/1059, October 29, 1948.
93. UNSCOR, 315th meeting, 1948, p. 9.
94. See remarks by Mr. Eban in *Id.*, at 8–15 and in UNSCOR 376th meeting, 10–22.
95. *Id.* Regarding the alleged intent of Britain in sponsoring the resolution, Mr. Eban stated that 'it is significant that the United Nations delegation, which has sponsored a resolution regarding the withdrawal by Israeli forces from their positions, is also committed to a political attempt to detach that part of Israel,' 376th meeting, p. 13.
96. See UNSCOR, 376th meeting, November 4, 1948, p. 6.
97. Security Council Resolution 61 of November 4, 1948, U.N. Doc. S/1070.
98. UNSCOR 374th Meeting, October 28, 1948, 1–9.
99. UNSCOR, 380th meeting, November 15, 1948, p. 2.
100. *Ibid.*
101. U.N. Doc. S/1079 of November 15, 1948.
102. UNSCOR, 380th Meeting, November 15, 1948, at 9.
103. UNSCOR, 380th Meeting, November 15, 1948, at 15–16.
104. *Id.*, at 23.
105. *Id.*, at 27.
106. UNSCOR, 381st Session, November 16, 1948, at 2.
107. *Id.*, at 7.
108. UNSCOR, 380th Meeting, November 15, 1948, at 6.
109. See remarks by Mr. El Khouri, Delegate of Syria, 381st Meeting, November 16, 1948.

When the Jews invited the Arabs to negotiate with them they were doing so on the basis of recognition of their state, and they were

> inviting the Arabs to recognize the existence of the Jews as a sovereign state, and to negotiate on that basis. How can they expect negotiation on that basis? Even in the Resolution which is now being submitted, it is suggested that the Acting Mediators should act on that basis, and here you meet the same thing, the negotiation of a truce or an armistice leading to a permanent peace would be recognizing the Jews as a separate state. . . The foundation that is essential for negotiations is not there. The Arabs want Palestine to be a single democratic state. . . .

See also remarks by Mr. Bey Fawzi, Delegate of Egypt *Id.*, at 21–2:

> I have stated more than once to the Council my point of view and the determination of my Government not to negotiate with the Zionists. We do not recognize them as a party. . . (I)t does not at all mean that my Government accepts the principle of an armistice. We unequivocally reject it.

110. See Appendix. For voting patterns on clauses thereof see UNSCOR 381st Meeting November 16, 1948, 53–6.

111. See statement of the Government of Israel to General Riley of the United Nations Truce Observation Commission just prior to initiation of the Israeli offensive:

> In view of the fact that the Egyptian Government has done nothing to indicate any desire on its part to achieve a peaceful settlement (conclude an armistice). . . the Government of Israel feels bound to reserve its freedom of action, with a view to defending its territory and hastening the conclusion of peace. U.N. Doc. S/1152 of December 27, 1948.

112. *Id.* During the Security Council debates, Israel made no attempt to justify its attack on the basis of specific Egyptian provocation. Rather, it was Arab refusal to start armistice negotiations which Israel gave as the reason for its actions. Arab intransigence revealed, the Israeli representative, Mr. Fischer stated, 'the determined desire of the Egyptian Government to resume hostilities,' UNSCOR, 394th Meeting at 16. Moreover, he claimed Israel had discovered from statements of captured Egyptian officers that a full scale offensive was to be launched by Egypt on December 27. *Id.*

113. See Letter, dated 24 December 1948, from the Permanent Representative of Egypt to the President of the Security Council, U.N. Doc. S/1151. Within one week after initiation of the offensive, Israeli forces were on the verge of destroying the Egyptian headquarters at El Arish in the Sinai.

114. See Appendix. The legislative history of Resolution 66 merits retelling for it sheds light on the motivations of the Big Powers. As will be recalled, Resolutions 61 and 62 of November 4, and 16, 1948, respectively, differed in that the first called for an Israeli withdrawal from territories gained in excess of the second ceasefire lines while the latter simply made the possibility of withdrawal an issue for discussion

in the proposed negotiations between the parties. Israel backed by the Soviet Union and the Ukrainian S.S.R. maintained that Resolution 62 took precedence. The Arab states, backed mainly by Great Britain, argued for the reverse. In fact, the Israeli justification for breaking the third cease-fire on December 22 was based almost wholly on the Egyptian refusal to abide by Resolution 62 and commence negotiation toward an armistice. Responding to Israel's claim, the President of the Security Council, the Representative of Belgium, stated 'To be quite frank, I cannot bring myself to accept his (the Israeli representative's) interpretation of the November 4 Resolution, which tends to make the implementation of that Resolution dependent upon that of the 16 November Resolution concerning a negotiated armistice.' UNSCOR 394th Meeting, p. 25.

Keeping the Belgian argument in mind, Britain, the sponsor of Resolution 66 stated, in defense of its call for compliance with Resolutions 61 and 62, that 'If a reference to the Resolution of 16 November is introduced, it should, I think, rather be done in such a way as to emphasize the fact. . . that the two resolutions are mutually interdependent and that it is incorrect to subordinate one to the other.' UNSCOR, 396th Meeting, p. 15. The Representatives of the Soviet Union and the Ukrainian S.S.R. strongly denounced any reference to the resolution of November 4. That resolution they asserted could only lead to resumption of war since it failed to recognize the only key to a peaceful resolution of the conflict—a negotiated settlement between the parties. Again, the argument was made that '(t)he chief purpose of the United Kingdom delegation, and of those delegations which supported it (Res. 61) was to serve the transfer of a considerable part of the territory of the State of Israel to the British puppet, King Abdullah. It was thus, in the first place, a question of preventing the implementation of the General Assembly Res. of 29 November, 1947 (181 (II)), on the frontiers of the State of Israel, and secondly, of obstructing the fulfillment of the provisions of that Resolution bearing upon the formation of an independent Arab State in Palestine.' *Id.,* at p. 17.

Resolution 66 was, nevertheless, adopted with its reference to the November 4 Resolution included. Three states abstained from the vote—the U.S.S.R., the Ukrainian S.S.R., and the United States. An Israeli withdrawal pursuant to Resolution 61 never took place, nor did the United Nations ever again refer to that Resolution. The Armistice Agreements became the only binding legal instruments between the two parties and those were taken pursuant to Res. 62.

115. UNSCOR 394th Meeting, Dec. 28, 1948, pp. 12–15, 17.
116. Gabbay, *supra* note 27 at 139.
117. *Id.* The ultimatum was a rather extraordinary political development. Britain threatened intervention on Egypt's behalf on the basis of the Anglo-Egyptian Treaty of 1936. At the same time, Egypt was seeking to annul the treaty.
118. See U.N. Doc. S/1187 of January 6, 1949.

119. 42 U.N.T.S. 251 No. 654.
120. 42 U.N.T.S. 287 No. 655 March 23, 1949 with Lebanon. 42 U.N.T.S. 303 No. 656 April 4, 1949 with Jordan. 42 U.N.T.S. 327 No. 657 July 20, 1949 with Syria.
121. See as representative of the provision in all the Armistice Agreements, Art. 5:2 of the Egypt-Israel Armistice Agreement, which provides:

    The Armistice Demarcation Line is not to be construed in any sense as a political or territorial boundary, and is delineated without prejudice to rights, claims and positions of either Party to the Armistice as regards ultimate settlement of the Palestine question.

    See S. Rosenne, *Israel's Armistice Agreements with the Arab States: A Juridical Interpretation* 4–10.(1951); statement by Dr. Bunche to the Security Council on Aug. 8, 1949, UNSCOR 433d Meeting.
122. See Maurice, *The Armistices of 1918,* Appendices (1943).
123. See *U.S. Foreign Relations, Japan: 1930/1941* p. 217.
124. IV *U.S. Foreign Relations, The American Republics: 1935,* (1953) p. 73.
125. See 39 *Am. J. Int'l L. Supp.* (1945) 88 (Rumania); 93 (Bulgaria); 97 (Hungary); 40 *Am. J. Int'l L. Supp.* (1946) 1 (Italy). See also so-called armistice agreements concluded during the course of World War II *Ibid.* 127 (Finland-U.S.S.R.); 173 (France-Germany); 178 (France-Italy).
126. See Levie, *supra* note I, 9 at 1, n. 1.
127. 42 U.N.T.S. 251, No. 654 (Feb. 24, 1949).
128. 42 U.N.T.S. 303, No. 656, (April 4, 1949).
129. See UNGA Res. 194 (III), Dec. 11, 1948. France, Turkey and the United States were elected as members of the commission.
130. PCC, 3d Progress Report, U.N. Doc. A/927.
131. U.N. Doc. A/927 p. 11, Annex A, B, p. 12.
132. See Gabbay, *supra* note 27 at 256–8.
133. U.N. Doc. A/992 at 6, 10.
134. See U.N. Doc. S/3373, March 17, 1955. Report by the UNTSU Chief of Staff to the Security Council. The report was adopted by the Security Council in Resolution S/3378 condemning the assault.
135. U. Ra'anan, *The U.S.S.R. Arms the Third World: Case Studies in Soviet Foreign Policy* 1–158 (1969). U.S. *News and World Report,* Nov. 4, 1955, 48, 50.
136. See the *Times* Nov. 11, 1955, *Middle Eastern Affairs,* Dec. 1955, pp. 390–2.
137. See Gabbay, *supra* note 27 at 518.
138. See 19 *Knesset Proceedings* (K.P.) of Nov. 15, 1955 at 325. Ben Gurion stated:

    (Eden's) proposal to truncate Israel for the benefit of its neighbors has no legal, moral or logical basis, and cannot be considered. Instead of fostering better relations and bringing peace nearer, it is likely to intensify the Arab States' aggression and to lessen the likelihood of peace in the Middle East. . . . History does not begin with the United Nations General Assembly Resolution of November 29, 1947.

139. M. Dayan, *Diary of the Sinai Campaign* 12–18 (1956).
140. *Id.*
141. *Id.*
142. *Id.*
143. For Israeli allegations at the U.N. that the Egyptian action was a serious infringement of its right to free navigation, see U.N. Doc. S/3442, Sept. 9, 1955; S/3653, Sept. 20, 1956; S/3673, Oct. 13, 1956. For allegations of Egyptian interference with shipping see U.N. Docs. S/3606, June 8, 1956; S/3611, June 28, 1956; S/3642, Sept. 5, 1956; and, especially, S/3652 of Sept. 19, 1956.
144. U.N.S.C.O.R. 538th meeting Sept. 1, 1951, p. 2.
145. See Dayan, *supra* note 139; see also *Haaretz,* Sept. 26, 1955 for declaration by Mr. Ben Gurion that Israel would open the Gulf of Aqaba for its use within a year, even if force were necessary.
146. *The Israel Yearbook,* 1957 at 41.
147. Thus the official Israel Yearbook, *Id.* cites the following factors as making the Sinai Campaign 'inevitable':
    a. The successful defiance of the Western powers offered by Nasser's regime in the Suez crisis.
    b. The increased pace of Egyptian military preparations, including the creation of substantial logistical bases and airfields for jet planes in the Sinai Peninsula.
    c. The gradual replacement of the Mig 15 by more modern Mig 17 fighters as soon as it became known that Israel possessed Mystere 4 planes.
    d. The signing of the Egyptian-Jordanian military alliance.

    'The Israel Government was therefore faced with the alternative of waiting until the coalition of aggressive neighbors under the leadership of Egypt had finished their preparations for a final onslaught, or anticipating the attack in order to destroy the offensive build-up before the attack could be launched.'
148. See regarding plans for British-French collusion with Israel, A. Nutting, *No End of a Lesson: The Story of Suez* 90–110 (1967). R. Bowie, *Suez 1956* 53–60 (1974); A. Beaufre, *The Suez Expedition: 1956,* 69–78 (1969). Israel would probably have attacked even without British-French collusion. See Dayan *supra,* note 139 at 10–15. C. N. Rostow in his excellent student paper, *Diplomatic Patchwork: The United States and the Settlement at Suez 1956–1967,* Yale History Dept. (1972) states on the basis of high calibre 'private information' that as access to the Canal was not a vital issue for Israel she would not have attacked without Anglo-French collaboration, at 6. *See* also for general treatments of the crisis, K. Love, *Suez: The Twice-Fought War* (1969); H. Finer, *Dulles Over Suez: The Theory and Practice of His Diplomacy* (1964).
149. U.N. Doc. S/3710.
150. U.N. Doc. A/3256.
151. U.N. Doc. A/3385/Rev. 1, Nov. 24, 1956; U.N. Doc. A/350/Rev. 1, Jan. 16, 1957; U.N. Doc. A/3517 Feb. 2, 1957.

152. Statement by Israel's U.N. representative, 12 UNGAOR Supp. 10 at 1275, Doc. A/PN666. Compare comments by the French U.N. representative *Id.,* at 1280, with the positions taken by Columbia and India, *Id.,* at 1291, 1302. In reference to the 1967 war, Prof. Eugene Rostow has written, 'it was clear from the international understandings of 1957 (that) Israeli military action under Article 51 (was justified) as an act of self-defense,' 'Legal Aspects of the Search for Peace in the Middle East' 64 *Proceedings of the Am. Soc. of Int'l L.* 64, 67 (1970). See regarding the 1957 agreements C. N. Rostow, *supra* note 148.

153. See especially W. Laqueur, *The Road to Jerusalem* (1968) and R. & W. Churchill, *The Six-Day War* (1969).

154 See Statement of the Permanent Representative of Jordan, Muhamed H. El-Farra, to the Security Council, June 8, 1967, Provisional verbatim record of the 1341st meeting, U.N. Doc. S/PV 1351 (1967); Statement by King Hussein of Jordan to the U.N. General Assembly, June 26, 1967: 'What is the duty of the United Nations? It can be nothing but the swift condemnation of the aggressor and the enforcing of the return of Israeli troops to the lines held before the attack of 5 June.' 22 UNGAOR, 5th emergency special session, 1546th meeting, U.N. Doc. A/PV 1536, at 6 (1967).

155 See Interview with King Hussein, *Der Spiegel,* Sept. 4, 1967 at 96. Shortly after 0630 Greenwich Mean Time sporadic fighting originated from the Jordanian sector of Jerusalem. At approximately 0930 Jordan opened fire along its borders with Israel, causing little property damage and no loss of life. At 1000 Jordan attacked the Israeli air base at Kefar Sirkin, destroying one aircraft. At 1100 the Israeli Air Force responded by attacking the airports at Amman, al Mafrak, and the radar station at Ajlun. By 1410, the strategically located U.N. Headquarters southeast of Jerusalem came under Jordanian occupation. At 1425 the Israeli Central Commander was ordered to counter-attack. R. & W. Churchill, *Supra,* note 153; Committee on Foreign Relations, United States Senate, *A Selected Chronology and Background Documents Relating to the Middle East,* 91st Cong., 1st Sess., 27–31 (1969).

156. King Hussein had signed a joint defense pact with President Nasser on May 30, 1967. Under the terms of the alliance, the Egyptian Chief of Staff would command both the Jordanian and the UAR forces in the event of war with Israel. Strategically, Egypt had established a pincer against Israel's most vulnerable point—the region where Jordanian territory jutted into Israel's narrow 10-mile waist—which could be manipulated from Cairo. Egypt realized that Israel would have to deploy the bulk of her armor in the south to ward off the potential Egyptian attack. On May 31 Iraq moved major troop concentrations and armor into Jordan. When the war broke out, an Iraqi division was about to cross the Jordan River to come under the command of Egyptian Gen. Riadh in Amman. On June 3 a battalion of Egyptian commandoes had arrived in Amman. See Churchill, *supra* note 153 at 51–52, 124–8.

157. Israel's initial public declarations were that Egypt had been the first to open fire. See Kol Israel broadcasts and newspaper accounts in Israel's major dailies of June 5–12, collected in Shiloah Center for Middle East Studies, *The Middle East Y. Bk.*, 215–16 (1967); Ayalon, 'The Six Day War,' *Maarakhot* 1, 6 (1967) (Hebrew, Israel Defense Forces Publication). See also Israeli Foreign Minister Eban's speech to the U.N. on June 19, 1967.

158. See Dinstein, 'The Legal Issues of "Para-War" and Peace in the Middle East,' 44 *St. John's Rev.* 466, 469, 470 (1970). Professor Franck writes:

> Perhaps only in the case of Israel's invasion of the Arab States in 1967 does it seem at all convincing, on the facts, that the use of force was truly preemptive in a strict sense, i.e. undertaken in reasonable anticipation of an imminent large scale armed attack of which there was substantial evidence. The territorial smallness of Israel, moreover, may make more plausible that country's case for striking first, lest a first blow even with conventional weapons by the other side be as decisive as a nuclear blow would be against a larger nation.

'Who Killed Article 2:4?', 64 *Am. J. Int'l L.* 804 (1970).

159. See interview with Gen. Weizmann of May 31, 1972, *Yediot Acharonot*.

> We had to attack because the enemy, intentionally or not, brought about a situation in which he tried to force upon us basic political decisions under the threat of military force. Perhaps the Egyptians would never have attacked. Perhaps we would have accepted the minority opinion not to go to war but to transport in the straits via a convoy under a Norwegian or Danish flag. Then we would have accepted second class statehood; and if the Arabs had attacked first they would have caused us more losses and the victory would have taken longer.

None of the other generals (Gavish, Peled, or Herzog) interviewed at the same time appeared to disagree with Gen. Weizmann's assessment of the facts. Gen. Rabin, then Commander-in-Chief of Israel's Armed Forces, expressed a similar opinion in a different interview, *Maariv* June 2, 1972. See, however, the text of the Cabinet decision to go to war made public on June 4, 1972:

> After hearing a report on the military and political situation from the Prime Minister, the Foreign Minister, the Defence Minister, the Chief of Staff and the head of military intelligence, the Government ascertained that the armies of Egypt, Syria and Jordan are deployed for immediate multi-front aggression, threatening the very existence of the state.
>
> The Government resolves to take military action in order to liberate Israel from the stranglehold of aggression which is progressively being tightened around Israel. . . .

*Jerusalem Post,* June 5, 1972, at 1. Supporting this view, see Interview with Gen. Chaim Bar-Lev, Deputy Chief of Staff in the 1967 War,

*Jerusalem Post,* July 3, 1972, at 1. See also observations by Western newsmen that Egypt and Jordan immediately prior to the outbreak of hostilities were not anticipating an Israeli strike, in *New York Times,* June 5, 1967, at 1, 3.

160 Reproduced in *Laqueur,* at 19. Eban also made the point that Israeli forces had struck in response to an Egyptian air and artillery attack in the Southern Negev. The major thrust of his speech was, however, an advocacy that the blockade was a *causus belli.*

161. Art. 16, Convention on the Territorial Sea and Contiguous Zones, done at Geneva, April 28, 1958, [1962] 15 U.S.T. 1606, T.I.A.S. no. 5639, 516 U.N.T.S. 205. See Gross, 'Passage through the Straits of Tiran and the Gulf of Aqaba,' 33 *L. & Contemp. Prob.* 125–46 (1968); Gross, 'The Geneva Convention on the Law of the Sea and the Right of Innocent Passage through the Gulf of Aqaba,' 53 *Am. J. Int'l L.* 564–94 (1959); Wright, 'The Middle East Problem,' 64 *Am. J. Int'l L.* 279 (1970); M. McDougal & W. Burke *The Public Order of the Oceans,* 209–212 (1961). For justification of the blockade as a defensive measure, see, Letter to the Editor of the *London Times* by El Shibib, Representative of the League of Arab States, May 29, 1972, at 9, col. 3; Letter to the Editor of the *New York Times* by Professor Roger Fisher, June 11, 1967 at 13. See also Lewan, 'Justification for the Opening of Hostilities in the Middle East,' 26 *Revue Egyptienne De Droit International* 88–106 (1970), concluding at 101:

> Even if Article 16 [of the 1958 Geneva Convention on the Territorial Sea and the Contiguous Zone] were a codification of an existing rule (and hence binding upon Egypt although not a party to that treaty), Egypt would have been legally justified in closing the Straits of Tiran to Israeli ships and all others which carried strategic materials destined for Israel at the time when Nasser announced the blockade.

The short answer to Lewan is that if an alleged state of belligerancy permitted Egyptian closure of the Straits, then it equally permitted Israeli opening of the Straits.

162 *See* E. V. Rostow, *supra* note 148 at 67.

> In 1957, in deference to Arab sensitivity about seeming publicly to 'recognize' Israel, to 'negotiate' with Israel, or to make 'peace' with Israel, the United States took the lead in negotiating understandings which led to the withdrawal of Israeli troops from the Sinai. The terms of that understanding were spelled out in a carefully planned series of statements made by the governments both in their capitals, and before the General Assembly. Egyptian commitments of the period were broken one by one, the last being the request for the removal of U.N.E.F., and the closing of the Strait of Tiran to Israeli shipping in May, 1967. That step, it was clear from the international understandings of 1957, justified Israeli military action under Article 51 as an act of self-defense.

See documents in Dept. of State, *U.S. Policy in the Middle East, Sept., 1956–June, 1957* (1957) 332–342; U.S. Cong. Senate Comm. on For.

Rela. *A Select Chronology and Background Documents Relating to the Middle East,* (1967, rev. ed., 1969); H. Finer *Dulles over Suez* (1964) Chs. 17 and 18; and C. N. Rostow, *supra* note 148 at 60.

163. It is important to focus on the nature of the all-out war threatened in response to any Israeli reprisal. President Nasser and other Arab leaders had made it clear that the war would not centre on the Arab right to control the Gulf of Aqaba. 'Taking Sharm al Shayk,' Nasser stated, 'meant that we were ready to enter a general war with Israel. It was not a separate operation.' Speech to Arab Trade Unionists, May 26, 1967, reproduced in Laqueur, *supra* note 153 at 175. See also Nasser's earlier speech before the UAR Advanced Air Headquarters, May 25, 1967, reproduced in Laqueur, at 169–172.

Cairo's propaganda campaign was more emphatic. The following broadcast of May 19, 1967, was typical of the ones preceding the war: 'It is our chance, Arabs, to direct a blow of death and annihilation to Israel, and all its presence in our Holy Land. It is war for which we are awaiting and in which we shall triumph,' Transcript of 'Voice of the Arabs,' reproduced in *Laqueur,* at 90. For a forceful argument that the Arab propaganda, even assuming that it did not always mean what it said, raised the expectations of both the Arab masses and leaders to a point where it had to be fulfilled, see *Id.,* at 71–108.

164. See Churchill, *supra* note 153 at 179–185. See also Lall's excellent study of the paralysis that ensued in the Security Council, 'The State of Belligerency and the Gulf of Aqaba: The Security Council Again Falters,' *The U.N. and the Middle East Crisis* 22–44 (1968).

165. Reproduced in *Laqueur,* at 179–85.

166. *Id.,* at 180.

167. *Id.,* at 184.

168. *Id.,* at 185.

169. See draft resolutions and voting patterns in U.N. Docs. A/L519, A/L52, A/2524, and A/L525, all rejected on July 4, 1967 by votes of 88 to 32, 98 to 22, 81 to 36 and 80 to 36, respectively.

170. See U.N. Docs. S/7951, S/7951/Rev. 1, S/7951/Rev. 2, S/PV 1360 (1967). See also Stone, *The Middle East Under Cease-fire* 10, (1967) viewing the Security Council's rejection of the Soviet resolutions condemning Israel as legally determinative of the defensive character of Israel's posture in the 1967 War.

171. G. A. Res. 337 A (V) Article 20 of the U.N. Charter served as the foundation for the resolution, the basic provisions of which are incorporated in Rules 8 and 9 of the Rules of Procedure of the General Assembly.

172. G. A. Res. 337 A. (V)., Part A., par. 1.

173. *See* regarding the General Assembly and subsequent Security Council debates on this issue, Lall, *The U.N. and The Middle East Crisis, 1967,* (1968).

174. U.N. Doc. S/Res/242, reproduced in Appendix.

175. *See* Lall, *supra* 230–79. Higgins, 'The Place of International Law in The Settlement of Disputes by the Security Council,' 64 *Am. Soc. of*

*Int'l L.* 7–8 (1970); Rostow, *supra* note 152; Stone, 'Security Council Resolution 242, Guideline or Pitfall?' 3 *Toledo L. Rev.* 43 (1971); Shapira, 'The Security Council Resolution of November 27, 1967—Its Legal Nature and Implications,' 4 *Israel L. Rev.* (1969).

176. Wright, 'The Middle East Problem,' 64 *Am. J. Int'l.* 270, 272 (1970).

177. Regarding this 'misunderstanding' by other international lawyers, Rosalyn Higgins is less kind, stating that in this instance, 'the notion of territorial acquisition has become deliberately blurred with that of military occupation.' *See* Higgins, *supra* note 175.

178. 'Article 2 (4) makes it clear by implication at least, that the aggressor should not be allowed to retain the fruits of his aggression. But this article provides no clear guidance on the problem of a state which has responded to a threat of annihilation and in so doing has taken the fight into the enemy's territory. . . . there is nothing in either the Charter or general international law which leads one to suppose that military occupation, pending a peace treaty, is illegal. . . Israel is in legal terms entitled to remain in the territory she now holds.'

Higgins, *Id.* at 7–8; see also Schwebel; 'What Weight to Conquest' 64 *Am. J. Int'l. L.* 344 (1970).

179. This becomes clear upon an examination of Security Council deliberations prior to reaching consensus on the text of Res. 242. Several states made repeated attempts to require 'withdrawal from all *the* territories,' which they interpreted to mean that only withdrawal from all of the territories would do. The defeat of these efforts makes it, therefore, incorrect to assert that withdrawal from *all* the territories is required. See Stone, *supra* note 170 at 14; Rostow, *supra* note 152; Weil, 'Territorial Settlement in the Resolution of November 22, 1967,' *Les Nouveaux Cahiers* 4–8 (Winter, 1970), English translation of text in J. Moore (ed) II, *The Arab-Israeli Conflict* (1974).

180. See *supra* note 121 and accompanying text.

181. Paragraph 3 of Security Council Resolution 242 called upon the Secretary General to designate a Special Representative 'to promote agreement and assist efforts to achieve a peaceful and accepted settlement in accordance with the provisions and principles in this resolution'. On the day after passage of the resolution, November 23, Ambassador Gunnar Jarring of Sweden was designated as the Special Representative.

182. In addressing himself to the territorial questions left unresolved by the 1949 Armistice Agreements, Abba Eban stated Israel's position as follows:

The peace negotiations would enable the parties to exchange proposals on the manner in which the armistice frontiers might be *mutually adjusted* for a peace settlement. One of the problems to be considered is the elimination of demilitarized zones, where division or obscurity of authority has caused great tensions at critical times.

> It would also enable adjustments to be made, by suitable exchanges, for reuniting certain villages with their lands and fields in cases where the armistice frontier now separates them.

A. Eban, *Voice of Israel* 108 (1957). Note, however, that the text of the Armistice Agreements is deliberately broader. Although Security Council Resolution 62, setting forth the conditions for the Armistice Agreements, stipulated that 'The agreements were to delineate permanent demarcation lines, beyond which the armed forces of the respective parties should not move' (para. c), the Arab states were able to successfully demand inclusion of the following term in the agreements: 'The Armistice Demarcation line is not to be construed in any sense as a political or territorial boundary, and is delineated without prejudice to the rights, claims and positions of either party to the armistice as regards ultimate settlement of the Palestine question', sect. 2, Art. V, Israel-Egyptian Armistice Agreement. Accordingly, Israeli interpretations of the agreements as allowing for only the most minor territorial adjustments go beyond a strict legal interpretation of the agreements in an attempt to present a moderate political position as an inducement to Arab negotiation. Nevertheless, after adopting such a stance between 1949 and 1967, and thus creating a pattern of community expectations as to settlement, Israel would seem legally estopped from now urging a more legalistic reading of the agreements' terms.

The American position has been that while the new boundaries to be arrived at need not be the same as those of the Armistice demarcation lines, allowance should be made for only minor territorial adjustments, with demilitarization rather than cession being the key to satisfaction of 'security considerations.' Speech by President Johnson, Sept. 10, 1968, 59 *Dept. of State Bull.* 348 (1968); Speech by Secretary Rogers, Dec. 9, 1969 62 *Id.* at 7, 218–9 (1970). This policy has remained unaltered under each of the succeeding administrations.

183. See para. 2 (c) of Sec. C. Res. 242 affirming further the necessity '(f)or guaranteeing the territorial inviolability and political independence of every State in the area, through measures including the establishment of demilitarized zones.'

184. The independence of Trans-Jordan was recognized formally by Britain in a treaty of alliance entered into at London on March 22, 1946, CMD. 6779 (1946). Sykes writes that '(t)he British government could hardly do anything else if it was to abide by the pledges of the League Mandate, or retain the goodwill of Abdullah who had been Britain's only active Arab ally in the war.' *supra* note 6 at 303. Riebenfeld attributes the move to a desire to dissassociate the question of Trans-Jordan's future from that of Cis-Jordan at a time when the Anglo-American Committee was beginning the consideration of the Palestine question. Riebenfeld (unpublished ms.), *supra* note 26 at 39-40. Regarding the validity of Britain's action of April 18, 1946 he states:

> It is an understatement to say that the step was of doubtful legality. 'The Mandate does not make provisions for the Mandatory Power to cede mandatory power to the people under tutelage. That is a change of the Mandate' (Wm. Rappard, Vice Chairman of the Permanent Mandates Commission. Minutes, vol. XIII, pp. 44-5) requiring consent of the League Council.

*Midstream, Id.* at 18. *See* also American-British correspondence and position papers on Trans-Jordanian independence in VII *For. Relats. of the U.S.* 794-800 (1946).

185. *See* Blum's position regarding Jordan's rights in the West Bank: 'the use of force having been illegal, it naturally could not give rise to any legal title *'ex injuria jus non oritur'.'* 'The Missing Reversioner: Reflections on the Status of Judea and Samaria', 3 *Israel L. Rev.* 279 (1968). E. Lauterpacht states 'Thus Jordan's occupation of the Old City—and indeed of the whole area west of the Jordan River—entirely lacked legal justification; and being defective in this way could not form any basis for Jordan validly to fill the sovereignty vacuum in the Old City.' *Jerusalem & The Holy Places* 47 (1968). See also J. Stone, *No Peace— No War in the Middle East* 39 (1968); Schwebel, 'What Weight to Conquest?', 60 *Am. J. Int'l L.* 344 (1970); Hearings on the Middle East Situation before the Subcomm. on the Near East of the House Comm. on Foreign Affairs, 92d Cong., 2d Sess. at 71 (1972).

186. The word 'ostensibly' is used advisedly as evidence exists that the member states of the Arab League, principally Trans-Jordan, although publicly maintaining between 1943 and 1947 that they favored the creation of an independent Palestinian state upon the Mandate's termination, were in fact planning for its incorporation into their respective states. For example, when the first Arab Unity Conference was held in Cairo in August 1943, Trans-Jordan's King Abdullah instructed his Prime Minister in a private memorandum to plan for a loose confederation of Arab states in which Palestine would be under his rule. *Memoirs of King Abdullah* 245-55 (1950). A public announcement of these intentions addressed to the people of Syria was prepared by Abdullah in April 1943. It was proscribed by the British, who feared that it would be detrimental to the cause of Arab unity. *Id.,* at 266-7. *See* also J. Marlowe, *The Seat of Pilate: An Account of the Palestine Mandate,* 221 (1959); Sykes, *supra* note 6 at 375-6.

On April 22, 1948, King Abdullah of Trans-Jordan, who had assumed the military leadership of the Arab League, called on 'all Arab countries to join my armies in a movement to Palestine to return the Arab character of that country when the British end their Mandatory rule on 15 May.' Reported in Marlowe, *Id.,* at 246. On April 25, 1948, after five days of talks on military preparation by the Arab League, a paper plan was produced by which (a) Trans-Jordan in cooperation with Iraqi forces would capture Haifa and the lower Galilee and (b) Trans-Jordanian and Egyptian forces in the south would join up near Hebron and jointly capture Jerusalem. *Id.* at 247.

Note also Kimche's assertion that this plan of invasion was communicated to the British Military Command in Palestine. J. Kimche, *Seven Fallen Pillars* 213 (1953). Trans-Jordan expressed its official justification for entry into the West Bank in 1948 in a cablegram sent by King Abdullah on May 16, 1948 to the Secretary General expressing a desire to curtail violence against the Arab population and to fulfill its 'national duty towards Palestine in general and Jerusalem in particular.' U.N. Doc. S/748.

187. Sykes, *supra* note 26 at 282.

188. Policy Statement of the Government of Trans-Jordan adopted by the Council of Ministers, Dec. 7, 1948 and affirmed by Trans-Jordan's Parliament, Dec. 13, 1948.
Reproduced in II *Whiteman,* at 1164.

189. A noted West Bank writer expresses the following opinion as to the voluntariness of that expression. Arguing 'that it would be more advisable to establish a Palestinian state before an Israeli withdrawal— if and when it materializes—than after such a withdrawal,' he states:

> Right now, no pressure exists and no threats are made at anybody. If, on the other hand, Israel evacuated the territories she occupied in 1967, and Jordan returned, then no one—be it the leader or the commoner—will be bold enough to say: 'I want a Palestinian government.' The reason is obvious and known to all Palestinians who lived under the Jordanian flag during the past twenty years. In such an eventuality all that would happen would be the convening of a Palestinian congress in which the people of Palestine would presumably decide its fate. During the congress, a speaker—who would be someone chosen from Amman among many willing ones—will stand up and say: 'The people of Palestine supports and demands the maintenance of the unity of the two Banks of the River Jordan'—exactly as what happened in the Jericho Conference held in the winter Royal Palace in that city in 1948, and in the course of which the Palestinian people were claimed merged with the Jordanian people. Needless to say, the Congress will be surrounded by Jordanian troops, tanks, and security personnel—so that no one will have dared to say 'No.'

See Nasaryya, 'The Palestine State Revisited.' 31 *New Middle East* 38 (1971). Sykes, *supra* note 6, at 382, refers to the West Bank representatives as 'picked notables.' For a similar assessment of the Jericho Convention, *see* Hammad, 'Palestinian Future—New Directions' 35 *New Middle East* 16-20 (1971). As the West Bank's future is still far from settled, statements against Jordan's right of reversion are understandably risky and should in the absence of clear proof to the contrary, be given substantial credence.

See also Ch. IIE, 'The Annexation as a Process of "Tacit Understanding" and "Antagonistic Collaboration"' in S. Mishal, *The Conflict Between the West and East Banks Under Jordanian Rule and its*

*Impact on the Governmental Administrative Patterns in the West Bank (1949-1967)* (Unpublished Ph.D. dissertation, Dept. of International Relations, Hebrew University of Jerusalem, 1974).

190. II *Whiteman,* at 1166.

191. See *supra* note 182. *See* also the following statement by Prof. Quincy Wright:

> Another complication may result from the *protracted* functioning of a cease-fire or armistice line within the territory of a state. While hostilities across such a line by the government in control of one side, claiming title to rule the entire state, seems on its face to be civil strife, if such lines have been *long continued* and *widely recognized,* as have those in Germany, *Palestine,* Kashmir, Korea, Viet Nam and the Straits of Formosa, they assume the character of international boundaries.
>
> (emphasis added)

Wright, 'International Law and Civil Strife' 1959 *Proceed's Amer. Soc. of Int'l. L.* 145, 151. As the armistice in Palestine did not concern itself with the division of an entity formerly existing as a unitary state but rather with the division of a mandated territory, which was continually racked by conflicting claims to eventual sovereign control by two different people, all the more reason would appear to exist for assuming that the armistice boundaries had assumed an international character. Accordingly, it was accepted by all parties concerned that hostilities across the armistice lines would constitute breaches of *international* peace and justify individual or collective defense.

192. von Glahn, *supra* note I, 14 at 273.

193. *See* Gerson, 'Trustee-Occupant: the Legal Status of Israel's Presence in the West Bank,' 14 *Harv. Int'l L. J.* 1, 39-40 (1973).

194. *Id.,* at 40.

195. See L. S. Kadi, PLO Research Centre, *Arab Summit Conferences and the Palestinian Problem* (1966).

196. *See* Hammad, *supra* note 189, at 16. S. Shye, *Israel Institute of Applied Social Research: Progress Report on Preparation of a Development Program for Administered Areas (The West Bank and Gaza Strip)* 19-21, 48-55 (1971).

197. Y. Harkabi, *Arab Attitudes to Israel* 433 (1971). Jordan had however little cause for concern. The Arab community in Mandatory Palestine had never succeeded in creating an institutionalized political center. Factional conflicts and their inability to develop a rallying ideological focal point was one of the prime reasons why an independent Palestinian state failed to be established in 1948. Power in the West Bank under British rule rested on traditional family status and wealth as maintained by the notables of the various towns of

the region. These same bases of power continued to exist under Jordanian rule. Rivalries continued and the possibility of the West Bank ever developing an authoritative center of its own remained dim. *See* Mishal, *supra* note 189.

198. See *supra,* note 185.

199. 14 *Harv. Int. L. Journ.* 1 (1973), *supra,* note 193.

200. See *supra* pp. 7–11.

## Chapter III

# Management: The Limits of Institutional Change

Israel's military occupation has been subjected to greater scrutiny and monitoring than any other instance of occupation in world history. Investigations have been conducted on a regular basis by U.N. commissions, various public and private organizations and, more generally, by the international mass media. The results have been less than harmonious or thorough and often replete with political passion. This chapter seeks to go beyond this reporting to present a cogent description and analysis of Israeli management practices and policies affecting the institutional structure of the West Bank. Specifically, reform of the governmental, property and educational system is examined; first, in light of the evolution of these policies and, secondly, in terms of their conformity with the purposes of contemporary international law.

### A. ISRAELI MILITARY OCCUPATION OF THE WEST BANK: FRAMEWORK OF AUTHORITY

#### 1. *Israeli Empowering Legislation*

Upon securing effective control of the West Bank, Israel divided its administration into two sectors: (1) security and short-term economic matters, which were left within the purview of the military command; and (2) political and long-term economic matters, for which policy was made by ministerial committees of the civilian government. The area was divided into six districts and headed by a military governor with army personnel, Arab administrators and a small civilian staff. By 1968, the civilian staff had been totally replaced by Arab officials.[1]

The Jordanian legal framework was retained, although Israel publicly stated that its maintenance was not necessarily mandated by the relevant international law—the Hague Regulations and the Geneva Conventions.[2] Their applicability was questioned on the grounds that they were only pertinent to conquered enemy territory, whereas it was at least uncertain whether the West Bank should not, in fact, be deemed 'liberated' territory to which Israel had a valid claim or at least one comparable in weight to that of Jordan.[3] On June 27, 1967, Israel's Minister of Justice, Y. S. Shapiro, stated in the Knesset that Israel should not view herself as a military occupant in territory which 'the Israel defense forces liberated from foreigners and which are recognized portions of Eretz Israel.'[4] The statement came in support of the proposed, and soon to be passed, *Law and Administrative Ordinance (Amendment No. 11) Law* which would permit the government to extend 'the law, jurisdiction and administration of the State of Israel to any area of Eretz Israel (Palestine).'[5]

The authority of the *Law and Administrative Ordinance Law* was shortly thereafter invoked to extend Israel's civil jurisdiction to East Jerusalem.[6] It was never invoked to extend Israeli civil jurisdiction to the West Bank proper, although that always remained a possibility. Measures were taken, however, which lent themselves to interpretation as implicit Israeli claims to sovereignty over the West Bank. On October 22, 1967, a provision in the military proclamations[7] specifying that the Geneva Convention would have superiority over security legislation was deleted.[8]

On February 29, 1968, the popular term, 'West Bank', was, by official fiat,[9] abandoned in favor of 'Judea and Samaria'—the historical and geographical designation of the region and one not without nationalist and religious overtones of association with the Jewish people. On February 29, 1968, the

Ministry of the Interior promulgated a regulation whereby the West Bank, the Golan Heights, the Gaza Strip and Sinai would no longer be considered as 'enemy territory'. Since the 1967 War, Israeli nationals had been allowed to enter the territories freely without committing the offense of entering 'enemy territory'. This regulation, the Ministry of Interior stated, simply recognized this fact and as such was purely administrative in nature, without any political implications regarding the future of the region. Nevertheless, Arab states chose to interpret the measure as an attempt to lay the groundwork for future annexation of the regions concerned.[10]

In interpreting claims invoking the authority of the Hague and Geneva Conventions, Israeli courts have refused to officially acknowledge their 'de jure' applicability to Israel's occupation. When faced with the issue, Israeli courts evaded it. The quotation below, from a recent decision, is illustrative:

> 2. Both submissions depend upon international conventions—the Hague Convention of 1907 and the fourth Geneva Convention of 1949. The latter was ratified by Israel by deposition of letter of ratification on July 6, 1951 whilst Jordan acceded to the ratification on May 29, 1951.
> 3. Regarding the application of the Convention to the outcome of the Six Day War as a case of 'partial or total occupation of a high contracting party' (Article 3 of the Convention) I have serious doubts whether the Convention has come into operation at all. But this is not the occasion for dealing with the matter. For the purpose of this judgment and because of the State of Israel's practice in observing the provisions of the Convention, which indeed serves as a guiding light in crystallizing the human principles of civilized people, I assume that I must resort to the Convention as if it were applicable.[11]

## 2. *Military Government*

Decision making on occupational matters became subject to the authority of three different levels of Israeli government: the cabinet level, the ministry level and that of the regional and district military commands. The Cabinet Committee, headed by the Prime Minister, assumed responsibility for formulating major policies. The Inter-Ministerial Committee for the Coordination of Activities in the Territories dealt with political and security problems. The Director-General's Committee for Economic Affairs was in charge of economic issues, and the Unit for Coordination of Activities in the Territories, a section of the Ministry of Defense, became responsible for coordination of all non-military operations in the territories. The Military Commander of the West Bank assumed full legislative and executive authority in the area. Administrative authority was delegated to regional and district commanders.

Routine administrative duties were left in the hands of previous or newly recruited indigenous Arab personnel. Health, welfare and other public service institutions were initially left intact, but gradual adjustment and modernization of services began to occur. The postal system, for example, was reorganized and expanded and required to use memoranda and stamps in both Arabic and Hebrew, as well as Israeli postal stamps and rates. The West Bank telephone system became linked to Israel's, with that of East Jerusalem becoming fully integrated into the Israeli telephone system.[12]

Regulatory changes aimed at standardizing West Bank license, weight and measure systems with those of Israel's soon were initiated. Arab tour guides, radio broadcasters, hoteliers and automobile drivers were required to obtain Israeli licenses. Automobile insurance covering the passengers as well as the driver became a mandatory condition for obtaining a license.[13]

### 3. *Indigenous Government*

The municipal governmental system that operated on the West Bank under Jordanian law was retained. Mayors were not elected directly, but rather were appointed by the Jordanian monarch from ten elected councillors in each large town and from five elected councillors in the smaller towns. The election of the councillors was limited to propertied tax-paying males.

Israeli occupation commenced just three months prior to expiration of the four-year mayoralty terms. When new elections became due on August 31, 1967, they were postponed indefinitely but finally held in 1972. Within that period of time, Israel replaced mayors in only three instances and each time for reasons allegedly unrelated to insubordination.[14]

The mayors acquired greater authority under Israeli military rule than they had had under Jordanian rule because the next highest level of government, the district, was not reactivated. Often they were used for contacts with the Amman Government; but they sought further elevation of their role beyond the purely local level. In ruling Israeli quarters, this was viewed as a step towards ultimate claims for full autonomy of the region. This was not favored and, as a result, any efforts by the mayors to establish themselves as politically representative of the West Bank became doomed from the start.[15] Whether the mayors would have assumed such greater authority had they been accorded the opportunity is questionable. Fear of being termed collaborators might have deterred them. Indeed, in May, 1968, West Bank leaders turned down an Israeli offer to hand over the Military Government's administrative functions to West Bank residents, since this would be tantamount to 'recognizing the occupation'.[16]

Day-to-day municipal government was left unhampered, but the Israeli Military Occupational Government always retained indirect leverage, particularly through financial controls such as the power to withhold or extend loans, development funds, tax rebates and permits and licenses for the city's residents.

### 4. *The Applicable Law and the Process of Claims*

Israel, as noted earlier, chose to leave open the question of the *de jure* applicability of the Geneva Convention to its occupation, although continuing *de facto* observance.[17] The basis for its denial turns on the issue of sovereignty over the region. Israel asserts that the rule of *status quo ante* of the Geneva and Hague Conventions is based on the supposition that the ousted power is the legitimate party entitled to reversion of the occupied territory, and that, accordingly, his political interests rather than the needs of the population are necessarily sought to be protected. Otherwise there would be little reason for preserving the occupied society's structure and prohibiting the introduction of beneficent reform. Thus, since in Israel's view Jordan was not a legitimate sovereign, the rule of *status quo ante*—the basis of the Hague and Geneva Conventions—need not be observed *de jure*.

There is no need at this point to decide the dispute as to whether the Conventions seek primarily to protect the political interests of the ousted sovereign or the humanitarian needs of the population. Suffice it to say that the Hague Convention's prohibition of any legislative change appears to have been promulgated to prevent the occupier's invocation of 'the welfare of the populace' to serve as a ruse for annexationist ambitions. But whatever the correct answer to this dispute may be, it is of little importance for our immediate purposes. This is because Israel stipulates, though believing it is not obligated to do so, that its military commanders and courts are bound by the Conventions. Thus, implicitly Israel agrees to be judged by the standard of conduct imposed by the relevant international conventions pertaining to belligerent occupation.

Yet, even where a military occupational government agrees to comply with the *status quo ante* policy of the Conventions, it will nevertheless be subject to numerous claims for alterations and reform of existing laws and institutions. The longer the occupation lasts, the greater the frequency and intensity of such demands can be expected to be. Elements among the inhabitants, disenchanted with the old order or dissatisfied with some of its particular policies, will attempt to use the occupation as a means for carrying out their own reformist measures. The military occupational government will call for reforms of particular laws and institutions that have allegedly hampered its ability to operate in safety and to protect the population. Finally, and perhaps most importantly, elements in the occupying power's population will urge elimination or revision of laws and institutions of the occupied territory which are perceived as ideologically or politically inimical or simply as obsolete. The salient point is that an occupational legal system, like any other, cannot easily remain, over long periods of time, static and immune from processes of change.

## B. THE GOVERNMENTAL SYSTEM

### 1. *Changes in the System*

#### a. *Legislative*

During the period of Jordanian rule, legislative bodies

indigenous to the West Bank did not exist. All legislative authority was vested in the central government in Amman. Although the municipal councils of the West Bank towns did resemble a system of subsidiary rule, their legislative role was confined to ordinances of minor patterns of public welfare.

Immediately following termination of the 1967 War, the Israel military command in the West Bank published, on June 7, 1967, *Proclamation No. 2 Concerning the Assumption of Government by the Israel Defense Forces.* Section 3 thereof stated:

> Every governmental, legislative, appointive and administrative power in respect of the region or its inhabitants shall henceforth vest in me [the West Bank Commander] alone and shall only be exercised by me or a person appointed by me for that purpose or acting on my behalf.

Although, by virtue of this legislation, all legislative capacity passed into the exclusive domain of the military commander, the Israeli military authorities were to make few additions or revisions to the laws and regulations in force at the time of their assumption of power. New or amending penal legislation was confined to security offenses. Legislative enactments and revisions on the civil side were generally concerned with the maintenance of public order and safety. Within the latter category, acts affecting banking, absentee property and requisitioning of private property were the first to be passed.

b. *Judicial*

(i) *Movement of the Court of Appeals and the Appearance of Israeli Advocates in West Bank Courts*

In late 1967, Israeli authorities transferred the Court of Appeals, then the highest court on the West Bank, from its seat in Jerusalem to Ramallah. The move was undertaken to indicate that Israel would consider Jerusalem as separate and apart in administrative matters from the West Bank proper. The 1st Report of the U.N. Special Committee to Investigate Israeli Practices Affecting the Human Rights of the Population of the Occupied Territories[18] found that this transfer 'seriously hampered the functioning of the court system' as it 'provoked a reaction on the part of the judiciary that brought activities of the Court of Appeals to a standstill.'[19] Accordingly, the Special Committee formally recommended that the General Assembly request the Government of Israel to 'restore the judicial system in the occupied territories to the status which it enjoyed before the occupation and in particular to return the Court of Appeals to its seat in Jerusalem.'[20]

To West Bankers, the movement of the Court of Appeals represented the symbolic incorporation or annexation of East Jerusalem.[21] Continuation of 'business as usual' in these circumstances was viewed as affirming the legitimacy of Israeli rule. A general strike of legal services was instituted. In response, the West Bank Military Commander authorized Israeli advocates to appear in proceedings before West Bank civil courts. When an Israeli advocate, pursuant to this order, attempted to appear in the District Court of Hebron, the Court refused to recognize him. It ruled that the order permitting his appearance exceeded the lawful authority of the Military Governor. The decision was referred to the Court of Appeals, newly situated in Ramallah.

Counsel for the appellant contended that the appearance of the Israeli advocates in West Bank courts was illegal under existing Jordanian law which restricts court appearances to advocates who are Jordanian nationals and members of the Jordanian Bar. The military commander was not competent, it was alleged, to reform regulations pertinent to the practice of law as such change was not absolutely required by either public welfare or military necessity—the only exceptions to Hague Regulation 43's general proscription of changes in the laws and institutions of held territory.

The Ramallah Court of Appeals refused to address itself directly to the merits of this issue, on the grounds that courts of occupied territories are 'not competent to consider whether or not an imperative need exists that requires additional or amending legislation . . .'[22] Nevertheless, in dictum, the Court upheld the validity of the military order.

> Even if we proceeded on the assumption that this Court is competent to examine the problem of such imperative need, we would decide that, as far as Order No. 145 is concerned, the present situation necessitated the issue of the Order because, of

> the dozens of advocates in the West Bank, a very small minority have agreed to practice, while the majority prefer to stay at home and have the inhabitants confused, with no one to turn to to represent them in the civil and military courts and with no one to defend them, or assert their rights.[23]

### (ii) *Military Courts: Operations and Right of Review*

Soon after commencement of occupation, military courts to try security offenses were established by decree of the Military Governor.[24] Procedural law and the law of evidence utilized in the military courts were the same as those that were applicable to criminal courts within Israel. Military officers, members of the Judge Advocate General Corps, served as judges.[25]

Before long, persons being tried began to assert that the acts they were accused of violating had been beyond the legislative authority of the occupier to enact. In *Military Prosecutor* v. *Zuhad* (Israel Military Court in Bethlehem, August 11, 1968)[26] the defendant was charged with violating a new traffic ordinance promulgated by the Military Government. In defense, he alleged that the military commander had exceeded the restrictions of Article 64 of the Geneva Convention, which provides that the laws shall remain in force unless 'they constitute a threat to security or an obstacle to the application of the present Convention' or unless changes are 'essential to enable the Occupying Power . . . to maintain orderly government of the territory . . .' Accordingly, he maintained that by virtue of Article 67 of the Convention, which provides that 'the courts shall apply only those provisions of law which were applicable prior to the offense, and which are in accordance with general principles of law . . .' the Court was required to refuse enforcement of the Traffic Law Order.

The Court stated that it could not find 'any precedent whatsoever' for a military court to examine the validity of the orders of an Army Commander, unless appearing invalid on its face.

> [E]very order issued by the Commander is presumed to be valid, and the presumption is rebuttable only when the order is on the face of it so unreasonable and extraordinary, is so contrary to the principles of natural justice and international morality

> common to civilized peoples, that it is intolerable and the Military Court must ignore it by virtue of its inherent powers because it was enacted on the basis of considerations deriving from malice and arbitrariness and not in order to achieve some lawful purpose.[27]

The ruling of non-review by military courts of military orders for conformity with international law has continued to apply. However, review has been made possible through institution of the novel procedure described below.

#### (iii) *Appeal to Israel Supreme Court by Occupied Population*

Shortly after the 1967 War, inhabitants of the West Bank, seeking review of adverse actions by the military courts, applied to the Israel Supreme Court, sitting in its capacity as a High Court of Justice, for writs of mandamus, habeas corpus and certiorari and for writs of prohibition. No objections to these applications were raised in the Supreme Court by the representatives of the Attorney-General or by any of the Justices of the Court. Israel Attorney-General Meir Shamgar gave as the purpose for permitting this practice the desire 'not to hinder inhabitants of the territory in making use of the legal remedies available in Israel against acts of the administration.'[28] In the larger context the move appeared as consistent with Israel's general aim of 'normalization of relations between inhabitants of the West Bank and Israel.'[29] Apparently motivated by enlightened self-interest, this grant of direct appeal by citizens of the occupied territory to the high court of the occupying power provides the first instance of such a right in the history of military occupation.

### c. *Executive (The Municipal Councils)*

Although regional West Bank rule never became manifest under Jordan's reign, the municipal councils of the various towns, composed of elected representatives, served as important means of political expression. Under Jordanian rule, the term of office for Municipal Council members was, since 1955, limited to four years.[30] The precise number of members permitted to serve on a Municipal Council was not specified[31] but was, rather, to be fixed by the Minister of the Interior, based on a system of proportional representation.[32]

Women were denied suffrage and were specifically prohibited from being candidates for seats on the Municipal Councils.[33] Suffrage was extended only to such male Jordanian citizens as had resided within the municipality's jurisdiction for at least one year prior to the preparation of the list of voters[34] and had made payment of a land or other municipal tax of a substantial amount.[35] The latter restriction effectively ensured that only the propertied class would be entitled to vote.

By a twist of the Jordanian law, it was possible to have a mayor appointed who had never been elected. The *1955 Town Municipalities Law* provides that the mayor be appointed by the Municipal Council from among its members, his appointment becoming effective upon approval by the Minister of the Interior. Moreover, the Minister of the Interior is authorized to appoint two additional members to the Municipal Council. As a result, individuals who have never been elected to serve on the Municipal Councils have been appointed as mayors.[36]

The last mayoralty elections held on the West Bank under Jordanian rule occurred in September 1963. According to Jordanian law, elections were scheduled to occur again in September 1967. However, the Israeli Military Government suspended the impending elections for an unlimited period of time,[37] claiming that the three months of occupation that had elapsed were not sufficient for the population to adapt itself to the new situation. Holding elections at this point would, it was claimed, necessarily involve campaigns and propaganda warfare that would be inimical to the maintenance of public order.

Demands for new municipal elections began, nevertheless, to be increasingly voiced, mainly by individuals aspiring to positions of leadership in the Municipal Councils.[38] After a great deal of hesitation, the Israeli government finally responded positively to this initiative. In November 1971, the Military Government passed the *Order Concerning Municipal Elections (Judea and Samaria)*[39] permitting the holding of elections according to Jordanian law. It stated:

> [W]hereas the term of office of the town municipalities, under the law, has expired, and whereas I am of the opinion that for regular public administration, and maintenance of the rights of the civil population, it must be permitted to hold elections for municipal councils . . . [it is so ordered].

In anticipation of the elections, the Military Government emphasized that the candidates would be vying only for assumption of administrative duties within the municipal framework and not for representation of the political interests of the West Bank. The newly-elected Municipal Councils were to play the same non-political role they had undertaken since occupation.

Elections were held in two stages: in the Samarians towns and in Jericho on March 28, 1972 and in the towns of Judea on May 2, 1972. Of the eligible population of 30,000, the participation percentage was high, both in the absolute sense and as compared to municipal elections held during the Jordanian period.[40] The Military Government assumed a low profile and chose not to utilize the provision in the Jordanian election law enabling the central government to appoint two additional municipal council members, one of whom might then be designated as mayor.

The Jordanian government gave the newly elected municipal officials at least 'de facto' recognition. Official congratulations were extended and the presence of their signatures on all official documents was requested.[41]

In late 1975 and early 1976 municipal elections were held again in the West Bank. They were immediately preceded by serious disturbances arising mainly from further moves to increase Jewish settlement in the West Bank. More militant anti-Israel candidates who supported the Palestine Liberation Organization were able to wrest majority control in the three major towns—Nablus, Hebron and Ramallah. For the first time the franchise was extended to women as well as all males regardless of their property-owning status, as had previously been the standard.[42]

2. *International Law Relative to the Occupant's Authority to Restructure or Otherwise Modify the Existing Governmental System*

a. *Legislative*

There is little disagreement in the law of belligerent occupation, both in practice and in doctrine, that the operations of indigenous, policy making legislative bodies may be suspended for the duration of the occupation.[43] Municipal Councils entrusted with 'day to day' municipal functions have been treated as an exception.

Although all legislative power vests in the occupant, he may promulgate new or amending legislation only where such action is made imperative by reasons of public order or military security (Article 43 of the Hague Regulations). In all other cases existing legislation is to be respected. Article 64 of the Geneva Convention reiterates this theme.

> The penal laws of the occupied territory shall remain in force, with the exception that they may be repealed or suspended by the Occupying Power in cases where they constitute a threat to its security or an obstacle to the application of the present Convention. Subject to the latter consideration and to the necessity for ensuring the effective Administration of justice, the tribunals of the occupied territory shall continue to function in respect of all offenses covered by said law.

Although Article 64 refers exclusively to penal legislation, it has been interpreted to extend to civil legislation as well. The official commentary to the Geneva Convention states:

> The idea of the continuity of the legal system applies to the whole of the law—civil law and penal law—in the occupied territory. The reason for the Diplomatic Conference making express reference only to respect for penal law was that it had not been sufficiently observed during past conflicts; there is no reason to infer 'a contrario' that the occupation authorities are not also bound to respect the civil law of the country, or even its constitution.[44]

The most significant difference between Article 64 of the Geneva Convention and the basic principle of respect for the existing legislation as formulated in Article 43 of the Hague Regulations relates to the occupant's right, now expressly recognized, to abrogate any legislation incompatible with humanitarian requirements. The official commentary states:

> The second reservation is in the interests of the population and makes it possible to abrogate any discriminatory measures incompatible with humane requirements. It refers in particular, to provisions which adversely affect racial or religious minorities, such provisions being contrary to the spirit of the Convention (Article 27),[45] which forbids all distinction based, in particular, on race, religion or political opinion.[46]

Under the Hague Regulations, an occupant could, arguably, have suspended the applicability of discriminatory legislation for the duration of the occupation, on the grounds that it is inimical to public order and safety.[47] The Geneva Convention gives the occupant the express power, although not the duty, to abrogate or annul such laws.

b. *Judicial*

(i) *Operation of the Courts*

In contrast to international practice relative to legislative bodies, judicial systems have generally been permitted to function, although not unhampered, during instances of belligerent occupation. In the codified law, Article 23 of the Hague Regulations and, more especially, Article 64 of the Geneva Convention, make specific reference to the judicial systems of occupied territory. Article 23 states:

> . . . it is especially forbidden . . . to declare abolished, suspended, or inadmissible in a Court of law the rights and actions of the nationals of the hostile party.

Article 64 of the Geneva Convention reiterates this theme, stating that:

> . . . subject to the latter consideration [security of the occupant's forces] and the necessity for ensuring the effective administration of justice, the tribunals of the occupied territory shall continue to function in respect to all offenses covered by said laws.

The official commentary thereon declares that:

> . . . the continued functioning of the courts of law also means that the judges must be able to arrive at their decision with

> complete independence. The occupation authorities cannot therefore, . . . interfere with the administration of penal justice or take any action against judges who are conscientiously applying the law of their country.[48]

Nevertheless, Article 54 of the Geneva Convention does permit removal of judges and officials from their posts at the occupant's discretion. Moreover, the commentary thereto states:

> This is a right, of very long standing which the occupation authorities may exercise in regard to any official or judge, whatever his duties, for reasons of their own.[49]

Oppenheim attempts to clear up the apparent contradiction inherent in the stipulation that the independence of judges need be respected while their retention is left at the discretion of the occupier. He reasons, essentially, that suspension of judges must be limited to instances of insubordination, express or indirect, and that in other cases they must be permitted to serve with their independence unimpaired.

> There is no doubt that an occupant may suspend the judges as well as other officials. However, if he does suspend them, he must temporarily appoint others in their place. If they are willing to serve under him, he must respect their independence according to the laws of the country.[50]

Writers on the subject generally agree that once a court in occupied territory reaches a decision, it must be handed down in the name of the law rather than in the name of either the ousted sovereign or the occupant.[51]

As a general rule, local courts are to be permitted to continue to exercise the jurisdiction conferred upon them by the laws that antedate occupation. There are two important exceptions. The first is that courts or tribunals which have been instructed to apply inhumane or discriminatory laws may be abolished. This is a corollary of Article 27 of the Geneva Convention, whereby an occupant is granted the right to abrogate institutions and laws which further discriminatory measures incompatible with humanitarian requirements.[52] Secondly, the jurisdiction of courts in occupied territory over soldiers of the occupying power and over inhabitants of the occupied region involved in security offenses may be abrogated. Breaches by soldiers will be tried by a courts-martial of the occupying power. Breaches by inhabitants may be tried by 'properly constituted, non-political military courts, on condition that the said courts sit in the occupied country' (Article 66, Geneva Convention). The obligation imposed on military courts to adjudicate in occupied territory is, in accordance with the principle of the territoriality of penal jurisdiction, designed to protect the accused from being brought before a court other than in the country where the offense was committed. Jurisdiction over nationals of the occupying power committing penal offenses in the occupied territory has been held to be within the exclusive purview of either the military courts or the regular courts of the occupant. This result is dictated by 'considerations of public order and the prestige and welfare of the occupying forces.'[53]

### (ii) *Judicial Review of Legislative Acts of the Occupant*

The rights of an occupying power in establishing and operating military tribunals in occupied territory are well established in international law.[54] It appears that international practice is uniform in establishing military courts in occupied territories. Although in many occupations military courts were 'properly constituted' and operated according to regular and recognized principles, in many other instances they served as special *ad hoc* tribunals, often concerned more with political or racial persecution than the administration of justice.[55] Yet reference to any right of review by military courts of legislative acts of the occupying power is singularly absent in the international law literature. Implicit in this lack of treatment is the assumption that military courts must enforce orders of their superiors unless appearing patently violative of international law.[56]

Some dispute arises, however, as to the right of indigenous courts to review, during the course of belligerent occupation, legislative acts of the occupant for the purpose of determining conformity with international law. A study of reported decisions by municipal courts during occupation reveals a general trend toward refusal to undertake judicial review. Where municipal courts have consisted of judges appointed by the occupying power, they will, of course, be anxious to uphold his decrees and deny any power of review to the court. Typical of such a situation is the decision of the Norwegian Supreme Court in the *Halvorsen* case, decided in 1941.[57]

> In approaching the question whether an Ordinance is in conformity with Article 43 of the Hague Regulations, we must note, first, that the occupant is empowered to enact new laws where the necessity arises. Whether such legislation is, in fact, urgently necessary is a question of political expediency which must be left to the judgment of the occupant who exercises legislative power in occupied territory. It cannot be subjected to judicial review. If courts had the right to examine the expediency of a law or to deny the necessity of its enactment, they would be liable to interfere in a field for which they lacked required qualifications, and in which the occupant must have the decisive voice, seeing that he is by international law both entitled and bound to ensure public order and public life in occupied territory.

Where municipal courts during occupation have affirmed the power of review, they have been reluctant to apply it,[58] fearful of the occupant's power to retaliate by forcing members of the bench to resign or by replacing the entire court.[59]

International law does not appear to uphold the right of judicial review of acts of the occupant by indigenous courts. Realistically, occupants will, of course, hardly be inclined to permit indigenous courts, with any measure of independence, to question the legitimacy of occupation orders.[60] Although Article 67 of the Geneva Convention requires courts in the occupied territory to 'apply only those provisions of law which were applicable prior to the offense, and which are in accord with general principles of law . . .', it would be incorrect to imply from this language that Article 67 grants a right of judicial review to courts of the occupied region. The Convention, as the entire law of belligerent occupation, seeks to protect the civilian population of occupied territory by minimizing potential confrontation between it and the occupying power.[61] To allow indigenous courts the right to review an occupant's act would require that they be permitted to pass on the validity of the 'military necessity' justification which the occupying power inevitably proffers in support of his act. To maintain that a right of review by indigenous courts exists during the course of occupation is then to speak not only of something incapable of practical effect, but of a practice destined to exacerbate tensions between the occupant and occupied populace. Accordingly, international law defers the right of review by courts of occupied territory until after termination of occupation.[62]

Does the occupied populace, however, have a right under international law to appeal to domestic courts of the occupant for the purpose of questioning whether military orders and promulgations were within the scope of the issuer's legitimate authority? In no instance of belligerent occupation, other than the Israeli case, is there any record of such practice. The literature of international law makes no reference to such a right. Israel's practice in granting the right to have military enactments reviewed by courts of the occupying power is an innovation in occupational rule which merits further adoption. Its effect promises to be the guarantee of a greater measure of respect by occupying powers for rights of the occupied population. Although the courts of the occupying power will probably be disinclined to overrule acts of the military government, nevertheless, in so far as such court decisions are reported, the occupant's courts will not be able to condone acts contravening international law without risking political and judicial embarrassment. In the quest for application of the rule of law in time of occupation, allowance of direct appeal by the occupied to the occupant's courts represents, despite possibilities of abuse, an important advance.

### c. *Executive*

#### (i) *Forced Retention or Resignation of Government Officials*

Local elected officials cannot, as a general rule, be forced to remain in office. Article 54 of the Geneva Convention provides:

> The occupying power shall not alter the status of public officials or judges in the occupied territories, or in any way apply sanctions to or take any measures of coercion or discrimination

> against them, should they abstain from fulfilling their functions for reasons of conscience.
>
> This prohibition does not prejudice the application of the second paragraph of Article 51. It does not affect the right of the occupying power to remove public officials from their post.

Article 51, to which reference is made regarding reservations, provides that the occupying power may requisition the work of men over eighteen years of age for use 'on work which is necessary either for the needs of the army of occupation or for the public utility services or in the feeding, sheltering, clothing, transportation or health of the population of the occupied territory.' Public utility services—the supply of gas, water, electricity and transport—are functions which are the direct responsibility of municipal officials. Thus, where resignation would seriously hamper supply of these services, the occupying power would appear justified in refusing to accept the resignation of municipal officials and in requisitioning their continued services. Professor Pictet, the official commentator on the Geneva Convention, states that the forced retention of mayors as well as judges is permissible because:

> . . . their resignation might well paralyse the whole administrative and judicial machinery, in which case protected persons would be the first to suffer . . . required continuation in office is all the more justified as the non-political nature of their duties is generally such as to remove any conscientious scruples they may have.[63]

Regarding those officials that are retained, voluntarily or not, in their posts, the occupant may exact an oath of sufficient and unprejudiced service but may not require of them an oath of allegiance.[64] The occupant must continue payment of their salaries, providing revenues for that purpose can be collected in the territory occupied.[65] There is no specific requirement that the pre-occupation salary rate be continued. Nor is there any specific requirement that the occupant pay pensioned officials rather than have individuals look for payment to the ousted sovereign.[66] Retained officials may, however, be declared ineligible for receipt of payment of salary from the ousted power and such payments may, if discovered, be confiscated by the occupying power.[67]

The right to demand resignation of government officials is even more encompassing than the right of forced retention. Article 54 of the Geneva Convention removes any restrictions from the occupant's authority to remove elected or appointed governmental officials. Emphasis is placed on the fact that any requirement that an occupying power retain 'political' officials of an adversary government is incompatible with the principle that an occupying power is entitled to obedience and respect for non-political orders by the civilian population.

(ii) *Appointments and Elections*

New officials may be appointed to fulfill non-political tasks. Whether, during the course of occupation, they may be elected to serve in a representative rather than administrative capacity is subject to question.

Unfortunately, international law has accorded the issue but scant attention. Professor Thomas Baty, one of the few writers on the subject,[68] has argued that any elections for representative political office need to be prohibited 'in toto' during the course of occupation. Determinative in his view is the fact that although elections could be honestly administered, dishonesty is too tempting and its use too difficult to prove.[69]

Posed against this contention is the fact that Article 43 of the Hague Regulations' requirement that pre-existing order and public life be restored, would seem to require elections to be held as initially scheduled as soon as possible. Article 54 of the Geneva Convention points, however, to a countervailing policy in so far as it permits an occupant to discharge elected political officials. But, if elected leaders may be lawfully dismissed, can elections under occupation rule ever purport to be free? And, if not, can or should international law require them to be held? Given the tendency of occupants to view themselves as liberators and not as invaders, elections under occupational rule become suspect. The temptation to manipulate elections, unsupervised by an international organ, will always be great. Where, as in the West Bank, a movement toward autonomy from the central government preceded occupation, the fixing of elections would appear to be even easier and thus all the more tempting.

Yet, it needs to be kept in mind that the abuses to which

elections under occupation are prone are well known. Accordingly, international law, insofar as it reflects state practice, attaches a rebuttable presumption of invalidity to elections under occupation on the grounds that they were permeated with duress. Hopefully the presumption of invalidity will spur the occupant to more scrupulous observance of fair election procedures. International law has not taken the stance urged by Professor Baty whereby elections are entirely prohibited. This is because contemporary international law, mindful of the political interests of the occupied populace as well as those of the ousted sovereign, disapproves of freezing all political dissent by the occupied populace against their former ruler, especially where dissent pre-dated occupation. Expeditious resolution of conflict is favoured but not at the price of basic human rights' deprivations: the peace-making process may be purposefully slowed to accommodate these interests.

Finally, if elections are to be sanctioned under occupation, insofar as the presumption of their invalidity is rebuttable upon a showing of a lack of coercion, may inequalities in the election laws be remedied? For example, Jordanian election rules applicable in the West Bank restricted voting eligibility to propertied males. Yet in the April 1973 elections, at the urging of many in the occupied populace who had long favored such reform, suffrage was extended to women. Was such reform permissible?

It has been submitted earlier that not all changes deviating from the *status quo ante* are prohibited. The ordinary processes of social life, especially where they antedate the occupation, need not be frozen. Where protection of fundamental human rights is involved, greater laxity in permissible social and political change exists. In each instance, the danger of hindering potential progress toward reconciliation between the occupant and ousted power must be assessed and weighed against the nature of the human rights' deprivation to be incurred. Formulation of the bounds of permissible change in the existing laws and institutions must never be mechanical.

### 3. *Assessing Israel's Management of Governmental Institutions*

#### a. *Legislative*

The caution exercised by the Israel Supreme Court in endorsing reform of Jordanian legislation is witnessed most clearly in the 1972 case of the *Christian Society for the Protection of Holy Places* v. *The Minister of Defense et al.*[70] At stake was the correction of a 'lex imperfecta', a statute failing to fulfill by its provisions the clear intent of the Jordanian legislature. The statute had provided that labor disputes be settled by arbitration, with arbitrators to be selected by management and labor organizations. The stipulated labor organization failed, however, to ever come into being. In its absence, the Military Commander permitted, at the request of an employee group, revision of the law to permit appointment of arbitrators directly by labor leadership or, alternatively, by the Military Commander. The Supreme Court concluded that the revision was justifiable under the 'ordre publique' exception to Article 43's mandate against legislative change.

The decision was not, however, without a strong dissent. Justice H. Cohn maintained that, 'The power [to reform legislation] is intended only for restoring such order and public life as may have existed prior to the occupation and for ensuring their continued existence . . .' and not for instituting 'order and public life as may appear to him [the occupant] better and more equitable.'[71] Only laws violative of the most fundamental human rights could be changed. The reform in question was deemed to be one which merely appeared in the occupant's eyes to be merited and equitable.

Reference to authoritative works on belligerent occupation indicates, however, that the dissenting opinion's concern for maintenance of the *status quo ante* was overdrawn. It is not change in any existing laws and institutions which is impermissible. Professor McDougal concludes: 'the principal thrust of the prohibition [of Article 43] . . . is the active transformation and remodeling of the power and other value processes of the occupied country.'[72] It is change in fundamental laws and institutions which is outlawed; and 'fundamentality' is gauged by the two-fold test of the degree of human rights violation it entails and its effect in injuring the reversionary interest of the ousted sovereign by the creation of vested interests inimical to a negotiated peace.[73]

Applying this test of 'fundamentality' or 'active transformation of values' to the military order in question in the *Christian Society* case, its promulgation appears clearly to be within the occupant's legislative authority. Nothing more dramatic than fulfillment of legislative intent of the Jordanian authorities was accomplished. The caution displayed by the Israel Supreme Court in ratifying the validity of this minor legislative adjustment reflects Israel's policy of minimal interference in existing legislation on the West Bank.

b. *Judicial*

It has already been stated that Israel's practice of allowing appeals by the occupied populace to the Supreme Court of the occupying power, to review the validity of military government legislation, represents an important precedent in the law of belligerent occupation. Of course, this procedure lends itself to abuse, especially by states with no history of divisible powers of government. They may exploit it in an attempt to add the color of legal validity to otherwise indefensible measures. Yet, as Supreme Court opinions are usually published nationally and, insofar as they touch upon matters of international importance, are reproduced in international legal digests, judicial opinions clearly inconsistent with international law make easy targets for adverse publicity. True, it might be maintained that availability of the occupying power's judicial system to the occupied population promotes 'creeping annexation' through integration of the two systems. But the independent functioning of the military tribunals, courts of the occupying power and courts of the occupied territory, preserves the separate identities of all three systems.

In this light, it is somewhat surprising to note the paucity of claims lodged by West Bankers in the Israel Supreme Court asserting the invalidity of acts of the military authorities. In part, this may be attributed to the belief of many West Bank attorneys that such action would constitute recognition of Israeli sovereignty over the region. Such an attitude may have been politically unwarranted and tactically unwise. Given the 'fishbowl' in which the Israeli judicial system operates, opinions found unfavorable could easily have been exploited to the occupied population's advantage. An Israeli Supreme Court decision viewed as wrongly confirming a military order's validity under international law could then have been used to expose the alleged usurpation of power by the Israeli authorities. But then this sword is double-edged. A well written and intellectually coherent Supreme Court decision denying a claim of alleged unlawfulness by the military government might only hurt those who would seek to embarrass Israeli rule.

The change in the Jordanian law to enable Israeli advocates to appear in West Bank courts for the duration of the strike by West Bank attorneys seems not to have been violative of Article 43 of the Hague Regulations. Availability of legal services is essential for the maintenance of public order and safety. Israeli attorneys acted in a representative and fiduciary capacity for West Bank clients and were bound by the regulations of the West Bank courts in which they appeared. The fundamental structure of the West Bank judicial system was certainly not altered by virtue of this reform.

The transfer of the Court of Appeals from Jerusalem to Ramallah presents peculiar questions which will be discussed in Chapter IV's section on 'The Special Problem of Jerusalem'.

### c. *Executive: The Question of Elections during Occupation*

The holding of regional elections during occupation is another welcome innovation in the law of belligerent occupation. Just as the practice of judicial review by the civil courts of an occupying power of acts of the military government abounds with the possibility of abuse, so too does the holding of elections during occupation. Yet, in both cases this possibility is kept under control by the intensity of public scrutiny to which both practices are subjected. The fact that the world public may well presume interference in the election process when held under the circumstances of occupation offsets the benefits to the occupying power of projecting the image of a 'freely elected' government. The burden will thus rest on the occupying power to rebut the presumption of invalidity. In this light the possibility of truly free elections need not be foreclosed on the grounds that although they may be honestly held, dishonesty would be too difficult to prove.

Elections under occupation circumstances will, however, continue to require the scrutiny of the world community. Hopefully, the Protecting Power arrangements of the Geneva Convention[74] will be implemented in future instances and thus provide the necessary supervision. In the alternative, 'ad hoc' means for international supervision of elections need be pressed.

In the 1972 elections on the West Bank an unusually large number of candidates ran, many of whom had never before served on municipal councils.[75] A remarkably high percentage of eligible voters participated—83·9% in the Samarian towns as opposed to 75% in the Jordanian period, and 87·8% in the Judean towns as opposed to 75·8% in the previous period.[76] A smaller, though not very disproportionate, turnout occurred in the 1976 elections.[77] While the extent of popular participation in elections does not in and of itself indicate confidence in a free unhampered electoral process, it does lend credibility to the claim of free elections. In fact, with the exception of the PLO, tampering with the electoral process has not been alleged by either elements of the occupied population or by Jordan. Nor has any interested third party made such allegations.[78] Indeed, the Jordanian government gave the newly elected members of the municipal councils endorsement going beyond 'de facto' recognition.[79]

In conclusion, Israel's decision to permit elections appears to be an example of democratic rule during occupation. The initiative for holding elections, it need be recalled, came mainly from various circles in the West Bank whose common feature was non-membership in the Municipal Councils.[80] Israel's positive response to their demands led to either new leadership or a stamp of popular approval for existing leadership. It allowed people to express their desire for leadership which would be equal to the task of the political, social and economic responsibilities foisted upon them by the events since June 1967, rather than to be stratified by an elite chosen to meet the responsibilities of the 1963 period, when elections were last held. And the elections of 1976, whereby a decidedly more anti-Israel leadership came to the fore, demonstrated that Israel was willing to meet the risk of adverse results in elections and to abide by them.

## C. THE PROPERTY SYSTEM: LAND SETTLEMENT AND ACQUISITION

### 1. *Settlement of Israeli Nationals in the West Bank*

#### a. *Search for a Policy*

Demands within Israel for civilian and paramilitary settlement in the West Bank arose almost immediately after the 1967 War. Security considerations were at first the predominant motive. The establishment of Nahal outposts—paramilitary agricultural centers—along troublesome border areas had long been a keystone of Israeli defense strategy. Soon, however, security considerations became interchanged and confused with reasons of 'historical continuity' and religion. The National Religious Party—the state's third largest—urged settlement in occupied areas having religious significance. The main opposition party, Herut, believing, in essence, in Israel's 'manifest destiny' to rule all of Palestine, campaigned on the slogan that 'settlement is a natural right of the Jews and is dictated by the national security situation.'[81]

On May 26, 1968, at the opening session of the Herut Convention, its chairman, Mr. Menachem Begin, Minister without Portfolio, called for 'large scale settlement in the areas of Judea and Samaria, the Golan Heights, Gaza and Sinai.' On July 11, 1968 the Party adopted a resolution to that effect.[82]

At the same time, the smaller Free Centre Party began to accuse the Government of following, in the words of its chairman, Shmuel Tamir, a policy of 'judenrein' on the West Bank. The sentiments of the religious and secularist annexationists became fused in a coalition movement called the '[Whole] Land of Israel Movement' (Hatnu'a Le'eretz Yisrael Hashlema). It was to gain increasing popularity in the years between the two wars, attracting among its leaders prominent personalities of almost all parties. By 1969, a public opinion poll was able to show that only 17% of Israel's population were ready to return the majority of the territories if a durable peace was reached with the Arabs, as compared with 78% who had favored doing so a year earlier.[83]

Those in the political community openly opposed to settlement argued that settlement would create vested interests and imply annexation, both of which would make more difficult, if not impossible, the task of negotiating a settlement. The Government tried to carefully tread a median line between the proponents and opponents of settlement. A pro-settlement policy ran the risk of deteriorating relations with the United States, which had made no secret of its opposition to Israeli settlement in the occupied territories.[84] Moreover, adoption of a pro-settlement policy would have been difficult to reconcile with Israel's commitment to honor, 'de facto', the Geneva Convention. Article 49 thereof expressly provides that 'The Occupying Power shall not deport or transfer parts of its own civilian population into the territory it occupies'. Finally, it was feared that a settlement policy might result in foreclosure of negotiation options with Jordan.

The middle course chosen favored paramilitary settlement, mostly along the frontier, while opposing the purchase and settlement of West Bank land by Israeli nationals. A stay on the West Bank for more than 48 hours was prohibited unless upon specific consent of the Military Governor.[85] Before long, however, the Israel Government was to succumb to pressures for allowing civilian settlement and land purchase.

### b. *The Beginning of Settlement*

#### (i) *Kfar Etzion*

In September 1967, the Israel Government decided to establish the first non-military settlement in the West Bank. The site was the region between Hebron and Bethlehem known as the Kfar Etzion bloc, named after Kibbutz Kfar Etzion, which in the 1948 War was overrun and razed by the Jordanian Legion. Very soon after the 1967 War a group of 15 men and 3 women, all children of the initial settlers of Kibbutz Kfar Etzion, requested Government permission to re-establish the Kibbutz which would ostensibly operate as a Nahal base. The Government quickly acquiesced and in the fall of that year the new settlers were welcomed by ex-Prime Minister Ben Gurion,

Prime Minister Eshkol, Defense Minister Dayan, General Uzzi Narkiss and Tourism Minister Moshe Kol.[86]

By September 1968, plans were laid for the founding of a second settlement at Gush Etzion to serve as a farming and absorption center for religious immigrants.[87] In continued furtherance of this aim, the Military Government, on June 16, 1969, ordered the eviction of two hundred Arab farmers and the requisition of 1,200 dunams (300 acres) of their land bordering the Kfar Etzion settlement. The stated reason said to justify the action was that a large number of terrorist incidents had occurred in the area, although it was not denied that the settlement may have been the cause of terrorist activity. The Arab farmers, determined to stay, rejected compensation offers and denied any complicity with terrorists. The mayors of Hebron, Bethlehem, Beit Jallah and Beit Sahur appealed to Prime Minister Golda Meir to rescind the order. Although temporarily lifted, it was after further study reinstated.[88]

The initial justification given by the Israel Government for permitting the Kfar Etzion settlement was that the area was a 'military strong-point'[89] and that, accordingly, 'the placement of Nahal in the Etzion bloc is motivated by consideration of military security.'[90] When interviewed, the settlers expressed different motivations, tied to redemption of an obligation to their parents and to the renewal of ties to the whole land of 'Eretz Yisrael'.[91]

(ii) *Kiryat Arba*

On April 10, 1968 about 80 religious Israeli Jews rented a hotel in Hebron to celebrate the Passover holiday. When the festival ended, many remained and declared their intention of settling in the city. The Land of Israel Movement supported them. The Military Government of Judea and Samaria rejected their application for permission to settle in Hebron on the grounds that it would create political and security problems. The Hebron municipality had earlier sent a note to the Israeli government warning that Jewish settlement would poison relations between the local population and the Israel authorities and that it would, in turn, lead to an escalation of terrorist activities. Nevertheless, Defense Minister Dayan supported Jewish settlement and declared publicly that the settlers' actions were not a breach of law.[92] In June, provision was made for the settlers to move from their hotel to the Military Government compound. Towards the end of July 1968, houses began to be built there for the settlers at government expense. In August 1968, additional applications to settle in Hebron were approved by the Israel Government. Then, in March of 1970, plans were announced by the Government for the establishment of an urban quarter for the settlers on the outskirts of Hebron on public land held by the Military Government.[93]

The urban quarter, established on the outskirts of Hebron, was called Kiryat Arba. It continues to be the largest and most controversial Israeli settlement on the West Bank. It should be noted that Kiryat Arba differs dramatically from the 17 other settlements established by Israel in the West Bank between 1967 and 1973. The others resemble para-military settlements, Kiryat Arba was planned and conceived as a city of close apartment blocks with a small industrial park on the edge. Between 1969 and October 1973 Israel spent more than $10 million on the project.[94]

Under a Government decision of early June 1973, the settlement was to be quadrupled in size, with work to be completed by 1975. In effect, the settlement was to be made into a small town complete with highways and modern shopping centers and schools with capacity for a population of more than 5,000 Israelis.[95] The October 1973 War and the ensuing change of the Labour Party's political platform were, however, to curtail implementation of these plans.

This decision of June 1973 to expand Kiryat Arba marked a victory for the political philosophy of Moshe Dayan of 'creating facts' in the region. Since 1968 Mr. Dayan had publicly argued that Israelis must have the right to settle anywhere on the West Bank—'an integral part of our homeland'—and that any peace agreement must guarantee that right. The minority of the Cabinet opposed the decision on the grounds that it would foreclose negotiating options with Jordan. Once established as a viable city, they maintained it might prove political suicide for an Israeli politician to suggest that Kiryat Arba be given up as the *quid.pro quo* for a settlement with Jordan.

(iii) *Other Settlements*

The relative success in establishing official settlement in Kfar Etzion and unofficial settlement in Kiryat Arba prompted groups of Israelis to attempt settlement in the major town in Samaria—Nablus. Here they ran into strong government opposition. In June 1969 a group of Israelis attempted to settle on Mt. Gerizim near Nablus. The Military Government forcibly removed them.[96] Nablus, much more than Hebron, remained a hotbed of strong anti-Israel sentiment and the government appeared un-anxious to try its hand there, at least until the experiments in Judea proved successful.[97]

By February 1973 sixteen Nahal-type settlements, in addition to Kiryat Arba, existed on the West Bank. All were affiliated with the various Kibbutz movements or had essentially become civilian farming cooperatives of one kind or another.[98] But, in the months preceding the outbreak of war in October 1973, a heated campaign was to be waged for vastly increasing the scale of Israeli civilian settlement in the West Bank. An understanding of the nature of that campaign and the manner in which the two opposing camps were counterposed is essential to an appreciation of the current debate, within Israel and without, over settlement activity in the West Bank. The subject is discussed in depth in Section 3, *infra,* 'The Galili Document and Post-1973 Settlement Policies'.

2. *Land Acquisition: Public and Private*

There are four basic modes which an occupying power may adopt relative to foreign real property: destruction, for reasons of security or punishment; confiscation; requisition, forced sales for reasonable compensation; or purchase, arrived at by a freely bargained-for exchange or its rough equivalent.

a. *Destruction*

There is no available record of the destruction of any public Jordanian real property. The destruction of private real property has, however, been utilized as a punitive measure. In addition, some non-punitive destruction has occurred in the case of the three villages of Yula, Beit Yuba and Emmaus—

'The Latrun Villages.' Situated in the middle of the Latrun route—the shorter formerly Jordanian-controlled road from the coastal plain to Jerusalem—the villages had formed a salient of Jordanian control challenging access to Jerusalem. Immediately after the 1967 War they were destroyed and their 4,000 inhabitants resettled. Military reasons certainly played an important role in the decision, yet perhaps not a decisive one. From the political viewpoint, the destruction of the villages was important to show Israel's determination to make access to the Latrun route an unnegotiable demand in any possible forthcoming negotiations with Jordan.[99]

The area was immediately resettled and cultivated by Israeli farmers, to whom the land was leased by the Government.

b. *Confiscation*

Israel has since 1967 confiscated substantial portions of former Jordanian public land. The reasons given have always been that appropriation was made necessary either for security considerations or to allow the army to carry out military maneuvers.[100] For example, on December 26, 1972, 10,000 dunams of public land between East Jerusalem and Jericho were expropriated by military order.[101] Defense Minister Moshe Dayan disclosed this fact in the Knesset and stated that he was not prepared to give specific reasons for the closing off of the area.[102] On January 2, 1973, a report appeared in *Ma'ariv* concerning a protest by farmers against the closing off by the army, since 1967, of 40,000 dunams of state land used for pasture and agriculture by the village of Tubas. According to the report, military government sources gave security as the reason for the closing.[103]

There is no record of confiscation—appropriation without compensation or the right thereto—of private property. Sometimes, however, access to property by anyone but their owners was prohibited. Military security considerations were the usual explanation.[104] As a matter of general policy, the Defense Minister made it known that military settlements would not be established on West Bank land unless it was (a) State or absentee property, (b) purchased against full payment, or (c) traded for other real estate with the owner's consent.[105]

c. *Requisition*

Typical of requisition of private land for military purposes was the order reported in the *Jerusalem Post* of August 16, 1973 regarding the closing off of 350 dunams of vineyards near Bethlehem for military purposes. The report stated that this was the third take-over of land in the Bethlehem area and that 'landlords were being told they could apply for compensation once they proved legal ownership.'

d. *Trusteeship (Absentee Property)*

Under the authority of Israel's Military Order No. 10 of July 23, 1967, *Abandoned Property of Private Individuals Order,*[106] the Military Custodian of Absentee Property seized the houses of all West Bank residents abroad at the outbreak of the 1967 War. In some cases the inhabitants were reportedly only temporarily away on a visit to Amman or to a nearby town. In other cases, a relative of the owner may have been present.[107]

Repatriation of refugees to their homes, once in possession of the Custodian of Enemy Property, has been permitted only in very limited circumstances. Israel maintains that repatriation is an issue to be negotiated in an overall settlement. In the interim, the military has not excluded the use of absentee property for its own purposes.[108]

e. *Purchase: The Campaign for Private Land Transactions*

Soon after the 1967 War, the Israel Government delegated authority to the Jewish National Fund and the Israel Lands Administration to purchase land in the occupied territories. By April of 1973, the Israel Lands Administration had, by its own account, succeeded in purchasing over 30,000 dunams in the West Bank and about 18,000 dunams in Jerusalem. The Jewish National Fund reported that between June of 1967 and April 1973 it had purchased over 10,000 dunams in the West Bank and stated it was prepared to purchase much more provided the Government approved.[109] Unofficial reports found that the Jewish National Fund and Israel Land Authority had in fact obtained several hundred thousand dunams and registered this extra land in the name of Arab agents against 'irrevocable' bills of sale.[110]

The purchase of land by individuals or companies was, however, prohibited by law. Nevertheless, it became an increasingly common occurrence, especially in the areas adjacent to Jerusalem—as far as Ramallah in the north and Bethlehem in the South—as individuals became convinced in 1972 and 1973 that the Israel Government would eventually annex these areas. Unlawful sales were carried out by means of granting an irrevocable power of attorney, and by postponing the registration of the transfer until such time as the Government would permit private land transactions. It was hoped that retrospective authorization would then be given to their transactions. The Government appeared to be following a policy of purposeful neglect. In March and April of 1973, Israeli individuals and companies began to make disclosures of large areas of land purchased in the West Bank which they requested they now be permitted to legally register. It was clear, the *Jerusalem Post* reported on April 13, 1973 that Israeli individuals and companies engaged in purchases were doing this on a large scale, with the money coming primarily from well-to-do land speculators and construction firms.

From early 1973, Defense Minister Dayan undertook a concerted campaign to revise Israeli legislation to permit the private purchase of land on the West Bank. In a speech to the Jewish Agency Convention in February, he stated:

> My personal approach to the subject is the more the better. We have the right to settle in each and every place in Judea, Samaria and the Gaza Strip—and I do not believe that anyone has the right to tell the Jews that they have no right to settle in the land of their fathers.[111]

At the same time he declared himself 'opposed on principle to the purchase of land in Israel by Arabs. We are in the process of creating a Jewish state and not an Arab state, and we have the duty to ensure the continuity of the Jewish community'.[112]

In March, 1973, Dayan attempted to force the governing Labour Party to adopt his position regarding the administration of the occupied Arab territories as part of its 1973 election platform. In addition to calling for more intensive Israeli settlement in the occupied territories, Mr. Dayan urged the creation of new towns at certain strategic points, greater Israeli investment in the areas and fuller integration of the economies of the West Bank and Gaza Strip with that of Israel. The proposal of the most immediate import was that individual Israelis be authorized to buy land from Arab landowners anywhere on the West Bank.[113]

The effect Mr. Dayan's proposals would have was, of course, recognized. They would commit Israel to making retention of Israeli-settled portions of the West Bank an unnegotiable item in any projected peace negotiations.

Dayan's proposal was immediately denounced as irresponsible by Prime Minister Meir, Finance Minister Sapir and Foreign Minister Eban. Each argued that indiscriminate land purchases by citizens would have the effect of making military and political policy for the Government. Furthermore, they maintained that such a move would foreclose the Government's potential negotiating options with the neighboring Arab countries.

Mr. Dayan countered by asserting that such negotiation was not on the horizon and that, as the 'status quo' might prevail for the next ten or fifteen years, there was no purpose in the Government's 'standing idle' in the occupied territories. To his domestic critics he maintained that 'anyone who says that Israelis do not have the right to buy land in Judea and Samaria had better stop teaching the Bible to his children.'[114]

Mr. Dayan's proposal soon came under heavy international as well as domestic criticism. The United States made diplomatic protests. At the United Nations, Secretary General Waldheim summoned the Israeli representative, Yosef Tekoah, to advise him of the protests he had received from the representatives of Jordan, Syria and Egypt. They had asked Mr. Waldheim to intercede to halt what they claimed was Israel's 'large scale appropriation of the Arab land and property' in the occupied areas.[115]

Due to this rising foreign and domestic opposition, a slim

majority of the eighteen member Israel cabinet decided on April 8, 1973 against the Dayan proposal for private land purchase. On the official level, the Government reaffirmed its existing policy of restricting private transfers of land by residents of the occupied territories to the Israel Land Authority for Government-approved settlement, and to the Jewish National Fund, the land-purchase agency of the World Zionist Movement, where specifically authorized.

Yet, despite the Israel Cabinet's rejection of General Dayan's proposal, private land purchase appeared to continue. *Haaretz* reported on April 4, 1973 that 'The punishment in the case of land transactions between Jews and Arabs in the occupied territories is five years imprisonment or a 14,500 fine . . . it seems that the Military Government ignores all these illegal transactions . . . as far as is known not one of the thousands who bought land has been brought to trial.' In the ensuing months before the 1973 War, land purchases continued to soar. For the Arabs, the economic temptation proved stronger than the fear of social ostracism or the threat of death either by operation of a newly enacted Jordanian law against land sales to Israelis or at the vengeful hands of terrorists. On May 8, 1973, *Haaretz* stated 'The wave of alarm among potential Jewish buyers, which reached its peak following the demand of Deputy Minister Yigal Allon that the feasibility of taking legal action against land purchases should be examined, has now subsided. It is now clear that nobody will be prosecuted for such purchases.'

### 3. *The Galili Document and Post-1973 Settlement Policies*

Mr. Dayan continued his campaign after the Cabinet had defeated his proposal for private land purchases. Realizing that he played a pivotal role in winning popular support for the Labour Party in the forthcoming national elections in October, he stated on July 24 that he was 'not certain if I can run for the coming elections under the banner of the Labour Party. If this will happen it will only be because of the present policy in the [occupied areas].' Sharply rejecting the approach of his party colleagues 'who see the [Israeli] presence in the areas as temporary and who therefore demand that we should take care not to overtie ourselves to the area, not to invest capital there, not to settle there and not to deal with the refugees,' he stated:

> The question is shall we or shall we not act in the areas in the next four years. The areas are not a security payment. We must do things there, especially industrial and urban settlement. . . . We must broaden settlement around Jerusalem, we must allow the purchase of lands in the areas. .
> We are not allowed to cross the 'Magic Green Line' and expand the State of Israel. The best course and that which will best bring peace closer is to develop mutual ties with the Arabs and invest in the areas. I don't care, if there is a platform or not, what I care about is whether or not we seriously intend to act in the areas. . . .This must be our top priority. We must decide now, and I am not at all certain that the majority in Labour and the Alignment will share my views . . . .Given the approach of Sapir and that of Mapam I cannot run for the Knesset elections or for the government under the banner of Labour[116]

The Finance Minister, Pinhas Sapir, was the strongest opponent of Dayan's views and had consistently spoken out against an annexationist trend. Speaking at the Knesset in May, 1969, he gave his views regarding the interrelationship between settlement of the territories, annexation and peace:

> Since the Six Days War it has been the Government's policy not to decide upon the destiny of the administered territories. This decision was wise and has brought us benefit. But this decision does not fit in with the wishes of settling in Hebron and uniting it, together with Gaza and Beersheba, in our economic unit; or that we should add the territories to the Israeli water and electricity nets and give the Arabs from the territories an opportunity to work in Israel. This is contrary to the Government's policy. They show a hidden intention to annex the territories.[117]

In formulating the party's forthcoming election platform, Sapir insisted that Israel make known her allegiance to the principle of temporariness of occupation of Arab territories. Only thus, he felt, could the occupation continue under conditions of relative quiet while preserving Israel's bargaining power.[118] Israel's permanent acceptance of the 1.2 million

Arabs from the territories would, he stated, 'strangle the nation.' Israel would have to bestow upon them all the rights of citizenship and, by so doing, 'the idea of a Jewish state would be exploded. The Arabs would be our partners in every area of life.'[119]

Sapir denounced statements by the National Religious Opposition Party that the territories were 'liberated' as being 'mystic' and irrational notions.

> The accomplishments of political Zionism have had nothing to do with mysticism. We rebelled against it and against those that advised we wait for the coming of the Messiah . . .[I]t is not the role of religion to determine in what territories we shall remain. In this, the second half of the twentieth century, we must speak in rational terms. I suggest we not make of religion a tool for prying in politics. I, too, was educated in the spirit of the Bible, no less than others. However, the thing we are talking about here is our nation, which we must protect as we would our most precious possession.[120]

Finance Minister Sapir did not, however, triumph. Dayan prevailed. On August 16, 1973, the Israeli press released the text of a thirteen point agreement regarding the policy to be adopted over the next four years in administering the territories under Israel's occupation. The agreement was ironed out by the executive of Israel's ruling Labour Party and termed by the press as the 'Galili Paper' after Minister-without-Portfolio, Israel Galili, who drafted a summation of the agreement. More realistically, it can be termed the Sapir-Dayan Agreement as it represented the relinquishment of Finance Minister Sapir's hopes for retaining the 'status quo,' so as not to close any doors to peace negotiations with Jordan and the other Arab states, to Defense Minister Dayan's wish to extend the borders of the State of Israel.

The following terms of the agreement merit closest attention.

4. Concession and benefits at the same rate given to investors in preference areas in Israel will be given to Israeli entrepreneurs with the purpose of encouraging them to set up industries of their own in the occupied areas.

8. . . .New settlements will be set up and the present network strengthened in the Golan Heights, the Jordan Valley, the Northern Dead Sea, the Etzion Bloc, the Rafiah Approaches, the Gaza Strip, Kiryat Arba, the Eilat Bay and Ophira (Sharm el-Sheikh) by the development of craft, industry and recreational centres. Non-governmental factors, both public and private will be co-opted in the development of the settlement areas in the occupied territories.

9b. The Israel Lands Administration (ILA) will lease lands to corporations and individuals for the execution of approved development programmes.

9c. The ILA will work to purchase land in every effective way through both corporations and individuals . . .

Article 4 of the Agreement articulated the increasing attention that had been focused on the possibility of establishing Israeli industrial sites on the West Bank along with continued Jewish agricultural settlement. Justifying this trend, the Minister of Commerce and Industry, Chaim Bar-Lev, stated in a press conference on August 29, 1973 that 'we regard Israel and the occupied areas as a single economic unit. This concurs with the needs of the present and is consonant with the prospects of a future political settlement. Whatever the settlement, I do not think that the area can once again be two separate economic entities.'[121]

Accordingly, Minister Bar-Lev had been proposing to extend Israel's Encouragement of Investment Law, offering grants for the establishment of industry in under-developed zones, to include the occupied territories. '. . .the shape of the aid given to Israeli entrepreneurs in the occupied areas does not meet the needs of 1973. The aid decided upon in 1969 grants every Israeli enterprise beyond the green line the status of an approved enterprise but without the grant given to approved enterprises in Israel.'[122]

The details of the proposal were published on August 2, 1973.

> All the areas in the occupied territories will be recognized as development areas and will be given all the concessions granted in Israel including an out-right grant of 20% of the size of the investment . . . The investments in the areas will also enjoy insurance from political risks through the government insurance company of Yaniv.[123]

The first industrial enterprise planned to be established under the new plan was at Kiryat Arba where an infrastructure was soon laid thereafter for a new industrial zone in an area of about 100 dunams with an investment of IL3 million.[124] Regarding the recipients of benefit from the proposed bill, which later became Article 4 of the Galili Paper, the August 15, 1973 issue of *Haaretz* wrote '. . .it will only be Israelis or foreigners: the local Arabs will only benefit as partners.'

Article 9 of the Galili Document permitted private land purchase through the conduit of the Israel Lands Authority. Article 8 provided for increased Jewish settlement on predominantly government acquired land.

Adverse reaction to the Galili Document was quickly forthcoming. The three Arab newspapers published on the West Bank were vehement in their opposition. All stressed a design in the actions of the Israeli authorities: first, permitting public institutions to purchase land, now extending that right to private parties and, in the future, full dispossession of Arabs from their land.[125]

Abroad, the *Washington Post* urged in its editorial of August 26, 1973, in response to the Galili Paper, that 'If the United States in fact retains a real interest in a Middle East settlement, it cannot stand by quietly or make only a token noise while Israel moves substantially further to annexing chunks of territory which it contends would be on the table in settlement negotiation. . .'

In Israel, the respected daily, *Haaretz,* editorialized in its September 4 issue that:

> Mr. Dayan can take credit for an impressive achievement particularly in the matter of the establishment of industries beyond the jurisdictional area of expanding Jerusalem. In this manner the government gave its approval to his demand to set up settlements and towns within Judea and Samaria without annexation and without changing its status as an occupied area . . .Through the initiative of Dayan it will be possible to take over the territories without annexing them and without granting their inhabitants, the Arabs, the rights of citizens of Israel.

When the Labour Party Secretariat of 160 members voted on the agreement on Sept. 5, 78 votes were cast in favor and none against.[126] Dayan had triumphed. Israel would act as the *de facto* Government of the West Bank and pursue policies that, *in time,* would allow Israel to digest the area. The most salient features of these policies would be Jewish settlement in urban and strategically important rural areas. Thus, although the Galili Paper left unchanged the political and legal status of the territories and that of its inhabitants, it marked a considerable weakening of Israel's position that all was negotiable. 'Creeping Annexation' became near-official policy.

With the outbreak of war in October 1973, the Galili Paper's future as an integral part of the Labour Party electoral program was left in doubt. As a result of the war, Israel's diplomatic isolation in the international community became more acute. Israel could not afford to appear to take a quasi-annexationist view regarding the future of the territories.

At its meeting on November 28, the Labour Party Executive did not specifically repudiate the Galili Paper but it did substantially disassociate itself from it. Its major proponent, Dayan, had lost political influence. As a result, the revised platform made it clear that the Labour Party had no wish to incorporate large numbers of Arabs in Israel as this would conflict with the declared aim of 'preserving the Jewish character of the State of Israel.' This implied a willingness to return the populated areas of the West Bank and the Gaza Strip, which between them held a million Arabs. The plans announced in the Galili Document for long-term industrial development projects and the escalation of Jewish settlement in the West Bank were never mentioned.

In the intervening years between 1973 and his rise to the Prime Ministership in 1977, the leader of the opposition bloc, Likud, Mr. Menachem Begin, continued to strongly condemn relinquishment of the West Bank, which his party regards as an integral and inalienable part of the 'historic homeland'.[127] The Israeli public was divided on the issue. In the general Election of December 31, 1973, the Labour Alignment was the predominant choice, but its representation in the Knesset was severely reduced, while that of the Likud increased. That left the National Religious Party, an opponent of the 'repartition of biblical Israel', in a pivotal slot. As a result, the Labour Government between 1973 and 1977 chose neither to actively pursue the escalated land settlement and purchase practices envisaged in the Galili Document, nor to disavow the Document. Instead, civilian settlement was allowed to continue at the general level of growth preceding the 1973 War. Land purchase activity decreased, however. Four additional para-military Nahal outposts were established, although the line between the military and civilian character of these settlements has continued to narrow. Land was cleared in a planned construction of an industrial type park, Maaleh-Adumin, on the Jerusalem-Jericho road.[128] Kiryat Arba was not expanded, although plans to do so had been announced in 1976—probably because existing quarters in the settlement were less than fully occupied.

The major post-1973 event relative to new civilian settlements has been the unauthorized action in late 1975 by the extreme nationalist Gush Emunim movement in settling near Nablus at Sebastian. At that time a Cabinet resolution, approved by a vote of 17 to 2 with 3 abstentions by the religious ministers, termed the attempted settlement illegal. Nevertheless, instead of calling for the forceful evacuation of the illegal squatters, the Government permitted them to stay for a few weeks at a nearby Army camp, Kaddum, until a permanent site could be selected for them. It was not disclosed where that site would be, although it was clearly implied that it would not be in Samaria, the heavily populated central portion of the West Bank, but rather in Judea, probably along the Jordan frontier.[129]

By August, 1976, the settlers were well ensconced at the army base, housed in semi-permanent structures with running water, electricity and playgrounds for the children. Yet, although the Kaddum settlement triggered off a host of bloody disturbances in the West Bank and became the cause of increasing friction,[130] the Rabin administration chose not to force the issue. Sentiments for the Gush Emunim ran high and thus any precipitous action against the settlers became too dangerous for the shaky Rabin coalition to undertake.

Under the new Likud Government the settlers at Kaddum have been encouraged to remain and promised more permanent quarters in Samaria. On May 19, 1977, on a visit there shortly after his inauguration as Prime Minister, Begin declared that 'We stand on the land of liberated Israel' and promised that there would be more such settlements in the area.[131] In July of that year the Begin government announced that it was according full legal status to Kaddum and Ofra, another fledgling settlement in Samaria, and to Maaleh Adumin, the industrial park on the Jerusalem-Jericho Road.

The settlers at Kaddum number a little more than 100. But their actual strength or size is not as important as what they symbolize. To many, Kaddum represents Israel's intention to retain the West Bank permanently. Not surprisingly, therefore, Kaddum and civilian settlements like it, have become the greatest source of friction between West Bankers and the Israeli authorities. And the Kaddum issue and all it stands for has become, as well, a major point of disagreement between Israel and its principal ally, the United States.

### 4. *Examination and Condemnation of Property Practices by the U.N. Special Committee to Investigate Israeli Practices Affecting the Human Rights of the Population of the Occupied Territories*

On December 19, 1968 the General Assembly adopted at its plenary meeting Resolution 2443 (XXIII) calling for the establishment of a Special Committee to Investigate Israeli Practices Affecting the Human Rights of the Population of the Occupied Territories. On September 12, 1969 Sri Lanka

(Ceylon), Somalia, and Yugoslavia were appointed to serve on the Committee.

On December 11, 1969 the General Assembly passed Resolution No. 2546 (XXIV) calling upon Israel:

> . . .to desist forthwith from its reported repressive practices and policies toward the civilian population in the occupied territories and to comply with its obligations under the Geneva Convention relative to the Protection of Civilian Persons in Time of War of 12 August 1949, The Universal Declaration of Human Rights and the relevant resolutions adopted by the various international organizations.

The Special Committee was requested by the Assembly to take cognizance of these provisions. On October 5, 1970 the Special Committee presented its first report[132] to the Secretary-General who made the report available to the General Assembly and referred it to the Special Political Committee for discussion. The Special Political Committe requested that the General Assembly renew the mandate of the Special Committee to investigate all Israel practices and the General Assembly so approved.[133] On September 17, 1971 the Special Committee transmitted its second and much fuller report[134] to the General Assembly through the offices of the Secretary-General.[134]

a. *Allegations of Annexation, Settlement and Denial of Self-Determination*

The Committee found that the evidence it collected 'supports the allegation that the government of Israel is following a policy of annexing and settling occupied territories in a manner calculated to exclude all possibility of restitution to lawful ownership.'[135] The Committee Report further found that:

> Every attempt on the part of the Government of Israel at carrying out a policy of annexation and settlement amounts to a denial of the fundamental human rights of the local inhabitants, in particular the right to self-determination and the right to retain their homeland, and a repudiation by the

Government of Israel of accepted norms of international law.[136]

The Committee based its finding that Israel was pursuing in the West Bank a policy of 'annexation and settlement'—terms which the Committee considered synonymous—on several asserted facts.

Firstly, it pointed to the existence, in the government of Israel, of a Ministerial Committee for Settlement of the Territories. This 'by its very existence' showed, according to the Committee, 'beyond doubt, that it is a policy of the Government of Israel to settle the territories occupied as a result of the hostilities of June, 1967.'[137]

It then made reference to 'the declared practice of land expropriation and settlement in East Jerusalem' and went on to tell of 'uncontradicted reports, appearing in the information media, of the planned establishment of Israeli settlements in the occupied territories.' Cited were reports of a new industrial site planned for Kiryat Arba on the outskirts of Hebron, additional commitments to civilian settlements in the Jordan Valley, planned construction of a settlement near Latrun, and the report that additional settlers would be moving to the Kiryat Arba quarter.

To substantiate its conclusion, the Committee made references to numerous announcements to this effect by Israeli ministers and leaders. While acknowledging that many of these statements purport to be personal opinions, the Committee found that 'their general tenor, the frequency with which they have been repeated and the various measures adopted by the Government of Israel, such as the establishment of settlements, justify in the Special Committee's opinion the conclusion that these statements are a faithful reflection of official Israeli policy.'[138]

The Committee found, on the basis of such statements, that 'the heart of the Middle East problem' is the 'Homeland doctrine' (Eretz Yisrael) as enunciated by the Government of Israel and supported by the Opposition. In light of this orientation, the Special Committee expressed that it 'has no doubt that the policy of annexation and settlement is dictated by considerations alien to those of national security.'[139]

On December 10, 1971 the Special Committee transmitted a supplementary report[140] to the Secretary-General for general distribution. It stated that further evidence had been found substantiating the Committee's conclusion that Israel was pursuing a concerted policy of settlement leading to annexation.[141]

(i) *Fifth Report of the Special Committee, October 25, 1973*

The fifth (and second major) report[142] of the Special Committee was presented to the Secretary-General and distributed to the General Assembly on October 25, 1973. It came in the wake of actions taken by the previous year's General Assembly in denouncing Israeli practices in the territories in even stronger terms. A resolution, then passed by the vast majority of the Assembly (86 to 7 with 31 abstentions), had deemed Israeli practices affecting the demographic structure and physical character of the occupied territories to be null and void and called upon all states to refuse to recognize such changes and the legitimacy of occupation generally.[143]

In presenting its fifth report, the Special Committee concluded, much as it had earlier, that

> . . . there is conclusive evidence that the Government of Israel is following a policy of establishing settlements in the occupied territories, populating them with Israeli nationals, some of whom are new immigrants and, with regard to certain parts of the occupied territories, such as Hebron (West Bank), Rafah and Sharm el-Sheikh (Sinai) and the Golan Heights, the Government of Israel has adopted long range plans for settlement.[144]

The Committee attempted, however, to substantiate more exhaustively than previously its assertions of Israel's pursuit of a policy of systematic settlement aimed at ultimate annexation. Reference was made to nearly every reported statement of Israeli government leaders[145] as well as all newspaper reports[146] supporting the Committee's conclusions. Alleged Israeli governmental plans to expand Kiryat Arba were given the greatest focus.[147]

(ii) *Subsequent Work of the Special Committee*

In the fall of 1974 and 1975 the Special Committee presented its sixth[148] and seventh[149] reports to the plenary session of the General Assembly. Each pointed to events tending to confirm conclusions reached in earlier reports. An eighth report[150] was issued in the fall of 1976. It found that Israel was continuing to implement a policy of annexation and settlement, citing new settlements established within the last year. The eighth report influenced the Security Council to issue a consensus statement in October 1976 unanimously condemning, for the first time, Israeli demographic practices in the territories. In particular, Israeli civilian settlement in the occupied territories was deemed a violation of international law and a hindrance to peace.[151]

5. *Israeli Land Policy in the Perspective of International Law and Politics*

> The investigating committee [The Special Committee] is staffed conspicuously, in some ways flagrantly, by anti-Israel people, and it was because of that imbalance that the United States, five years ago declined to vote for its constitution . . . The trouble with Israeli apologists is that they concede nothing. In the instant case [The Report of the Special Committee] . . . it was actually debated in the Knesset all year long whether a building program clearly intended to fasten down, over the very very long haul—generations maybe—Israel's hold over the West Bank, and over parts of Sinai, should be undertaken, with a not inconsiderable minority of Israeli legislators voting most ardently against what they denounced as moves that could not reasonably be interpreted as other than imperialist in design. But somebody like Abba Eban would rot in hell before admitting that there was the least suggestion of any truth in the assertion that the leaders of Israel had it in mind to squat down in the West Bank, and the Golan Heights, forever.
>
> . . . An Israeli minister recalled to me . . . that when the United States returned Okinawa to Japan, Secretary of State Rogers announced that it was not often in world history that the victor

returned to an aggressor a territory which had been used as a military offensive base, after only twenty-five years. 'By these standards', the Minister said, 'we have only twenty years more in the Sinai'. A perfectly respectable argument, in my opinion; but not one that requires one to believe that, during those twenty-five years, no activity is being taken by the occupying power which is proscribed by the Fourth Geneva Convention.

My feeling was that perspective is important. If the Fourth Geneva Convention has been enacted solely to govern the activities of Israel and South Africa, and whatever Western states choose voluntarily to abide by it, then that should be known.

William F. Buckley, Jr.,
*United Nations Journal—*
*A Delegate's Odyssey* (1974)
175, 176, 182

a. *The U.N. Special Committee: Legal Competence and Impartiality Examined*

(i) *Selection of Membership*

The very manner in which the U.N. Special Committee was established has been challenged as unlawful under the procedural rules of the United Nations. It is to be noted that by Resolution 2443 calling for the establishment of the Special Committee, the President of the Assembly, Dr. Emilio Arenales of Guatemala, was to appoint the members of the committee. He died, however, before completing this task. As a result, the General Assembly decided that the Vice Presidents of the Assembly designate among themselves a successor to Dr. Arenales. Dr. Luis Alvaro of Peru was chosen. He, in turn, requested the governments of Sri Lanka, Somalia and Yugoslavia to serve on the Special Committee. Each of these states pursued a hostile policy toward Israel. Somalia considered itself to be in a 'state of war' with Israel, Yugoslavia severed diplomatic relations after the 1967 War, and Sri Lanka broke off diplomatic relations with Israel soon after the Committee's formation.[152]

The procedure utilized upon the death of Dr. Arenales to select the membership of the Special Committee was, in Israel's view, unprecedented and *ultra vires* and thus terminated the mandate of Resolution 2443. Dr. Arenales was chosen because of his reputation of impartiality. His successors were accused of failing to live up to this standard. The Special Committee responded, in justification, that in an area of as vital concern as human rights, flexibility in procedure is desirable and that the new constitution of the Special Committee had been subsequently ratified by the General Assembly.[153]

In assessing these opposing claims, it would appear that Resolution 2443 did not have to be interpreted so literally as to exclude the possibility of implementation of an alternative procedure for the selection of the Committee's membership upon the death of Dr. Arenales. The new mode agreed upon for the selection of the Committee's chairman by vote of the vice presidents of the General Assembly was not in and of itself an irrational or unjust procedure.

(ii) *Usurpation of the Geneva Convention's Protecting Power System?*

The procedure of an *ad hoc* U.N. Investigation Committee to investigate occupation practices may, however, be proscribed by the 'Protecting Power' provisions of the Geneva Convention. Article 9 of the Geneva Convention provides for the institution of Protecting Powers, whose duty is to safeguard the interests of the ousted and occupying powers as well as those of the inhabitants of the occupied population. The Protecting Power may be a neutral state or organization, agreed upon by the belligerents.[154] Article 11 further provides that where such agreement is impossible, the occupying power should accept the offer of a neutral organization, such as the International Committee of the Red Cross, to fulfill this role.[155]

At the end of the 1967 War, none of the belligerents took any steps towards nominating a Protecting Power. The International Committee of the Red Cross (ICRC) sent a note to Jordan, Egypt, Syria, Lebanon and Israel on April 4, 1968, drawing their attention to 'the contractual possibilities and obligations of Governments concerned' and stating that 'they should designate a Protecting Power or a substitute for it.'[156] Only Jordan bothered to reply and then only to state that it would not accept the ICRC's suggestion.[157]

In the absence of the selection of Protecting Powers, the ICRC began increasingly to undertake functions extending beyond its traditional role of caring for disaster victims.[158] Tasks normally reserved for the Protecting Power were assumed,[159] although the precise role of the Protecting Power was clouded by the fact that in its twenty-four years of formal existence the Protecting Power system had never been invoked by any party to a conflict. The ICRC began by inquiring into Israeli penal legislation and procedures on the West Bank. Later the ICRC displayed no hesitancy in stating that Israeli settlement of civilian population in the West Bank, not being justified by the 'security of the population or imperative military reasons', was in contravention of Article 49 of the Geneva Convention.[160] Furthermore, the ICRC delegation in Israel began to 'intervene with Israeli authorities' for the purpose of obtaining full information regarding land expropriation to determine whether it could be justified by military reasons.[161] The line distinguishing the role of a Protecting Power from that assumed by the ICRC became exceedingly thin.

Given the Protecting Power system of the Geneva Convention and the gradual assumption of its role by the ICRC, we may ask at this point whether creation of the 'ad hoc' Special Committee was warranted. Indeed, it has been maintained that '[t]he establishment of the Special Committee was to a large extent a reaction of the United Nations to the failure of the enforcement mechanism outlined in the Convention.'[162] This view seems misconceived. If genuine concern for implementing the 'enforcement mechanism' of the Convention existed, then the logical step would have been to call upon the belligerents to select Protecting Powers. In the absence of an affirmative response, the ICRC should have been designated by the U.N. Secretary General, upon Security Council approval, to assume that role.[163] A Protecting Power would have had the same rights of investigation granted the Special Committee and would have been able to carry out this task with greater competence and much less obstruction. But the General Assembly refused to call for invocation of this mechanism and the Security Council took no action on its own. Instead of enforcing the policing procedures of an important multinational treaty, a new untried study group was created. Most importantly—without yet touching upon the question of bias—the members were unacceptable to the belligerent parties. This in itself assured that the Committee's results would have little more than propaganda value. In light of the fact that (a) the General Assembly failed to make any reference to invocation of the Protecting Power system for the purpose of performing the investigatory task assigned to the Special Committee, and that (b) the Committee's membership was totally unacceptable to Israel, the creation of the Special Committee was most inappropriate and perhaps, legally speaking, *ultra vires* the authority of the General Assembly.

(iii) *Bias*

As stated earlier, the states designated to serve on the committee were all publicly adverse to Israel. Two of those states, Sri Lanka and Yugoslavia, had severed all diplomatic relations with Israel. As a result, there was a basic lack of trust and credibility in the purpose and composition of the Special Committee from the start. Many of its findings and procedural means confirmed, as we shall see in the next section, this presumption of bias. Most scholars have taken the position that the Committee was biased from the very beginning.[164]

b. *Management of Public Real Property*

(i) *The Usufructuary Rule*

Central to the control of both public and private property is the prohibition of the destruction or seizure of enemy property, except where 'imperatively demanded by the necessities of war,' (Article 23(g) of the Hague Regulations). This principle has been amplified by Article 53 of the Geneva Convention which states in relation to the destruction of real or personal public and private property, that such activity is prohibited, 'except where such destruction is rendered absolutely necessary by military operations.'

Real property of the former sovereign passes to the occupant for the duration of the occupation but does not confer ownership upon him. In relation to such property, Article 55 of the Hague Regulations specifically provides that:

> The occupying state shall be regarded only as administrator and usufructuary of public buildings, real estate, forests and agricultural estates belonging to the hostile state and situated in the occupied territory. It must safeguard the capital of these properties and administer them in accordance with the rules of the usufruct.

Where necessary for reasons of military security, the occupant may destroy, use or modify the property according to his needs, as all acts prohibited by the laws of war are qualified by the doctrine of 'military necessity.'[165] Article 55 cannot be read in isolation bereft of the military necessity exceptions of the aforementioned Articles 23(g) of the Hague Regulations and Article 53 of the Geneva Convention. Professors McDougal and Feliciano emphasize this point.

> The limitation of Article 55 presses but lightly upon the military necessities of the occupant, since the utilization ('utendi, fruendi') of such resources does not depend upon the recognition of legal interest in the occupant. As a practical matter, the applicable specific prohibitions are simply that the occupant may not wantonly dissipate or destroy the public resources and may not permanently (i.e., for the indefinite future) alienate them.[166]

Short of alienation of ownership, the belligerent occupant may lease state property providing its term does not extend beyond the duration of the occupation. The 'fruits' of the public land—crops, timber, minerals—may be exploited and sold, providing their production does not deplete existing resources and is carried on in a manner mindful of ecological imperatives.

Certain public real property must be treated according to the rules applicable to private property. Within this class are institutions that may be roughly classed as cultural—churches, hospitals, schools, museums and libraries. Such property may be used temporarily for military purposes, but unlike public property, compensation for any damage done is required.[167] Where the public or private character of property is in doubt, it is presumptively public, pending a final determination of ownership.[168]

As military necessity may justify the destruction or seizure of enemy public real property, its definition becomes most important. It is agreed that a military commander does not have sole discretion to determine whether acts of seizure or destruction are indeed justified by military necessity. The 'kriegs-raison' doctrine of early 20th century German international law advocating this approach has been rejected by international law.[169] Its acceptance would have withdrawn the rule of law from the province of war as the code would have become a matter of 'military convenience, having no further sanction than the sense of honor of the individual military commander or chief of staff.'[170] But any definition of 'military necessity' with a measure of precision has yet to be formulated. Simply stated then, 'military necessity' must be judged contextually, based on the reasonableness of the action under the individual circumstances, not as perceived by the active participant but by the 'neutral' observer.[171]

(ii) *Compliance*

Applying these principles to the Israeli occupation, we note that all public property acquired by the Israel Military Government was obtained through confiscation decrees signed by the Military Governor specifying that their use was essential for military purposes. The expropriated public property has generally been used as the sites of military and 'para military' encampments. Keeping in mind that 'military necessity' is read in a more liberal light when reference is made to public rather than private property, it appears that Israel's expropriation of public real property for conversion into military camps was permissible.

Expropriated public property was, however, also used in the instance of Kiryat Arba for the purpose of civilian settlement. Such use is in contravention of Article 55 of the Hague Regulations requiring the occupant to act as administrator and usufructuary of enemy public property. Although in his capacity as a usufruct, the occupant may lease or utilize lands or buildings for the duration of the occupation, he cannot use the property in such a manner as impairs its corpus. Construction of new buildings of a permanent nature would seem to do harm to this principle because although they may be given or sold to the ousted power upon termination of occupation, the very fact of their existence creates vested interests in their retention, except under conditions of transfer which the ousted power is likely to find unacceptable.

### c. *Management of Private Real Property*

#### (i) *Destruction*

Destruction of private property is prohibited by article 23(g) of the Hague Regulations 'unless such destruction or seizure be imperatively demanded by the necessities of war.' Article 53 of the Geneva Convention reiterates the prohibition of destruction of private real property 'except where such destruction is rendered absolutely necessary by military operations.'

Israel engaged in an open policy of demolition of homes which served as the bases for acts of terrorism. Demolition occurred, however, only where individuals connected with the offense resided in the building. In other circumstances, residents were evicted and the building closed without being destroyed. There is little evidence to support charges that Israel's demolition policy was in contravention of the prohibitions in Article 50 of the Hague Regulations and Article 33 of the Geneva Convention against *collective punishment*. Can, however, the destruction of a house undertaken as a punitive measure to discourage further acts of terrorism be deemed 'imperatively demanded by the necessities of war' or 'rendered absolutely necessary by military operations'?

An affirmative answer appears appropriate. The destruction of homes in such instances has been shown to bear a direct relation to the legitimate end of deterring terrorist activity. Moreover, in the context of alternative deterrent means at a government's disposal, demolition appears as a reasonable mode.[172]

In addition to the claim discussed above against the permissibility of the demolition of private homes as a punitive measure, the major claim lodged against Israel regarding destruction of property concerns the three villages (Yula, Beit Yuba and Emmaus) in the Latrun area. All were razed during June and July of 1967. The declared purpose of the action was to ensure Israeli access to the Latrun route to Jerusalem. It would be difficult to justify such action, given the prohibitions of Article 23(g) and 53 of the Hague Regulations and Geneva Convention, respectively. For 'military necessity' to be properly invoked, there must be a proximate nexus between the private property destroyed and the aim of ending hostilities against the army of occupation and ensuring the safety of the population. Unlike the situation of punitive demolitions, such a nexus would not appear to exist here. Indeed, the prime aim of the property's destruction appears political rather than military, *viz.*, to prove categorically that Israeli control of the Latrun salient was not negotiable.

(ii) *Confiscation*

Private property may not be confiscated, such action being expressly prohibited by Article 46 of the Hague Regulations. Mssrs. McDougal and Feliciano write: 'these protective prescriptions [Articles 46 and 47 prohibiting pillage] only provide that (a) as in the case of public property, there must be a legitimate reason for appropriation and (b) the occupant must pay compensation for the appropriated property.'[173] Private property may not be confiscated but it may be requisitioned where necessary for military purposes.[174]

No record exists of confiscation, as opposed to requisition of private property on the West Bank, inclusive of East Jerusalem.

(iii) *Requisition*

Where property is requisitioned, payment is to be made at once or if not possible, as soon as the occupant is so able. Article 52 of the Hague Regulations provides 'contributions in kind shall be given and the payment of the amount due shall be made as soon as possible.' Thus, it has been held that a lawful requisition becomes unlawful if fair compensation is not paid within a reasonable period.[175]

Regarding the standard of compensation, the commander must ensure, by whatever method, that the fair value is paid for any requisitioned goods.[176]

Of course, the same problems posed in reference to the parameters of 'military necessity' for expropriation of public property exist for requisition of private property.

The reported cases record only the most obvious cases of what is not 'military necessity'. For instance, the requisitioning of property for the purpose of supplying material resources to the population of the occupying power has been held unlawful.[177] Requisitioning for purposes of selling the property at a profit, rather than for direct use of the occupation forces, has also been declared unlawful.[178] The more difficult but unlitigated issues are whether requisition of real property to provide food for the occupying army or cash for the purchase of weapons is unlawful, and if so, in what particular circumstances.

Some guidance is provided by reference to the language of Article 52 of the Hague Regulations which prohibits requisition 'except for the *needs* of the army of occupation,' rather than as required by the 'necessities of war.' The former term has, contrary to probable popular initial impression, been interpreted as more restrictive in meaning and, therefore, more favorable to the inhabitants.[179] Article 55 of the Geneva Convention continues this line of interpretation. Requisitions may not be carried out unless 'for use of the occupation forces and administrative personnel, and then only if the requirements of the civilian population have been taken into account.'

There is no reported record of private property which, having been requisitioned for military use, was not put to that end. The Special Committee Report cites no cases of such activity.

### (iv) *Trusteeship (Absentee Property)*

Regarding absentee property, Israeli policy is expressed in Military Order No. 10 of July 23, 1967, *Abandoned Property of Private Individuals Order*.[180] Such property may be taken into custody only if both owner and occupier are absent from the region. The officer-in-charge safeguarding such properties is required to preserve its value for the owner. When the rightful owner returns he is entitled to reacquire his property. Sale in the interim of such property is permitted only where there is no other way to ensure that the lawful owner can receive a return for the value of his property.

There are no reported sales of absentee property nor are there any reported cases of their use for civilian or military settlement purposes.

Closely tied in with the issue of absentee property is the issue of refugee repatriation so that ownership of such property may be reclaimed. Israel has permitted refugee repatriation only in instances involving separation of members of an immediate family. Neither customary nor conventional international law expressly requires the repatriation of refugees during the course of belligerent occupation. The 1951 Convention Relating to the Status of Refugees,[181] which is declarative of the relevant international law, is silent on this point. Article 45 of the Geneva Convention states that:

> This provision [against the transfer of protected persons to a Power not a party to the Convention] shall in no way constitute an obstacle to the repatriation of protected persons, or to their return to their country of residence *after the cessation of hostilities*.

It remains questionable whether post-1967 Arab-Israeli relations fall within the latter phrase.

Proponents of such a right cite in their favor paragraphs one and two of Article 13 of the Universal Declaration of Human Rights. Article 13(1) states that 'everyone has the right to freedom of movement and residence within the borders of each state.' Article 13(2) states 'everyone has the right to leave any country, including his own, and to return to his country.' In the 1968 case, *The Military Prosecutor* v. *Khali M.M.K. Bakous and Others,*[182] the defendants, members of the Palestine Liberation Organization, were charged with infiltrating from the East to the West Bank. They asserted that they were entitled to freely enter the West Bank from Jordan by virtue of the provisions of Article 13(1). The Court ruled that even assuming that the Universal Declaration has binding force, the provision in question could not confer the right to freedom of movement between the two Banks, since those two areas are not situated in the same state. In reference to freedom of return to one's country, whatever the legal parameters of that right are, they are not sufficiently wide to encompass such a right where hostile relations continue between the ousted power and occupying state.

### (v) *Purchase*

One of the most interesting legal questions to arise from the Israeli occupation is the permissibility of purchase by the occupant's nationals of land owned by nationals of the occupied territory. International law has paid surprisingly little attention to the difficulties posed by this issue. No mention of purchase is made in either the Hague Regulations or Geneva Convention, and writers on the subject of belligerent occupation appear to have ignored it.[183]

The U.N. Special Committee to Investigate Israeli Practices in the Occupied Territories came to the conclusion in its final major report that

> The Fourth Geneva Convention and the Hague Regulations made it abundantly clear that, irrespective of whether the land belongs to the State or to private individuals, the occupying power has no right under international law to acquire ownership of such property. Any such acquisition there is *ipso jure* invalid.[184]

The Committee's conclusion in regard to acquisition by the occupying power is clearly incorrect. 'Military necessity' and the 'needs of the occupying forces', respectively, justify confiscation of public property and requisition of private property. Nevertheless, there is sufficient merit in the Committee's assertion regarding the illegality of private land transactions to warrant quotation of its reasoning.

> The Special Committee is of the opinion that any transactions for the acquisition of land between the State of Israel and Israeli nationals on the one hand, and the inhabitants of the occupied territories on the other, have no validity in law and cannot be recognized as legal changes in ownership. Even the payment of compensation does not render such transactions valid or confer legal title. The Special Committee's reason for expressing this opinion is that the inhabitants of the occupied territories, in the absence of the protection and guidance of the regime under which they lived before the occupation, are not acting as free agents. The disposal of the property of individuals in any State is liable to control and regulation by the State in accordance with State policy. This indispensable factor does not exist in the occupied territories. It is incumbent on the United Nations to state, unequivocally, that these transactions are not recognizable. They would create a formidable obstacle to restoration of the *status quo ante* the hostilities of June 1967. If it is the intention or desire of the United Nations that the territories under occupation by the State of Israel as a result of the hostilities of June 1967 should be vacated and not be subject to

> acquisition by Israel, the United Nations cannot allow conditions to be created which would leave in the heart of these territories after the cessation of military occupation, large areas and settlements which are claimed to have been acquired by the State of Israel or its nationals.[185]

The Special Committee appears to have concluded that the inhabitants under any occupation cannot be deemed to act as free agents in land transactions with the occupying power. If the Committee's intent was to state that the inhabitants in the particular case of Israel's occupation were deprived of such freedom of action, it certainly failed to make this clear and offered no proof. However cogent the Committee's reasoning may be in condemning land transfers during occupation, it is addressed to the political rather than the legal merits of such actions. Juridical expressions on the subject, although scant, support the lawfulness of voluntary private land transactions between opposing nationals in an occupation context.

The most authoritative statement on the subject is the judgement of the U.S. Military Tribunal at Nuremberg in the I.G. Farben Trial.[186] Addressing itself to the question of economic exploitation as a war crime, the Tribunal made reference to the applicable sections of the Hague Regulations:

> [W]ith respect to private property, these provisions [Articles 46 and 47] relate to plunder, confiscation, and requisition which, in turn, imply action in relation to property committed against the will and without the consent of the owner. We look in vain for any provision in the Hague Regulations which would justify the broad assertion that private citizens of the nation of the military occupant may not enter into agreements respecting property in occupied territories when consent of the owner is, in fact, freely given . . . If, in fact, there is no coercion present in an agreement, even during time of military occupancy, and if, in fact, the owner's consent is voluntarily given, we do not find such action to be in violation of the Hague Regulations. The contrary interpretation would make it difficult, if not impossible, for the occupying power in time of war to carry out other aspects of its obligations under international law, including restoration of order to the local economy in the interests of the local inhabitants (Article 43, Hague Regulations). On the other hand, when action by the owner is not voluntary because his consent is obtained by threats, intimidation, pressure, or by

> exploiting the position and power of the military occupant under circumstances indicating that the owner is being induced to part with his property against his will, it is clearly a violation of the Hague Regulations. *The mere presence of the military occupant is not the exclusive indication of the assertion of pressure.* Certainly where the action of private individuals, including juristic persons, is involved, the evidence must go further and must establish that a transaction otherwise apparently legal in form was not voluntarily entered into because of the employment of pressure. Furthermore, there must be a causal connection between the illegal means employed and the result brought about by employing such intimidation.[187]

The prosecution had contended that private land transactions constituted an element of the punishable offense of plunder and spoliation and that they could not be properly viewed as 'individual actions.' Rather, a broader perspective encompassing the 'cumulative' effect of such actions was urged. In this light, private land purchase was contended to be 'a crime against the country concerned in that it disrupts the economy, alienates its industry from its inherent purpose (and) makes it subservient to the interests of the occupying power . . .'[188] 'As far as this aspect is concerned,' the prosecution continued, 'the consent of the owner or owners, even if genuine, does not affect the criminal character of the act.'[189] The Tribunal rejected the view that private land transactions be viewed as part of a comprehensive cumulative process of coercion in favor of examining the issue of voluntary transfer on a case by case basis.

Yet the basis of the Tribunal's decision left room for doubt. True, the Tribunal had made it clear that 'the mere presence of the military occupant is not the exclusive indication of the assertion of pressure'. Farben was, however, found guilty, not because of evidence that it had individually coerced the will of sellers but because

> In many cases in which Farben dealt directly with the private owners, there was the ever present threat of forceful seizure of the property by the Reich or other similar measures, such, for example as withholding licenses, raw materials, the threat of uncertain drastic treatment in peace-treaty negotiations or

> other effective means of bending the will of the owners. The power of the military occupant was the ever present threat in these transactions, and was clearly an important if not a decisive factor.[190]

In the subsequent Krupp Trial,[191] the Nuremberg Tribunal leaned even further toward the proposition that in determining the voluntary nature of an individual transaction, the ultimate outcome of all the transactions on the economy of the occupied territory need be considered. There the Tribunal stated that:

> Spoliation of private property, then, is forbidden under two aspects: firstly, the individual private owner of property must not be deprived of it; secondly, *the economic substance of the belligerently occupied territory must not be taken over by the occupant* or put to the service of his war effort—always with the proviso that there are exceptions to this rule which are strictly limited to the needs of the army of occupation insofar as such needs do not exceed the economic strength of the occupied territory.[192]

The official notes to the United Nations War Crimes Commission Report of the Trial state, however, that it is probable 'that the Tribunal tacitly excluded from the meaning of the phrase, "must not be taken over by the occupant," transfers of property effected by freely arrived at agreements.'[193]

It is suggested that a fair conclusion to be reached from the judgements of the *Farben* and *Krupp* cases is that private, voluntary land transactions are prohibited by international law only where the magnitude of the transactions is of a scale equivalent to the systematic plunder of the resources of the occupied territory. Nevertheless, private land transactions between opposing nationals in an occupation context, if not unlawful, are nevertheless highly undesirable. Almost inevitably they will tend to complicate and perhaps retard the peace-making process. Even where purchases are neither coerced nor the product of unequal bargaining power, acquisition of property in occupied territory may provide an irresistible incentive for retention of occupied territory, even at the price of foregoing movement towards a negotiated full peace settlement.

### d. *The Settlement by Nationals of the Occupying Power on Occupied Territory*

The Hague Regulations neither permit nor forbid civilian settlement by the occupying power's nationals in the occupied country. They do not address themselves to the issue. The Fourth Geneva Convention of 1949, drawing upon the experience of the Second World War, expressly provides in Article 49, however, that:

> Individual or mass forcible transfers, as well as deportations of protected persons from occupied territory to the territory of the Occupying Power or to that of any other country, occupied or not, are prohibited regardless of their motive. (Para. 1)
>
> The Occupying Power shall not deport or transfer parts of its own civilian population into the territory it occupies. (Para. 6)

Oppenheim states that this prohibition was 'intended to cover cases of the occupant bringing in its nationals for the *purpose of displacing the population of the occupied territory.*'[194]

Nevertheless, civilian settlement on a more sporadic basis may, like private voluntary land transactions discussed earlier, be viewed as contrary to the spirit of the Hague Regulations and the Geneva Convention. The basic duty of the occupant is to preserve the existing situation in the occupied territories. Only minimal changes essential and unavoidable for the maintenance of military security and the preservation of the public order and welfare of the inhabitants are permitted. The operative premise of such regulation is that other changes may not only be directly inimical to the best interests of the population but make more difficult the peace-making process by creating vested interests in the maintenance of occupation.

One civilian settlement creates the demand for another, and inevitably a formidable obstacle to peace negotiations is created. Relations between the occupier and occupied are exacerbated and the prospects of rapprochement are diminished. Vested interests on the one side and greater embitterment on the other pull the parties farther apart.

Proponents of settlement in Israel argued that settlement would encourage movement toward a peace settlement. The theory was that by being apprised that the longer they wait, the less there will be to negotiate, Arabs would turn to negotiation.

Moreover, it was suggested that with the advent of a peace treaty, Jewish factories and settlements should be permitted to exist in Arab territories as the only 'peace' Israel could agree to would be one calling for such 'normalization.' The warning that 'settlements are continuing and time is against you' is at best, however, a dubious incentive to negotiating peace. Far from acting to alleviate Arab intransigence, such statements may have further led the Arab states to resolve that lost lands could be regained only by force. Arab declarations to this effect then completed the vicious circle. Israeli listeners found in them justification for increasing settlements in the occupied territories on the grounds that prospects for peace were simply not in sight.

e. *Conclusions*

The gradual shift from security settlements adjacent to the Jordan River to settlements having a civilian rather than para-military character and the prospering of the Jewish enclaves in Etzion, Hebron and Ramallah pointed in the direction, even before ratification of the Galili Document, of a strong Israeli commitment to permanent occupation of major parts of the West Bank, despite disclaimers of such intention. Vested interests and ties were created in the region that were and continue to be difficult to uproot.

The Arab-Israeli dispute has always essentially revolved around the question of ownership and control of land in a small and poor territory. It is, therefore, of little surprise that, in the course of a decade of occupation, Israeli settlement on the West Bank proved to be the greatest source of friction between Arabs and Israelis. Despite the goodwill that accrued from the Government's 'indirect rule' in economic and other matters, Israeli settlement aroused, among all segments of West Bank society, deep resentment and distrust of the Israeli authorities.[195] The escalation of private land transactions and the campaign to legalize these purchases only accentuated Arab fears. Although the land transactions appear, in fact, to have been the product of free bilateral bargaining, the sale of Arab land to an Israeli Jew was fundamentally different from the sale of Arab land to an Arab or a foreign investor. The

Israeli purchasers and settlers posed indirectly, if not directly, a threat to the continuation of the West Bankers' conservative and traditional society. The less land remained in Arab possession, the more rapid appeared the nearly inevitable process of 'modernization'—the transformation of the Arab from petty farmer to worker, in this case for Israel. The predominent fear of political, economic and cultural subservience to an alien and Western society was grounded in what appeared, with good reason, to be an unofficial Israeli policy of creeping annexation.

On the international level, Israel's land settlement policy lowered the credibility of its statements that the occupied territories were negotiable. The Arab world, insofar as it was amenable to negotiation, and most Afro-Asian countries, viewed Israel's settlement policy as a major obstacle to a peace agreement.[196] Regardless of its validity, the concept that in 1967 Israel was not merely defending her existence but was fighting a carefully planned campaign to gain more territory was accepted as truth by many in the Arab 'non-aligned' world. Israel's policy of 'creating facts', as referred to by Defense Minister Dayan and others in the Government,[197] helped confirm this suspicion.

Mr. Dayan, especially, and other cabinet members and ministers as well, had made it well known at the very outset of occupation that Israeli withdrawal from the West Bank, at least in full, would not be considered. For example, Premier Levi Eshkol in June, 1968, stated that in determining the new 'political border' of Israel, the government would have to bear in mind the historical rights of the people of Israel in the land of Israel, without ignoring the fact of Arab population concentrations in certain areas.

To the Arab inhabitants of the region, these statements aroused fear that they might one day all become refugees.[198] Jordan, the state most disposed of all Arab regimes to make peace with Israel, viewed the land acquisition and settlement problem as such a serious bar to regaining its territory that it passed legislation imposing a death penalty on any Arab citizen or intermediary voluntarily selling land to an Israeli.

Thus, the settlements, limited as they were, were nevertheless substantially responsible for maintaining a charged atmosphere in relations between Israel and its neighboring Arab states. Using the conquered territories as a pressuring device, Israel has in effect been telling the Arab world that unless territorial concessions via a peace treaty were soon offered, there would be increasingly less territory to negotiate about. It was and remains a gamble. The Arab states could also decide that 'no loaf is preferable to half a loaf' and opt for war. Before 1973 Israel was confident that its military superiority would dissuade the Arab States from this route. This is not to say that Israeli settlement policy bore a direct relation to the Arab attack of 1973.[199] Arab unwillingness to make peace, even for the reward of full territorial concessions, was an independent factor. Nevertheless the period surrounding the passage of the Galili Paper marked the height of Arab-Israeli tension preceding the war. To the Arabs, it demonstrated Israel's unequivocal intent to effect permanent settlement of at least major parts of the occupied territories. The least that can be said is that Israel, by offering less, did not act to reduce Arab intransigence and further the prospects of peace.

Jewish settlement in Palestine aroused Arab hostility from the very beginning of the Mandate as it symbolized potential domination by a rival culture with alien religious and social values. Regardless of the validity of the moral and legal arguments behind the creation of the Palestine Mandate and the state of Israel, the indigenous Arab population perceived the Jewish presence in Palestine as a theft of their land.

Yet by 1967, the allegations of Israel's 'expansionist and colonialist ambitions' had assumed for many Arabs a rhetorical quality. Israel's post-1967 policy of increasing land acquisition and settlement in the administered territories helped give new life to these slogans. Thus Israel's land policy only dimmed the prospects of Arab-Israeli rapprochement[200]. Nevertheless, in the perspective of contemporary international law, Israel's land acquisition and settlement policy was not unlawful as it neither aimed for, nor neared, a stage involving displacement of the existing population as a prelude to future annexation. Settlement and land acquisition were more in the nature of incipient *ad hoc* populist trends than the outgrowth of established government policies. Their proportions were insubstantial; after a decade of Israeli rule fewer than 2,000 Israeli civilians, or roughly half of one per cent of the region's population, reside in the West Bank.[201]

Under the Labour Government, Israel has repeatedly stated that civilian settlement and annexation are not to be considered as opposite sides of the same coin. Israel intimated that its territorial demands in the West Bank would be limited to the populated areas of the region and to buffer zones along its borders. Opponents of Israel's stance, insisting that it was annexationist in nature, had an opportunity to test Israel's real intention with no risk of harm to themselves by proceeding to the negotiations table. This they refused to do. Whether Israel, in the aftermath of the defeat of the Labour Party in May 1977, will be as amenable to broad territorial concessions remains to be seen.

## D. THE EDUCATIONAL SYSTEM

### 1. *Administration under Israeli Military Government*

#### a. *Textbook and Curricula Reform*

Soon after commencement of occupation the task of administering the West Bank educational system was delegated by the Military Government to the Israel Ministry of Education and Culture. The Ministry of Education and Culture decided to reopen the schools as scheduled for the forthcoming academic year and to maintain the basic Jordanian structure of public education. The Ministry also made it clear that some change would be required:

> . . . Of course, the teachers must recognize that there will be change. All teaching of the hatred of peoples and the destruction of states, including, of course, the State of Israel, must be eliminated. Those teachers who cannot accept this principle will be asked to leave.[202]

Change centered around reform of the West Bank curricula and replacement of textbooks. The existing curricula and texts were soon revised to reflect those in use in Arab schools within Israel. Of the 134 Jordanian texts in use on the West Bank, 78 were considered by Education Ministry officials to be so politically biased as to be unacceptable.[203] The only texts found to be unbiased were foreign language and scientific textbooks published abroad.[204]

In July and August 1967, teachers' groups on the West Bank drew up petitions threatening to strike in opposition to the proposed Israeli curricula and text reforms which, in their view, contravened international law's mandate to maintain and preserve the existing institutions of the occupied territory without interference unless absolutely prevented by immediate security or welfare needs. Most of the passages excised from the school texts dealt, in the view of West Bank educators, merely with the affirmation of their Palestinian identity and membership in the greater nation of Islam.[205]

The Military Government, concerned about the threatened strike as the first organized opposition to Israel's authority in the region, exerted its influence on the Ministry of Education to retract the proposed curricula reform. The Ministry agreed to maintain the Jordanian curriculum—except in Jerusalem—but rejected 78 books altogether, reprinting the remaining 56 only after deletion of objectionable passages.[206] Similar deletions were required of texts in use in private and UNRWA schools.[207]

The concessions came too late (two weeks before the opening of schools on September 4) to quell the resentment that had been aroused among Arab educators and the population generally at having educational policy imposed on them. A call for a strike by teachers and boycott by students of the schools was issued. As a result, nearly three-quarters of all the state schools on the West Bank were unopened.[208]

The Israeli authorities reacted by taking punitive measures against some strike leaders[209] and by publicizing its position to the population. A letter circulated by the Military Governor to parents of school children stated:

> The school structure, curriculum and courses remain exactly as they were. Neither is there any truth to the rumors that the study of religion has been prohibited. All that has happened is that scurrilous anti-Israel and anti-Jewish material has been deleted from the textbooks . . .
>
> The Military Government does not intend to take any action to bring about the opening of the schools.[210]

The teachers' strike was finally resolved through a compromise arrangement whereby a joint committee of Israeli and Arab educators was established for the purpose of supervising textbook revision. The individual responsible for the proposal, Nablus Mayor Hamdi Canaan, stated that while deletion of anti-Israel material was justifiable, 'such changes should be made by mutual agreement and not unilaterally, presenting us with a "fait accompli".'[211]

The Arab representatives agreed to drop the subject, 'The Palestinian Problem,' from the school curriculum, and the Ministry of Education agreed to disqualify only six of the partially approved texts. Teachers and educational officials arrested because of strike-related activities were released.

The schools were reopened in mid-November, 1967 and despite the periodic recurrence of wildcat strikes, remained in operation throughout the 1967–8 academic year. They reopened the following fall without incident.

While the compromise settlement of the textbook controversy ended the two month strike, its repercussions would continue to be felt. Because the strike had been successful, schools became the focal point for expression of discontent with Israeli rule.

b. *Higher Education*

Toward the middle of 1973 demands for the creation of an Arab university on the West Bank, which had been rather meekly voiced since 1971, began to increase in intensity. A representative West Bank committee was formed for the purpose of pressing and cajoling the Military Government to establish such a university. Its chairman, Azis Zahadi, a prominent West Bank attorney situated in Ramallah, had gained early notoriety by attempting to represent the Palestinian cause at the 1949 Armistice discussions between Israel and Jordan at Rhodes. His efforts were in vain, but he remained throughout Jordanian rule a strong proponent of an autonomous Palestinian state on the West Bank.

Serving also on the committee for a West Bank university was E. Freij, the Mayor of Bethlehem. Although an opponent of Zahadi's views calling for Palestinian autonomy—Freij had always favored continued amalgamation with Jordan—he agreed on the importance of establishing an Arab university on the West Bank, regardless of who the acting sovereign might be.

One West Bank institution of higher learning had already existed under Jordanian rule and continued to function under Israeli occupation. This was Bir Zeit College, located in the town whose name it had adopted. Bir Zeit College had an enrollment of about 400 students on a relatively spacious campus. All instruction was in English, and a number of its students were annually accepted by Arab universities in the adjoining Arab countries. The College was a Christian-operated institution and was dependent for its support almost entirely on charitable contributions from abroad.

Under Jordanian rule, Bir Zeit was a two-year junior college. After the start of Israeli occupation, its president, Dr. Hannah Nasir,[212] decided to revamp the school and change it into a four-year institution granting the bachelor of arts degree. Without asking for prior permission from the Military Government, he instituted this change. The Military Governor subsequently sent him a letter threatening disciplinary action unless all unauthorized changes were rescinded. Dr. Nasir ignored the letter. Disciplinary action was not taken, and the school, since 1972, has functioned as a four-year degree-granting institution.[213]

When the Committee for Formation of a West Bank University was formed, the possibility of accomplishing this goal through the expansion of Bir Zeit was first explored. The idea was rejected on the grounds that the entire present curriculum was in English, and that the task of introducing an Arab curriculum—many of the teachers at Bir Zeit were from abroad—would prove too difficult.[214]

Freij concentrated his efforts on obtaining Jordanian approval for the project. According to Jordanian law, institutions of higher learning could not be established without obtaining an express grant of permission from the Minister of Education. Zahadi concentrated on gaining Israeli approval.

The majority of the West Bank political elite, however, seemed opposed to the idea. Whereas its proponents maintained that a university would diminish Israeli control over all spheres of social and political life, its detractors argued that Israeli interference in the life of the university would be inevitable, and thus Israeli control would only be increased.

The Committee scored a limited success when in 1974 a West Bank College of Moslem Studies was established near Hebron.[215] Since then, further demands for a West Bank university have not been made.

2. *International Law Relative to the Scope of an Occupant's Authority to Interfere with the Educational System*

Perhaps the most powerful instrument an occupying power has at its disposal in attempting to permanently redefine existing institutional and social structures of occupied territory is the power to initiate broad educational reform involving curricula, texts and teachers. Despite the importance of the issue of permissible authority to interfere with educational systems, the Hague Regulations and the Geneva Convention are silent on this point, providing only the general prohibition against 'institutional' change.[216]

An occupant is permitted to utilize political propaganda warfare to popularize his views among the occupied population.[217] This is an invariable fact of life under occupation and it would be of little avail to attempt to proscribe it. As schools and universities are often the centers for the articulate and political segments of any population, and as they assume primary responsibility for perpetuating community doctrine and myth, they will naturally be the focal point of propaganda warfare.

Little scholarly work has been done on the limits, if any, that can be imposed on the exercise of propaganda warfare in school settings. There is general agreement that the occupant may exercise supervision over the schools and prevent the teaching of subjects which either prove a threat to the security of his forces or encourage passive resistance by the civilian population. Beyond this, there is confusion.

Reference in the international law literature to the permissible scope of the occupant's authority over the educational system first occurs regarding the German occupation of Belgium during the First World War. The German military government in Belgium passed a considerable amount of legislation aimed at preventing anti-German teaching in the schools and at suppressing nationalistic exercises and demonstrations by students. A German ordinance provided that '. . . teaching staff, school managers and inspectors, who during the period of occupation, tolerate, favor, provoke or organize Germanophobe manifestations or secret practices will be punished by imprisonment for a maximum term of one year.'[218] Another ordinance provided that 'the German authorities have the right to enter all classes and rooms of all schools existing in Belgium and to supervise the teaching and all manifestations of school life with a view to preventing secret practices and intrigues directed against Germany.'[219] Textbooks containing any statements offensive to the Germans were forbidden. Dismissal of the classes in honor of the King and similar patriotic manifestations were prohibited. Legislation was promulgated aimed at recognizing Flemish rather than French, and in some districts German, as the official language of instruction in universities.

The German authorities justified the increased prominence they gave to Flemish on the grounds that they were merely aiding the liberation of the long-oppressed Flemish race from the Walloon yoke and providing them with a medium for development of their own culture. The reorganization of the University of Ghent was described as motivated by a desire to meet the long-standing demand of the Flemish population for a university of their own. Indeed, the Flemish population had long before the War frequently petitioned the Government to provide them with an institution of higher learning in which the medium of instruction would be Flemish.

Commenting on the lawfulness of German interference with the Belgian educational system generally, and the University of Ghent in particular, Professor Garner wrote:

> While it would seem to be within the lawful rights of a military occupant to exercise supervision within the territory occupied, so far as it may be necessary to prevent seditious teaching calculated to provoke and instill hostility to his authority, it may be doubted whether he has any lawful right to forbid such

> exercises, as the singing of national anthems or whether he may justly abrogate the language to be employed in the schools . . . no considerations of public order or safety required the forcing of the Flemish or German language into the schools; its obvious purpose was to 'Flemishize' or Germanize a portion of the country occupied by the enemy . . .
>
> [Regarding the reorganization of the University of Ghent] Its courses of instruction, the language in which they were given, and the selection of its professors were matters of no legitimate concern to the military occupant so long as the conduct of the university and the character of its teaching were not such as to endanger the military interests of the occupant or threaten the public order. The pretext that the measure was in the interest of the oppressed race ceased to have any weight as soon as the leaders, as well as the great majority of those in whose interest it was alleged to have been undertaken, united in protest against it.[220]

Measures taken by the Russian military government during the First World War in administering the educational systems of occupied territory proved even harsher than those undertaken by the Germans. When Russian forces occupied Poland, all schools with the exception of vocational institutions were closed. Although private schools were permitted to reopen, they were permitted to operate only under the following specific conditions:

> . . . Changes in the staffs require the approval of the Governor. Both teachers and textbooks are to be removed at his request or at the request of his Deputy. The Russian language will be taught for five hours each week. History, geography, the Polish language and Polish literary history may be taught only on the basis of texts which are permitted to be used in Russia or which have been approved by the Governor-General or his Deputy . . . Violation of one of these orders will result in the closing of the institution concerned.[221]

During the course of the Second World War, the German military governments in Europe, and the Japanese occupation authorities in China and in the Philippines, interfered, as is well known, with educational systems for reasons totally divorced from military considerations. In German-occupied Poland, schools were permitted to reopen only after the curricula had been reorganized to entertain a pro-German bias. All institutions of higher learning were closed for the duration of the German occupation. Institutions which remained open were under the complete control of the German military authorities.[222] In Holland, as one example, all texts suspected of containing a 'spirit' incompatible with 'friendly' relations between the two countries were confiscated and destroyed. The same process was applied to all public libraries.[223]

During the Allied occupation of Germany, the German policy of text and curricula control was applied in reverse as part of the Allied denazification program.[224] Nationalist Socialist elements were purged from teaching staffs, Nazi texts were eliminated and curricula were reorganized to present the Allied viewpoint.[225]

It is submitted that in instances of post-surrender occupation, where the Hague Regulations are inapplicable, the occupant may lawfully control and supervise any aspect of an educational system. In other instances, interference must be limited. The traditional tests of 'military security' and the 'welfare of the population' provide, however, little guidance as to the scope of permissible interference. Nor does state practice provide an admirable model for fashioning doctrine. In nearly every major instance of belligerent occupation in recent history, the occupying power has quickly taken steps aimed at rigid and total control of the curricula and personnel of schools and institutions of higher learning.[226]

The difficulty in establishing standards in reference to permissible educational reform is that propaganda warfare, especially among states professing competing ideological systems, is the norm during the course of 'peaceful coexistence.' Thus, upon assumption of the occupation of the territory of an ideological opponent, there will be the strongest proclivity toward the excision of doctrinally adverse material and the dismissal of educators likely to continue to adhere to it. If the standard the Geneva Convention applies to the judiciary and executive, whereby members thereof suspected of being potential subordinates may be summarily dismissed from their positions, is equally applied to the educational system, then it would seem that institutions, curricula and personnel ideologically adverse to the occupant need not be retained. Whether the occupant may then introduce in their stead new material, institutions and personnel, ideologically acceptable to him but repugnant to the occupied populace, is a different question.

Where revision of existing educational structures is undertaken for promotion of fundamental human rights and the lessening of tension conducive to resumption of war, it is clearly permissible. In more ambiguous situations, the preferable standard would appear to be one whereby revision is limited to rendering material 'politically neutral'. The Protecting Power system of the Geneva Convention, were it invoked, might play an important role in this area by mediating disputes revolving around the reasonableness of revisions. Indeed UNESCO has already played a noteworthy role in this respect.

### 3. *Assessing Israel's Educational Policy in the West Bank*

All major reports of the U.N. Special Committee to Investigate Israeli Practices Affecting the Human Rights of the Population of the Occupied Territories failed to make any allegation, directly or indirectly, of undue interference by the Israeli authorities in the educational system on the West Bank. Given the critical and partial nature of the Committee and its reports, Israel's educational policy must be deemed at least presumptively lawful in all its particulars.[227]

Although Israel's Education Ministry attempted at first to introduce the use of the pro-Israel texts employed in Arab schools within Israel, a compromise was reached whereby political discussion of the 'Palestinian Question'—mainly the 1948 War—would be eliminated, but the pro-Israel texts used in Arab schools within Israel would not be adopted. The compromise was sensible. Most importantly, its means of achievement—through the mediation efforts of UNESCO—provides an admirable example for future conflict resolution of this type.

The West Bank College, newly created in 1974 in Hebron, was the product of indigenous demand rather than the designs of the occupying power aimed at training a subservient educated class. Its operation, too, by all accounts has remained unhampered by Israeli rule. As such, it provides a striking example of how the processes of social life under occupation need not become static, frozen at the pre-occupation level, but may continue to operate dynamically and be realized within the exigencies of occupation rule.

Since 1968, the educational system has been allowed to function smoothly and relatively undisturbed. However, this fact has been lost sight of in the escalation of the political war against Israel within all United Nations organs. Thus, for example, on November 18, 1976, UNESCO passed a resolution at its general conference accusing Israel of 'systematic Judaization of education and cultural life' in the occupied territories.[228] No change in Israeli policy had occurred in the educational sphere between 1968 and 1976 and that policy was one which left little room for fault-finding.

NOTES

1. *See* Israel Ministry of Defense, *The Military Government's Civil Administration,* 1–10 (1968); *The Jerusalem Post,* Dec. 8, 1967, Feb. 16, 1968.
2. For a seasoned argument on behalf of the non-applicability of the traditional law of belligerent occupation, *see* M. Shamgar, then Attorney-General of Israel, 'The Observance of International Law in The Administered Territories,' *1 Israel YRBK on Human Rights,* 151 (1971).
3. *Id.* See, for earlier formulations of this view, J. Stone, *Between the Ceasefires* (1967) and Blum, 'The Missing Reversioner: Reflections on the Status of Judea and Samaria,' *Israel L. Rev.,* 289 (1968).
4. 49 *Records of Knesset Proceedings,* 2420 (1967) (hereinafter K.P.) (in Hebrew; translations are by author).
5. 21 *Laws of the State of Israel* (hereinafter LSI) 75 (1967).
6. *Administrative and Judicial Order No. 1,* June 30, 1967. *Kovetz Hatakanot (Subsidiary Legislation)* (hereinafter *K.T.*) (in Hebrew) 2690 (1967). Note that Jerusalem's annexation could have been affected under existing legislation. Israel's *Area of Jurisdiction and Power Ordinance* I *LSI* 64 (1948) permits the Minister of Defense to apply any or all of Israel's law 'to any part of Palestine which the Minister of Defense has defined by proclamation as being held by the Defense Army of Israel.' Passage of the *Law and Administrative Ordinance Law (Amendment No. 11)* came under severe criticism during the debate over the bill in the Knesset as being procedurally unconstitutional in the light of the 1948 Law. *See* 49 *K.P.* 2423 (1967). The 1948 Law, in contrast to the 1967 *Administrative and Judicial Order,* speaks of defining the 'area of the State of Israel' rather than of 'the extension of Israel's administrative and judicial jurisdiction.'

7. Paragraph 35, Proclamation No. 3. *1 Proclamations, Orders and Appointments of Israel Defense Forces in Judea and Samaria* 12 (1967) (in Hebrew) (hereinafter *P.O.A.)*.
8. Israel Defence Forces Order No. 144, October 1967, Security Amendment No. 9, 2 *P.O.A.* 303 (1967).
9. *Amendments to Entry Into Israel Law of 1953* and *Amendments to Orders Extending Applicability of the Emergency Regulations of 1948, K.T.* 910-11 (1968).
10. *See* Nahumi, 'Policies and Practices of Occupation,' *New Outlook,* May 1968. 35.
11. *Military Prosecutor* v. *Suhadi S. H. Zuhad,* Israel Military Court, Bethlehem, August 11, 1968. *47 Annual International Law Reports,* (E. Lauterpacht, ed.) (hereinafter *Annual Reports*) 490 (1974).
12. *The Military Government's Civil Administration, supra* note 1 at 148.
13. *See,* regarding early regulatory changes, Israel Foreign Office. *The Israel Administration in Judea, Samaria and Gaza,* 18-20, 50-3. (1968).
14. *Jerusalem Post,* June 8, 1968 regarding the Mayor of Jericho; January 2, 1968 regarding the Mayor of Jabud and May 18, 1968 regarding the Mayor of Nablus.
15. *See* Raphaeli, 'Military Government in the Occupied Territories: The Israel View,' *The Middle East Journal,* Spring, 1969, 185.
16. *See,* regarding Arab claims of Israeli pressure on the Arab authorities to cooperate with the Israeli authorities in setting up civilian government in place of a military government, 1968 *Middle East Record* 445.
17. *See* Shamgar, *supra* note 2.
18. *See infra* Section C4.
19. U.N. Doc A/8089 (1969), 60.
20. *Id.*
21. Personal interview with Justice Jihad Jarallah, President West Bank Supreme Court, Summer 1973.
22. *Al-Ja'bari* v. *Al-'Awiwi* Court of Appeals of Ramallah, June 17, 1968, 42 *Annual Reports* 484, 486 (1971).
23. *Id.,* 487. The Jordanian government took various steps to deter Arab lawyers and judges from collaborating with the Israeli authorities. In January 1968, the President of the Hebron District Court and two East Jerusalem judges were dismissed for such collaboration, *Ha'aretz* January 22, 1968. In April three lawyers were expelled from the Jordanian Bar Association for agreeing to serve as judges under the Military Government. At the end of June, the Jordanian government suspended another eight judges, *Jerusalem Post* March 3, 1968, and had five others reprimanded, *Radio Israel* July 7, 1968. At the Arab Lawyers Conference in September 1968, West Bank lawyers were urged to persist in their boycott of the courts, *Middle East News Agency* September 4, 1968. Additionally, Jordan directly supported the Arab lawyers in their strike by providing monthly payments, *Jerusalem Post* March 4, 1968, until July of 1968, *Lamerhav* July 15, 1968.

24. *Order Regarding Entrance into Force of Security Measures* 1 *POA*, Order no. 14, p. 5 (1967).
25. *See* generally regarding scope of authority and procedural aspects of Israel military courts, M. Drori, *Legislation in Judea and Samaria* (unpublished in Hebrew), 13-16.
26. 47 *Annual Reports* 490 (1974).
27. *Id.* at 492. As an example of a military order which a military court could overrule as 'clearly and manifestly unlawful,' the Court cites an order which would prohibit the bearing of children. *Id.*, at 495.
28. *Shamgar, supra* note 2, at 273. Note that the Israel Supreme Court never asserted its jurisdiction to review legislative acts of the military government on the basis of international law integrated into Israeli law, but rather referred to the source of its jurisdiction as the mutual stipulation of the parties that international law would govern.
29. Drori, *supra* note 25, at 73, n. 569.
30. Art. 64(1) *Town Municipalities Law, No. 29*, 1955, *The Jordanian Official Gazette*, No. 1225, May 7, 1955, repealing and replacing the Town Municipalities Law, No. 17 of 1954, *Id.* No. 1183, June 6, 1954. Prior to 1954 the British Mandates Municipal Corporation Ordinance of 1934, *The Official Gazette*, No. 414, January 12, 1934, Supp. 1, p.1 was in effect.
31. The minimum number was seven and the maximum twelve, Art. 7, *Town Municipalities Law of 1955*.
32. Supplement No. 1. *Jordanian Official Gazette*, No.1231, June 16, 1955.
33. Article 12, *Town Municipalities Law of 1955*. *See*, on the inferior status of women in Jordanian law, Shitrit, 'Civil Rights in Jordanian Law,' *Mishpatim* (Israel Bar Assn., Hebrew) 113, 115 (1968).
34. Article 2 (6), *Id.*
35. Article 12(3) specifically requires the payment of land tax or other municipal tax of at least one Jordanian dinar.
36. Sheikh Mohammed Ali El'Jaabari, the Mayor of Hebron, is the most prominent example of a mayor appointed in this manner.
37. *See Order Concerning the Extension of Term of Office of the Administrations of Local Authorities, POA* No. 80, 200-1 (1967).
38. Interestingly, however, the first prominent West Bank personality to call for elections was an already existing mayor, Hamdi Cana'an of Nablus. *See* article in the East Jerusalem daily *El-Quds* December 15 (1968).
39. *POA* No. 19, p. 1099 (1971).
40. In Samaria the voting percentage increased from 75% in the Jordanian period to 83.9%; in Judea the increase was from 75.8% to 87.8%. *Davar* May 3, 1972. The PLO urged West Bankers to refuse to participate in the elections. However, guerilla activities aimed at frightening the electorate away from the polls did not take place. It is unclear whether this occurred as a result of recognition of military impotence or as a matter of calculated choice. *See New York Times*, March 2, 3, 1972. *See also* 18 *Keesing's Contemporary Archives* 25293 (1971-2).

41. *See Al Hamishmar* May 8,9, 1972. Initially, however, Jordan opposed the holding of elections, calling on West Bank Arabs to boycott the election or face economic sanctions. Israel responded to the threat by expanding the elections to include 23 West Bank municipalities rather than only four towns as originally planned. Apparently convinced that its proposed boycott would be self-defeating by causing opponents of the King to be elected, Jordan was reported to have dropped its opposition several months before the scheduled elections. *See* 1971 *Facts on File* 15.
42. 22 *Keesing's Contemporary Archives* 28033 (1976). Note that in April of 1973 Jordan's civil law had been changed to extend the franchise to women. Jordan Information Office, Washington, D.C.
43. *See* von Glahn *supra* I, 14, at 136, 137.
44. J. Pictet, *Fourth Geneva Convention Relative to the Protection of Civilians in Time of War* (Commentary, International Committe of the Red Cross) 335 (1956).
45. Article 27 of the Geneva Convention provides '. . .all protected persons shall be treated with the same consideration by the Party to the conflict in whose power they are, without any adverse distinction based, in particular, on race, religion or political opinion.'
46. Pictet *supra* note 44, at 335.
47. *See,* regarding attempted justification of Allied denazification measures as permissible under the Hague Regulations, Oppenheim, who states:

    [T]he principle laid down in Article 43. . . could hardly apply to an occupied state the law of which denied fundamental human rights and the very notion of legal order as developed in civilised society. The Hague Convention did not envisage—and was therefore not applicable—to the perversions of the idea of law as manifested themselves in the practice of Nationalist-Socialist Germany.

    II *Lauterpacht-Oppenheim* (7th ed., 1952) at 603, n.2.

    This argument is moot, however, as the Hague Regulations are not applicable to instances of post-surrender occupation; *see supra* pp. 5-6.
48. Pictet *supra* note 44, at 336.
49. *Id.* at 308.
50. II *Lauterpacht-Oppenheim* (7th Ed.) 447.
51. *See* von Glahn *supra* note I, 14, at 107.
52. Pictet *supra* note 44, at 336.
53. *See* Freeman, 'War Crimes by Enemy Nationals Administering Justice in Occupied Territory,' 41 *Am. J. Int'l L.* 579, 600 (1947).
54. *See* generally, Wolff, 'Municipal Courts of Justice in Enemy Occupied Territory,' 29 *Grotius Society,* 99 (1943). See also 'German Military Courts in Occupied Areas,' 17 *Ohio B.A. Rep.* 479 (1944).
55. *See* Morgenstern, 'Validity of the Acts of the Belligerent Occupant,' 28 *Br. Yrbk. of Int'l. L.* 290, 295 (1951).
56. For application of the 'patently unlawful' test, *see* Y. Dinstein, *The Defense of 'Obedience to Superior Orders' in International Law* (1964).

57. II *Zeitschrift für ausländisches öffentliches Recht und Völkerrecht* 604 (1942-43). See Morgenstern, *supra* note 55 at 306-307.
58. See the *Overland's Case,* Norway, 12 *Annual Digest* 446 (1943–45); see, also, *In re Lecoq, et al.* (1944), Conseil d'Etat, France, where the asserted right of review existed 'only if and so long as such determination does not involve the interpretation of acts of an international nature, and does not touch upon the rights of the occupying power.' *Id.* at 452; *Requisition of Private Property (Austria) Case* (1949), Constitutional Ct. Austria, *Id.* at 504 (1949).
59. Thus, for example, the Norwegian court deciding on the *Halvorsen* case, *supra* note 57, was composed of judges appointed by the Nazis upon the resignation of the entire previously presiding bench. The cause of the resignation was a correspondence between the former Supreme Court and the German Commissar in the first year of occupation. The Supreme Court had disagreed with the Commissar and taken the view that courts in an occupied country can pass on the validity of the occupant's legislative measures according to international law, *See* note, 12 *Annual Digest,* 1943-45 at 447.
60. 'During the occupation and within the occupied area, to raise questions about the scope of the occupant's competence to prescribe and apply policy for the territory occupied *is perforce a somewhat tenuous enterprise'* McDougal and Feliciano *supra* note I, 10, at 771.
61. *See* Gerson, *supra,* note II 193 at 4.
62. To be discussed in detail in *infra,* Chapter IV, Section B.
63. *See* in accord Pictet *supra* note 44, at 36.
64. Article 45, Hague Regulations; II *Lauterpacht-Oppenheim* (6th ed.) at 348.
65. Article 48, Hague Regulations.
66. *See* von Glahn *supra* note I, 14, at 134.
67. *Id.* at 135; II Garner, *International Law* 63 (1923).
68. *See* Baty, 'The Relations of Invaders to Insurgents', 36 *Yale Law J.* 966 (1927). See also, Drori, 'Municipal Elections in Occupied Areas', 9 *Israel L. Rev.* 92 (1974). Drori assumes, without elaboration or substantiation, that elections are permissible, if not required, by the Hague Regulations.
69. *Id.* Although posing his analysis in a belligerent occupation context, Baty inexplicably made no reference to the relevant international rules but sought instead to examine the issue in a more abstract vein.
70. Israel High Court of Justice (HCJ) 337/71 VI *Decisions of the Israel Supreme Court* (1972). See case comment by Dinstein in 2 *Iyunei Mishpat* (Tel Aviv University Law Review—in Hebrew) 505 (1972).
71. *Id.* HCJ 337/71 at 588.
72. McDougal and Feliciano *supra* note I 10 at 768.
73. *See* Stone *supra* note I, 9, at 698 and McDougal and Feliciano *supra* note I 10 at 767–71. See discussion in Chapter I on the problem of defining the scope of an occupying power's authority. Prof. Y. Dinstein, commenting on the case, has suggested that the validity of an

occupying power's orders be determined under the criterion of whether the occupying power would legislate a similar law in its own state. If so—the order is valid; if not—it may be assumed that the order has not been intended for the welfare of the population and is therefore invalid. 'The Legislating Power in Occupied Areas', 2 *Iyunei Mishpat* (Tel Aviv Law Review, in Hebrew) 505 (1972).

74. *See infra* notes 154, 155.
75. *Davar* May 3, 1972. *See supra* note 40.
76. *El-Quds* May 3, 1972.
77. In a total electorate of 62,998, 71% voted compared with 85% in 1972. However nearly half of the electorate was composed of two classes who had never been given the right to vote previously—women, and males without property. *See* 22 *Keesing's Contemporary Archives* 28033 (1976).
78. The policy of the Jordanian government was aimed at freezing any political initiative for an autonomous West Bank. The legitimate representatives of the West Bank were, in Jordan's view, the Government of Jordan and, in a more specific sense, the members of the Jordanian Parliament from the West Bank.
79. *See* Fahri, 'Political Positions in Judea and Samaria', 231 *Maarachot* (Israel Defense Forces publication, in Hebrew) 9 (1973).
80. *See* Horowitz, 'Political Adaptation under Military Occupation: The Case of the West Bank, June 1967–October 1973', Paper at Round Table, *International Political Science Association,* Jerusalem, Sept. 9–13, 1974. As noted earlier, the initial demand was, however, raised by the then Mayor of Nablus, Mr. Hamdi Cana'an, in an article in *El Quds,* December, 1968.
81. Jerusalem Domestic Service Broadcast (Hebrew), October 10, 1968.
82. The *Jerusalem Post,* July 12, 1968.
83. *Id.,* June 20, 1969.
84. *See,* for example, the statement by Robert McCloskey, U.S. State Department spokesman, maintaining that settlement in occupied areas would be 'inconsistent with Israel's position, as we understand it, that they regard the occupied territories and all other issues . . . as matters of negotiation'. The *Jerusalem Post,* September 27, 1967.
85. The *Jerusalem Post,* May 20, 1968.
86. The Israeli action at Kfar Etzion was criticized by the U.S. State Dept. in a statement of Sept. 27 which stated: 'If accurately reported, the plans for establishment of permanent Israeli settlements would be inconsistent with the Israeli position as we understand it that they regard occupied territories and all other issues arising out of the fighting to be matters for negotiation.' In a protest note filed on Sept. 28 with the U.S. British, French and Soviet embassies in Amman, Jordan's Foreign Minister condemned the action as a violation of international law. *See* 1967 *Facts on File* 413.
87. *Id.,* September 6, 1968.
88. *Id.*
89. The *Jerusalem Post,* September 27, 1967.

90. Press conference of Israel's Ambassador to the United States, Avraham Harman, *The New York Times,* September 29, 1967.
91. The *Jerusalem Post,* September 27, 1967; Personal Interviews.
92. *Id.,* May 20, 1968.
93. *See* 1970 *Facts on File* 158.
94. The *Jerusalem Post,* October 20, 1973.
95. *Id.,* June 11, 1973.
96. *Id.,* June 24, 1969.
97. *Id.,* editorial.
98. See list in *New Outlook,* February 1973, 58, 59.
99. See statement by Israeli officials to the Deputation of the National Churches of Christ that, under no circumstances, would the villages be rebuilt or the inhabitants be allowed to return to their land. Nat'l. Council of the Churches of Christ, *Report of the Deputation to the Middle East* 6, 7 (1968).
100. Several hundred thousand dunams of land were declared closed for military purposes between June of 1967 and April 1973. The exact figures are difficult to ascertain. *See Jerusalem Post,* April 9, 1973.
101 *Ma'ariv,* Dec. 27, 1972.
102. *Id.*
103. *Id.,* Jan. 2, 1973.
104. See statement by Defense Minister Dayan on January 9, 1973 that 70 square kilometers of privately owned land northeast of Bethlehem had been closed off by military authorities, but were not confiscated. According to the report, the land was mostly rocky and uninhabitable and landlords were to be permitted free access to their property. The *Jerusalem Post,* January 10, 1973.
105. *Id.* August 16, 1973.
106. See *infra* note 179. The equivalent law applicable within the State of Israel is Israel's *Absentee Property Law* (1950), LSI 68.
107. Report of the Secretary-General under General Assembly Resolution 2252 (ES-U) and Security Council Resolution 237, U.N. Doc. A/6797; U.N. Doc. S/8158 (1967).
108. *See* policy statement by Minister Dayan in *supra* note 107. As of April 1973 Israel controlled 328,789 dunams of abandoned property and 10,402 buildings. *Jerusalem Post* April 9, 1973.
109. *See* Israel Radio Report of April 1976 claiming that in 1975 50 million Israeli pounds (about $2 million) had been spent on land purchases. 22 *Keesing's Contemporary Archives* 28033 (1976).
110. *Id.* April 9, 1973. In addition to land acquired by purchase Israel controlled 730,214 dunams of cultivated Jordanian public land and 300,000 dunams of desert lands stretching along the Judean hills. The West Bank has a total size of six million dunams, *Id.* April 9, 1973.
111. *Ma'ariv,* Feb. 2, 1973. On Feb. 7 he further explained his position as follows:'The West Bank—I prefer to call it Judea and Samaria—is part of our homeland. Being our homeland, we should have the right to settle everywhere without visas or passports from anyone else. The Israeli government should make sure that any peace agreement it signs

includes that right.' 1973 *Facts on File* 122. This approach was consistent with Dayan's earlier insistence on a permanent Israeli presence in the West Bank, the Gaza Strip and Sinai. On August 19, 1971 he caused an international stir when he announced: 'We should regard our role in the administered territories as that of the established government—to plan and implement whatever can be done, without leaving options for the day of peace—which may be distant.' The U.S. State Dept. reacted by deeming the statement 'harmful' and 'completely inconsistent with Israel's acceptance of the United Nations Security resolution of Nov. 22, 1967'. Prime Minister Golda Meir, Foreign Minister Abba Eban, Deputy Premier Yigal Allon and Finance Minister Pinhas Sapir all denounced the statement. See 1971 *Facts on File* 654.

112. *Haaretz,* April 6, 1973; May 8, 1973.
113. 1973 *Facts on File* 267.
114. *Haaretz,* April 12, 1973.
115. *New York Times,* April 6, 1973.
116. *Ma'ariv,* July 24, 1973.
117. *Id.,* May 20, 1969.
118. *See* 16 *New Outlook* (May 1973) 57–8.
119. *Id.*
120. *Id.*
121. *Yediot Achaaronot,* August 29, 1973.
122. *Id.*
123. *Al Hamishmar,* August 2, 1973.
124. *Yediot Achaaronot,* August 29, 1973.
125. The first reaction came from *El-Sha'ab,* which appeared the next day with the headline 'Arab Land Dissolves Before Encroachments of Zionist Law'. In the paper's view, the new proposal not only constituted a violation of local law but also reflected contempt for international law and U.N. resolutions. *El-Sha'ab* asserted that this 'playing with the law' over the land issue began back at the time of the British Mandate when the Jewish Agency conspired with the British authorities. The mentality of Israel's statesmen was alleged to operate on a single track: first they take, then justify; and finally they attack anyone who dares to criticize or condemn the actions, labeling them Nazis and anti-Semites. 'In terms of Israel's one-track policy, the rule is "Do whatever you like; take whatever you want; establish facts as you see fit." Only afterwards is this followed by the legislation that explains and facilitates the acts, giving them a legitimate form and calling them law.' *El-Sha'ab,* August 16, 1973.

The weekly, *El-Fay'r,* viewed the Defense Minister's proposal as an indication of Israel's reluctance to return a single square millimeter of the territory conquered in 1967. Talk of peace by Israel was, in light of the proposal, deemed merely an attempt to throw sand in the eyes of the Arabs in order to gain time and allow Israel to strengthen its hold on the occupied lands. Referring to Mr. Dayan, it stated:

We have gotten used to his majesty, the new king of the West Bank,

> who, since he was sent by divine Providence to help us with technology and to increase our crop yields, knows more than anyone else about events there. We have to take his words seriously . . . There may be those in the Arab world who believe Israel's declarations about peace; but we here, who have been blessed with a 'most liberal Israeli occupation', do not believe them. *El-Fay'r,* August 19, 1973.

The editorial in the daily, *El-Quds,* ran a headline stating 'The Authorities Will Not Rest Until All the Land Has Been Taken from the Arabs'. Israel's purpose was portrayed as the swallowing up of Arab land to encircle the Arabs and to cause them to emigrate from their own country. *El-Quds,* August 18, 1973.

126. Although none of the members voted against the agreement, voices of opposition were raised, most notably by A. Eliav, M.K.:

> This document is brought to us with the lash of the time whip and the scourge of panic and haste . . . It gives the stamp of approval to what one of its signers [Sapir] called the strangulation of Zionism. In this hall, in this country, and in this entire movement there are many whose souls weep secretly at this document . . .

127. On January 12, 1975 Herut opened its national convention at Kiryat Arba, where its leader, Menahem Begin, stressed that all of the West Bank is part of the ancestral homeland and should be incorporated into Israel. The *New York Times,* January 13, 1975.

128. The settlement at Maaleh-Adumin is located ten miles northeast of Jerusalem on the Jericho road. On January 12, 1975, the Government approved a first year appropriation of 10 million Israel pounds for the construction of the industrial complex. *See* 21 *Keesing's Contemporary* Archives 27312 (1975).

129. *See* 22 *Keesing's Contemporary Archives* 28033.

130. Unrest occurred as soon as the settlers squatted in Sabastian in December, 1975. It escalated into two weeks of bloody riots in Nablus, Bir Zeit, Ramallah and Hebron, and Jerusalem starting March 7, 1976. On April 20th, thousands of marchers organized by Gush Emunim converged on Sabastian in Samaria to urge annexation of the West Bank by Israel. *See New York Times,* April 1, 1976. Arab counter-demonstrations resulted in one Arab being killed and several hurt in Nablus and Jenin. *See Ibid.*

131. *See* 1977 *Facts on File* 401.

132. U.N. Doc. A/8089.

133. UNGA Res. 2727 (XXV).

134. U.N. Doc. 8389.

135. *Id.* at 27. The report stated at p. 53 that

> The evidence that the Special Committee has received reflects a policy on the part of the Government of Israel designed to effect radical changes in the physical character and demographic composition of several areas of the territory under occupation by

the progressive and systematic elimination of every vestige of Palestinian presence in these areas. It would have the effect of obliterating Arab culture and the Arab way of life in the area, and, contrary to international law, transforming it into a Jewish state. Measures taken under this policy include the establishment of settlements for Israeli Jews in, for example, occupied Jerusalem, Hebron, certain parts of the Jordan Valley, the Golan Heights, Gaza, Northern Sinai and Sharm El-Sheikh. Such a policy will render more difficult any eventual restoration of the Palestinian people's property and other rights. Besides denying the right of Palestinians who have fled the occupied territories to return to those territories, it also threatens the right of Palestinians who have remained in the occupied territories to continue to live there. In the Special Committee's view the right of the inhabitants of the occupied territories to remain in their land is unqualified and inalienable.

136. *Id.* at 28. Moreover, the Report concluded:

> . . . the practice whereby Israeli nationals are transferred to the occupied territories as is the case in East Jerusalem, Hebron [and] . . . certain parts of the Jordan Valley [is] part of a *total* policy of depriving the people of the occupied territory of their right to remain in their homeland. *Id.* at 53.

137. *Id.* at 29.
138. *Id.* at 29.
139. *Id.* at 33.
140. U.N. Doc. A/8389/Add.
141. *Id.* The Supplementary Report took special cognizance of an article appearing in the *Jerusalem Post* of September 28, 1971, detailing the intention of Israel's Housing Ministry to expand the Kiryat Arba settlement to provide accommodation for 900 families. In this connection, the Special Committee noted that such an action would contradict the espoused policy of the Government of Israel as contained in an earlier letter to the Security Council, justifying limited settlement at Kiryat Arba. The Israeli letter stated:

> A small group of pious Jews and their families have on their own spontaneous initiative taken up residence in Hebron, a town with venerable Jewish historical and religious associations . . . There is no good reason why their neighbors should not live on peaceful and amicable terms with them and so help to heal the tragic memories of the massacre of Hebron Jews in 1929.

142. U.N. Doc. A/9148 (1973). A fourth report was issued on December 25, 1972, U.N. Doc. A/8828. It reaffirmed the conclusion of the previous report without making any substantially new allegations.
143. U.N.G.A. REs. 2949 (XXVII), December 8, 1972, U.N.G.A.O.R. 27th Session, Supplem. 30.

> (The Gen. Ass.) Declares that any changes carried out by Israel in the occupied Arab territories in contravention of the Geneva Convention of 12 August 1949 are null and void, and calls upon

Israel to rescind forthwith all such measures and to desist from all policies and practices affecting the demographic structure or physical character of the occupied Arab territories;

Calls upon all States not to recognize any such changes and measures carried out by Israel in the occupied Arab territories and invites them to avoid actions, including actions in the field of aid, that could constitute recognition of that occupation.

144. U.N. Doc. A/9148 (1973) at 21.

145. Typical of the statements quoted was the speech delivered in the Knesset by Prime Minister Golda Meir on July 25, 1973 that:

These outposts and settlements are seeds which will develop in the future, growing in population and becoming more firmly rooted. This settlement activity has deepened our roots in the land and strengthened the foundations of the State [and] preparations and plans are under way for the continuation of this important activity, whether rural or urban settlements . . . (The *Jerusalem Post,* July 26, 1973), *Id.* at 24, 25.

146. Regarding newspaper accounts of new settlements, the examples of the evidence seen by the Committee as proof of a settlement policy are the following:

A report appeared in *Ha'aretz,* and the *Jerusalem Post* on 12 October 1972 of an announcement of six new settlements to be established during 1973, three of which were planned for the Golan Heights, two in northern Sinai and one in the Jordan Valley.

A report appeared in the *Jerusalem Post* on February 4, 1973, of a statement by Mr. Auni, Deputy Director General of the Housing Ministry, to the effect that seven rural settlements were planned in the occupied territories for 1973 and that in all, since 1967, 40 such settlements had been established in the occupied territories.

A report appeared in *Ma'ariv* on 29 January 1973 of 10 settlements having been established in the West Bank between the Beit Shean Valley and Jericho. According to the same report, the possibility of establishing one or two regional centres was being discussed in view of the increasing number of settlements in the Jordan Valley.

A report appeared in *Ha'aretz* in January, of the establishment of a Nahal settlement, called Kur, on 1,000 dunams of land belonging to 'absentees of a neighboring village', while the village itself was given 4,000 dunams belonging to absentees from the same village. According to the same report, no more Israeli settlements were to be built in the Jordan Valley because almost no land fit for agriculture was left in the area.

*Id.* at 25, 26.

147. *See* as typical of citations relative to Kiryat Arba the following:

A statement was made in the Knesset by Housing Minister Z. Sharef, as reported in *Ma'ariv* and the *Jerusalem Post* on 28 February 1973, to the effect that, by 1974, 600 housing units would be constructed in Hebron. According to the report in the *Jerusalem Post,* 634 apartments would be constructed under phase one of the plan and 1,000 under phase two. Housing Minister Sharef made another statement in the Knesset, reported in the *Jerusalem Post* on 12 April 1973, that a commercial centre was to be constructed in the Jewish Settlement in Hebron.

A statement was made in the Knesset by Absorption Minister N. Peled, as reported in the *Jerusalem Post* on 12 April 1973, inviting settlers in Hebron to try and persuade immigrants in absorption centres to make their homes in Kiryat Arba. According to the report, the Absorption Ministry would give every help to immigrants wishing to settle in Hebron, but it could not force them to go there by administrative order.

*Id.* at 28.

148. U.N. Doc. A/9817 (1974).
149. U.N. Doc. A/1027 (1975).
150. U.N. Doc. A/31/218 (1976).
151. The statement, in relevant parts, states:

> . . . the measures taken by Israel in the occupied Arab territories that alter their demographic composition or geographical nature and particularly the establishment of settlements are accordingly strongly deplored. Such measures which have no legal validity and can prejudice the outcome of the search for the establishment of peace constitute an obstacle to peace;

12 *U.N. Monthly Chronicle* 5 (1976).

152. For allegation by the Chairman of the Committee that its members were non-partisan, *see* Amersinghe, 'The Work of the Special Committee to Investigate Israeli Practices Affecting Human Rights of the Population of the Occupied Territories', 10 *U.N. Monthly Chronicle,* 70, 75.
153. *See* Amersinghe, *Id.* at 70. Note, however, that in each of the subsequent two 'ratifications' of the Special Committee's constitution and its mandate, the total of abstaining and negative votes constituted a majority of the membership, i.e. G.A. Res. 2727, 52 yes—20 no—43 abstentions, 1970 *YRBK of the United Nations* 251; G.A. Res. 2951, 53 yes—20 no—46 abstentions, 1971 *Id.* 195.
154. Article 9:

> The detaining Power shall request a neutral state, or such an organization, to undertake the functions performed under the present Convention by a Protecting Power designated by the Parties to the conflict.

155. Article 11:

> If protection cannot be arranged accordingly, the detaining Power shall request or shall accept, subject to the provisions in this Article, the offer of the services of a humanitarian organization, such as the International Committee of the Red Cross, to assume the humanitarian functions performed by Protecting Powers under the present Convention.

At the time of the drafting of the Geneva Convention, the ICRC expressed its reluctance to act as a Protecting Power for fear 'that the independence which must characterize its action would not permit of its acting as the agent of a particular Power', Pictet *supra* note 44 at 102. The Convention had specified the duty of the Protecting Power as being 'to safeguard the interests of the Parties to the conflict'. The Secretary-General has pointed out that 'more modern concepts would probably require that Protecting Powers, just like the international organizations which may be substitutes for them, should be considered not only as agents or representatives of the respective belligerents, but also as the agents of the international community which would express through them in a concrete manner its concern for the respect for certain basic human rights.' U.N. Doc. A/7720 at 67.

156. ICRC, 'The Middle East Activities of the ICRC', 10 *International Rev. Red Cross* 425, 429 (1970).

157. *Id.* at 429.

158. The ICRC was granted permission by Israel to move about freely in pursuit of its tasks throughout the occupied territories. *Id.* at 445. These centered in (1) expediting the transmission of family news, (2) facilitating the return of displaced persons to the West Bank (for a limited period of time in 1967 and then again in 1968) and the operation of 'Family Reunion' schemes, (3) observing and protecting where necessary deportation and population movements, (4) observing and protecting where necessary the destruction of property, (5) ensuring and maintaining the hygiene and public health of the population and controlling relief and donations toward that end, (6) assisting protected persons who are the subject of penal prosecution and visiting detainees and internees to assure observance of minimum standards, (7) tracing of missing civilians and finally (8) visiting and assisting interned Jews in Arab countries since 'the provisions of the Fourth Geneva Convention should, at least by analogy, apply to those persons in view of the fact that measures affecting them were taken as a direct result of the conflict between Israel and the Arab states.' *Id.* at 508.

The ICRC was usually careful to specify that its task was limited to humanitarian objectives and for that reason could not, for example, 'intervene when the Occupying Power transferred some of its own civilian population to the occupied territories unless such transfer were immediately detrimental to the Arab residents.' *Id.* at 159.

159. The role to be played by the Protecting Power as embodied in the Geneva Convention finds its clearest expression in Article 143 thereof:

> Representatives or delegates of the Protecting Power shall have permission to go to all places where protected persons are, particularly to places of internment, detention and work. They shall have access to all premises occupied by protected persons and shall be able to interview the latter without witnesses, personally or through an interpreter.
>
> Such visits may not be prohibited except for reasons of imperative military necessity, and then only as an exceptional and temporary measure. Their duration and frequency shall not be restricted . . .

Article 30 establishes the right of every protected person to make application to the Power protecting his interest. The official commentary to the Convention states that the Protecting Power must supervise the application of the whole Convention and ensure that it is better applied. Pictet *supra* note 44 at 81.

160. *Id.* at 457.

161. *Id.* at 459.

162. 'Protection of Human Rights in Israeli Occupied Territories', 15 *Harvard International Law Journal,* 470, 478 (1974).

163. Since ratification of the Geneva Convention, the Protecting Power system has never been invoked by any party to international conflict. An explanation is offered in the 1971 Secretary-General Report, *Respect for Human Rights in Armed Conflict:*

> Many reasons have been advanced for this. The relatively small number of States which could be considered as truly neutral to all parties to the armed conflicts; the cumbersome and time consuming procedure of appointment of Protecting Powers which calls for the agreement of the belligerents as to these Powers at the time when hostilities are raging; the fact that the military phases of some of the conflicts were over before Protecting Powers could be appointed. The burden in terms of material and human resources which is imposed upon States solicited as potential Protecting Powers has also been mentioned as a deterrent vis-a-vis the parties to the conflict. U.N. Doc. A/7720, 66.

The Secretary-General strongly suggested that what was needed was the development of an international organization offering all the guarantees of impartiality and efficiency to serve as a potential Protecting Power. Of course, the ICRC already meets this criterion. In the 1974 Geneva Diplomatic Conference on the Reaffirmation and Development of International Humanitarian Law in Armed Conflicts, draft resolutions were adopted calling for an increased role for the ICRC, approximating essentially that of a Protecting Power. *See* Forsythe, 'Who Guards the Guardians: Third Parties and the Law of Armed Conflict', 70 *Am. J. Int'l. L.* 41 (1976).

See also Paust, 'An International Structure in Implementation of the 1949 Geneva Conventions: Needs and Function Analysis', 1 *Yale Studies in World Public Order* 148 (1974); Freymond, 'The International Committee of the Red Cross within the International System', 12 *Int'l. Rev. Red Cross* 245, 249 (1972).

164. *See* Baxter, 'The Law of War in the Arab-Israeli Conflict on Water and on Land', 6 *Towson State Journal of International Affairs* 1, 13 (1971), finding the Special Committee investigations to have been 'politically colored' and 'inspired by the Arab states'. See statement by Professor von Glahn: 'I have no trust whatsoever in the two United Nations investigations of the conduct of military government in the occupied territories.' Discussion, 'Compliance with International Conventions, Destruction of Houses and Administrative Detentions', I *Israel YRBK of Human Rights* 387 (1971).

165. J. Westlake, *International Law* 57 (1907).
166. McDougal and Feliciano *supra* note I, 10 at 812, 813. *See,* regarding the application of Article 55, *Etat Fran çais* v. Lemarchand, *Annual Digest* 1948, Case No. 198 where the Court of Appeal held that the dismantling by the German occupying forces of certain buildings owned by France and the use of their material in the construction of a German Army training school had violated the occupant's duty as a usufructuary to preserve the capital. See also *Administrator of Waters and Forests* v. *Falck,* Court of Cassation, France *Id.,* 1927–28, Case No. 383.
167. *See* Article 56, Hague Regulations; Article 5 of the Hague Convention for the Protection of Cultural Property in the Event of Armed Conflict.
168. *British Manual of Military Law,* Part III, para. 614 (1958); Department of the Army, *Law of Land Warfare,* para. 394 (1) (FM27–10, 1956); M. Greenspan, *The Law of Modern Land Warfare* 292 (1959); Rennell, *British Military Administration of Occupied Territories in Africa* 423–436 (1948).
.169. *See The War Book of the German General Staff* (J. Morgan, trans.) 69–73, 153, 161–163 (1915). For the assertion of this doctrine by a German court in 1922, see VI Hackworth, *Digest of International Law* 409.
170. *See* C. Fenwick, *International Law* (3rd Ed.), 547 (1948); *see* 'The Krupp Trial' [*United States* v. *Krupp et al.* (1948)], U.N. War Crimes Commis. X *Law Reports of Trials of War Criminals.*
170. *See* for general statement of this principle in the application of the laws of war, *The Hostage Case (U.S.* v. *List et al.)* (1949), U.S. Mil. Tribunal, VII *Law Reports of Trials of War Criminals* 68–9; in *re von Lewinski* (1949), Brit. Mil. Ct. Germany 16 *Annual Digest* 509, 521–3 (1949).
172. *See* Dershowitz in 'Discussion: Human Rights in Time of War', *Israel YRBK on Human Rights* 377 (1971).
173. McDougal and Feliciano *supra* note I, 10 at 809; Jessup, 'A Belligerent Occupant's Power over Property', 38 *Am. J. Int'l. L.,* 457–458 (1944).
174. Note that the law of invasion, dealing with ongoing military conflict, requires no payment or compensation for use or damage of enemy private property. *British Manual of Military Law,* Part III, 592; *U.S. Rules of Land Warfare* 324.
175. *Karmatzucas* v. *Germany,* Germans-Greek Mixed Arbitral Tribunal 3 *Annual Digest* 380 (1925-6) held:

    That such requisitions were lawful as complied with the provisions of Article 52, namely, that the payment of the amount due should be made as soon as possible after the requisition; and that as nearly nine years had elapsed since the requisition and full payment had not been made, the requisition was contrary to International Law and afforded a good ground for the recognition of the competence of the Tribunal and an award of compensation.

    In a note on the case, the editors, Lord McNair and Hersch Lauterpacht, state that:

> . . . the reasoning of the tribunal is open to objection as it is difficult to see how subsequent failure to pay rendered the requisition unlawful 'ab initio'. It would have sufficed to hold that the subsequent failure to pay was illegal.

See also *Goldenberg et Fils* v. *Germany* (1928) Special Arbitral Tribunal between Romania and Germany, 4 *Annual Digest* 452, 1927–1928.

176. See Article 55 of the Geneva Convention.
177. *See Scotti* v. *Garbagnati and Marconi,* 15 *Annual Digest* 604 (1948).
178. *Siutta* v. *Guzkowski,* 1, *Id.,* 480, 1919–1922.
179. *British Manual of Military Law,* Part III, para. 598, *U.S. Rules, Land Warfare Field Manual* FM27–10, 338 (1938).
180. *See* for reproduction and English translation, I *Israel YRBK on Human Rights,* 443–447 (1971).

Relevant sections thereof are reproduced below:

> 1(a) 'Abandoned Property' means property the legal owner or occupier of which left the region on or before the appointed date or subsequently thereto, leaving such property within the region, provided that property the occupier of which is not the owner shall not be considered as Abandoned Property, unless both the owner and the occupier are absent from the Region;
>
> 8(a) The officer-in-charge shall safeguard the Abandoned Property, by himself or by means of others authorized by him in writing, with a view to preserving it or the full amount of the proceeds thereof, as far as possible, on behalf of the owner or occupier as the case may be
>
> 9(a) The officer-in-charge may sell Abandoned Property consisting of movables, or the yield of Abandoned Property, if in the circumstances he considers that this is the only way properly to ensure that the owner or any person lawfully occupying the property can receive a return for the value of his right in the property
>
> 13(a) Where a person who was the owner or lawful occupier of Abandoned Property returns to the Region and proves his ownership of the property, or, as the case may be, his right to occupy the same, the officer-in-charge shall transfer to him the property or the value thereof, whereupon that property shall cease to be abandoned. Property and any right which any person had in that property immediately prior to its vesting in the officer-in-charge shall be restored to such person or any person taking his place, but subject to any rights acquired over the property by another party as a result of any act of the officer-in-charge and subject to the provisions of section 9.

181. U.N. Doc. A Conf. 2/108.
182. I *Selected Judgements of the Military Courts* (S.J.M.C.) (in Hebrew) 371, June 10, 1968.

183. Only Greenspan mentions the issue, but devotes less than one paragraph to its discussion. *See* Greenspan *supra* note I, 11 at 294–5.
184. U.N. Doc. A/9148, 11, 22 (1973). And later, 'the Government of Israel acquires no right of ownership whatsoever by the acquisition, *through appropriation, barter or any other measure, over any area* in the territories occupied during the June 1967 hostilities.' *Id.* at 22.
185. *Id.,* 44–5.
186. 'The Farben Case', (*United States* v. *Krauch et al.* (1948) U.N. War Crime Commission X *Law Reports of Trials of War Criminals.*
187. *Id.* at 46–7.
188. *Id.* at 46. The stance taken by the prosecution was consistent with the Inter-Allied Declaration of January 5, 1943, a warning directed especially at neutral countries, which stated the intention of the Allies 'to do their utmost to defeat the methods of dispossession' practised by the Axis Powers and to 'reserve all of their rights to declare invalid *any* transfer of, or dealings with property, rights and interests of *every description whatsoever* which are, or have been, situated in the territories which have come under the occupation or control, direct or indirect of the . . . [Axis Powers] . . . which belong or have belonged to persons (including juridical persons) resident in such territories. This warning applies whether such transfers or dealings have taken the form of open looting or plunder, or of *transactions apparently legal in form, even when they purport to be voluntarily effected'* (emphasis added). Inter-Allied Declaration Against Acts of Dispossession Committed in Territories under Enemy Occupation or Control, January 5, 1943, CMD. No. 6418 (1943); 8 *Department State Bulletin* 21 (1943).
189. *Id.*
190. *Id.* at 50.
191. 'The Krupp Trial' *(United States* v. *Krupp von Bohlen et al.)* (1948), U.N. War Crimes Commission X *Law Reports of Trials of War Criminals*
192. *Id.* at 135.
193. *Id.* at 163.
194. *Lauterpacht-Oppenheim* (7th ed., 1955) at 452.
195. Author's interviews with West Bank leaders, Summer 1973 and 1976. Among those interviewed, expressing the same reaction, were the mayors of Hebron, Beit-Jallah, Jericho, Bethlehem, Ramallah and Nablus. Other prominent West Bank personalities, strongly expressing the same sentiments, were Azis Zahadi, a leading Ramallah attorney leading the movement for West Bank autonomy in peaceful cooperation with Israel; Abu Shilbayeh, former editor of Jerusalem's Arab daily, *El Quds;* Anwar Nusseilsah, former Jordanian Defense Minister; Anwar Katib, a leading East Jerusalem figure; and Dr. H. Nasir, President of Bir Zeit College. *See also supra* note 129 and accompanying text regarding Arab disturbances in March to May of 1976 in protest against Israeli settlement policy.
196. *See* Cooley, *The Christian Science Monitor,* May 30, 1973.

197. General Dayan was the person most responsible for the switch in Israel government policy from prohibition of any private settlement in the region to encouragement of civilian settlement in selected regions. Mr. Dayan spoke of such settlement as 'trees rooted in the soil, not pots of flowers which you can move from one place to another'. In 1968, he stated at a public press conference, 'where we have settled, we shall not budge'. In 1971, he said, 'any place where we establish an inhabited settlement, we will not give up either the settlement or the place it is in'. *Davar,* December 29, 1968.

198. *See* Cooley *supra* note 196 at 7.

199. *See* W. Laqueur, *Confrontation: The Middle East and World Politics* (1974), seeing a causal connection, and critical review by Gerson in 10 *Towson State J. Int'l Affairs* 27 (1975).

200. A note on the domestic effect of Israel's settlement policy may be in order. In an open letter dated August 29, 1973, novelist Amos Oz wrote on the consequences of Israel's creeping annexation policy for Israel in particular and for Arab-Israeli relations in general.

> To rely on ourselves alone, to push, grab, 'let's clobber them', and who cares what they say, and others are not any better so they better not tell us what to do, and an aberration here and another there with some smooth phraseology . . . In brief the regime acts on the presumption that the Arabs, in fact all Gentiles, only understand the language of force. And many citizens are translating this into the language of their relations with their neighbours and speak to each other in the language of force bereft of niceties and restraint. I don't know if another policy on the part of the government would bring us peace with the Arab states, but I don't hesitate to say that meanwhile this policy is corrupting our citizens and is contaminating them with brute force, cynicism and tearful righteousness . . . let things be and thats it, what the hell, others are not better, liberated areas will not be returned, nothing will be returned, what is mine is mine and whoever has nothing, has nothing. Only this and only with force. I think that if those people who tell me that our position was never better, if those people are not obtuse, then they are lying. The situation is not better nor is it good; it is bad and it is getting worse. Our support should be extended to those who perceive this and are ready to try and rescue the labour movement from those who have brought her to its present impasse.

201. *Israel Economist* July 1976. *See* also Van Arkadie, *Benefits & Burdens: A Report on the West Bank and Gaza Strip Economies Since 1967* (1977).

> As far as the Israeli settlements are concerned this decision can be justified at least partly because available evidence suggests that their political importance notwithstanding, the post-1967 settlements are still a relatively minor part of the pattern of purely economic connections at interactions that have evolved between Israel and the occupied territories to date.

At xi.

202. The *Jerusalem Post,* August 15, 1967.
203. *Id.* In an interview given to the *Jerusalem Post* Mr. Gadish, Assistant Director General of the Ministry of Education, in charge of Arab education within Israel and since 1967 coordinator of West Bank education, stated his reasons for rejecting every second textbook on the West Bank and Gaza as unsuitable. 'Not only history, geography and literature, but even grammar was full of hate propaganda. A West Bank Arab Grammar for the fourth to sixth grades read: 'The homeland has been stolen', 'the Arabs will not rest until their Paradise is returned to them', 'Holy war is duty', 'the enemy was routed', . . . 'The number of survivors is very small', 'We shall not allow the enemy to enjoy the benefits of our goodness'.
204. *Id.*
205. *See* A. Safadi 'West Bank Teachers Still Repeat Old Lessons' *Jerusalem Post* Sept. 29, 1967; The Institute for Palestine Studies (Beirut), *The Resistance of the Western Bank of Jordan to Israeli Occupation,* 45–60 (1967); *See* also Jordan's protest of Israeli ban of books as being aimed at 'killing the Arab schoolchild's national Spirit and religious beliefs'. *Jerusalem Post* Sept. 27, 1967.
206. *The Jerusalem Post,* August 30, 1967.
207. *The New York Times,* December 7, 1969.
208. *Id.,* Sept. 16, 1967; The *Jerusalem Post,* Sept. 5, 6, 1967.
209. The head of the Education Department in Nablus, the principal of the two main high schools in Jerusalem and the director and assistant director of the Jerusalem District Education Office were arrested and kept under administrative detention.
210. The *Jerusalem Post,* Sept. 28, 1967.
211. *Id.,* Sept. 24, 1967.
212. Dr. Nasir was deported to Jordan shortly after the 1973 War for allegedly failing to cooperate with the Israeli authorities in preventing the teaching of anti-Israeli and anti-Jewish material.
213. Personal interview with Dr. H. Nasir, September 1973.
214. Personal interview, Mayor Freij, Bethlehem, September 1973.
215. On March 13th, the Israeli authorities had approved the proposed establishment of a Palestinian Arab university on the West Bank. The school was to be funded by international sources and wealthy Palestinians. The Israeli government was to provide no financial aid. As originally planned, the university was to be opened in 1974 with 1,000 students from the West Bank and the Gaza Strip. 1973 *Facts on File* 267.
216. Article 50 of the Geneva Convention provides that 'The Occupying Power shall, with the cooperation of national and local authorities, facilitate the proper working of all institutions devoted to the care and education of children.' The language used in the article implies that higher education is not intended to be covered. Moreover, it provides no further guidelines as to permissible scope of interference by the occupant.
217. Propaganda is nearly always a method of warfare among ideological

opponents. For a Soviet rationalization of this tool, *see* Taracouzio, *The Soviet Union and International Law* (1935):

> These [propaganda] methods cannot be considered as violations of international law, for there are no rules of war known in relation to the issue. Furthermore, the Hague Regulations prohibiting the compulsion of 'the nationals of the hostile party to take part in the operations of war directed against their own country' . . . is not applicable here. For it is compulsion which is proscribed, whereas the effect of propaganda manifests itself in a free decision to those who voluntarily accept the ideas sponsored by such propaganda. at 336.

218. Ordinance of June 26, 1915, issued by Governor-General von Bissing, Text in J. Massart, *Belgians under the German Eagle* 280 (1916).
219. *Id.*
220. J. Garner, II, *International Law and the World War* 73, 78 (1920). The German policy of attempting to win Flemish support and drive a wedge between them and the Walloons manifested itself in a great many spheres beyond that of educational control. German proclamations were printed in Flemish; theatres and movies were required to print their program in Flemish; Flemish offenders were let off with lighter punishments than those imposed on the Walloons. *See* Massart *supra* note 218 at 284.
221. Cybichowski, 'Die Besetzung Lembergs im Kriege 1914/1915', 26 *Zeitschrift für Internationales Recht* 434–5 (1916).
222. See text of German Legislation in, Republic of Poland, Ministry of Foreign Affairs, *German Occupation of Poland,* 102–106 (1942).
223. Kollewijn, 'The Dutch Universities under Nazi Domination', 245 *Annals of the American Academy of Political and Social Science* 118–128 (1946).
224. Von Glahn makes the following observation:

> Interestingly enough, reports of these proceedings outraged public opinion in Allied countries, yet when virtually identical measures were adopted by the Allied occupation authorities in Germany, they were greeted with approval as concrete evidence of the denazification of the Reich! *Supra,* von Glahn note I, 14 at 66.

From the legal viewpoint, the German occupation of Europe was one of belligerent occupation. Even where nations were totally defeated, their allies continued to wage war. By contrast, in the American occupation of Germany, the applicability of the Hague Regulations was at least subject to serious doubt because of Germany's total defeat. See discussion in *supra,* note I, 17.

Professor von Glahn himself makes the following point later in his work:

> . . . only limitations resting on grounds of humanity could be said to have been binding on the victorious Allies during the post-surrender period. Beyond such humanitarian restrictions, ill defined as the concept must be, no valid bounds could be discerned for policies and acts of the Allied Powers for that period of the

German occupation which began with the surrender and disappearance of the German government and ended with the recognition of the Bonn administration by the Western Allies. *Id.* at 283.

225. *See* Zook, 'Japan and Germany: Problems in Reeducation', 427 *International Conciliation* 3 (1947); H. Zink, *American Military Government in Germany* 147–65 (1947).
226. *Id.* at 64.
227. *See,* regarding this approach, Morris Greenspan, author of the influential text, *The Modern Law of Land Warfare* (1959) in his exploration of the findings of the U.N. Special Committee in 'Human Rights in the Territories Occupied by Israel', 12 *Santa Clara Lawyer* 377 (1972) stating:

    Both of these bodies [the U.N. Special Committee and the Special Working Group of Experts, U.N. Economic and Social Council, report in U.N. Doc. E/CN. 4/1016 (1970)] . . . . .

    . . . reached similar conclusions, with the work of the Special Committee being much more comprehensive than that of the latter. Both have issued reports critical of Israel, and it is mainly on the basis of these reports that the author proposes to examine the real status of human rights in these occupied territories. While this may seem to be a rather negative approach to the question, it has this advantage: since these reports embody every accusation that the Arabs believed they could bring against Israel for infringement of human rights, the areas of controversy are defined; and it can be fairly assumed that, in matters in which no charges have been made, Israel's conduct of the occupation is not open to serious criticism.

228. *New York Times,* November 19, 1976.

Chapter IV

# Disposition: Sovereignty and Postliminium Problems

## A. SOVEREIGNTY RE-EXAMINED

### 1. *Jordan: Still the Legitimate Negotiating Partner?*

The question of sovereign rights to the West Bank, currently so hotly debated, is often examined without attention to historical perspective. The claim is increasingly heard that the principle of 'self-determination' is dispositive of the issue and that, accordingly, the West Bank Arabs have a right to creation of a state of their own. This is a simplistic view of the problem. It fails to adequately consider the issue in its full setting of history, law and politics, in the light of the Jordanian and Israeli interests at stake, as well as the interests of the international community in a fair and principled resolution of the Arab-Israeli dispute.

Chapter II's inquiry into the historical background giving rise to competing claims to sovereignty over the West Bank considered the problem of sovereignty in mandated territories generally, and that of the Palestine Mandate in particular. It concluded that the international community had authoritatively and repeatedly recognized and assured Jewish rights in Palestine under the Palestine Mandate; that upon its termination two states emerged as successors to the sovereignty of Turkey—Israel and Jordan; and that these states should make peace with each other in accordance with the terms of certain Security Council resolutions, with respect to the entire territory of the Palestine Mandate, exclusive of the Gaza Strip, whose future was to be negotiated between Israel and Egypt. This consensus of the international community and the parties directly affected was embodied most explicitly in the 1949 Armistice Agreements.

### a. *Post-1967 Jordanian-West Bank Relations*

In the years immediately after the 1967 war there was international understanding that Jordan possessed a reversionary interest in the West Bank and was the legitimate negotiating party for conclusion of a treaty of peace with Israel whereby the West Bank, with allowance for minor territorial adjustments, would finally become, *de jure,* a recognized part of Jordan's national territory. In Security Council Resolution 242 reference was made exclusively to the 'states' of the region as the parties responsible for negotiating a peace. Jordan, in its relations with the West Bank, made it clear that the negotiation of Israeli withdrawal from the West Bank was Jordan's responsibility; the legitimate representatives of the West Bank were deemed to be its ministers in the Government of Jordan,[1] and any indigenous political initiative for a non-Jordanian solution would not be tolerated. This was acceptable even to bitter opponents of the Hussein government. They realized that only Jordan held a meaningful bargaining position capable of leading to termination of Israeli occupation.

Yet, free from Jordanian control, many West Bankers critical of the Hussein regime and now able to give vent to their feelings, began to openly voice their estrangement from the Amman regime.[2] The civil war which raged in Jordan in 1971 and the strong hand shown by the government helped to deepen this estrangement between large segments of the West Bank population and the Jordanian government.

Despite these developments, Jordan managed to retain its influence over the bases of power in the West Bank. Money was the main instrument of Jordanian control. It was distributed liberally to local leaders loyal to the Jordanian authorities. West Bank civil servants on the Israeli payroll remained on the Jordanian payroll as well.[3] Economic and family ties between the two Banks were preserved by the 'open bridges' policy mutually agreed upon between Israel and Jordan.[4]

Gradually, the Jordanian government reconciled itself to the existence of daily contacts between the Israeli authorities and the West Bank mayors and notables. It still prohibited all contact with Israel not related to administrative duties, so as to prevent local initiatives which could influence the political future of the West Bank. But there was a growing acceptance of the new modus vivendi that had been established between Israeli authorities and West Bank mayors. Thus, for example, although initially bitterly opposed to the municipal elections of 1972, Jordan eventually reconciled itself to their taking place and to their consequences.

In 1971, Editor Haykal of Cairo's *El Ahram,* writing in the aftermath of the Jordanian civil war, stated: 'It is certain that the West Bank does not want to remain under Israeli occupation, but neither is it ready, after all that has happened to the Palestinians, to go back to King Hussein.'[5] Since the October, 1973 War, the estrangement between King Hussein and the Palestinians has escalated dramatically. In December, 1973, *Newsweek,* following the 1973 Algiers Arab summit conference, stated: 'Arafat has begun to eclipse Hussein in the battle for the hearts and minds of the Palestinians—and, in the process, he has made it unlikely that Hussein will ever gain back the West Bank.'[6]

At the Arab summit conference in Rabat in October, 1974, the Palestine Liberation Organization (PLO) was able to gain recognition by the assembled Arab delegations, including Jordan's, as the 'legitimate' representative of the Palestinian people.[7] Essentially the same status was accorded the PLO by a majority of the General Assembly in October, 1974 when it invited the PLO to participate in upcoming debates on the Middle-East situation. On November 9, 1974, the Jordanian Parliament, by an overwhelming majority, amended its constitution in a move which has been interpreted by some as a prelude to waiving all Jordanian claims to the West Bank. The approved amendment permitted King Hussein to reorganize the government to exclude Palestinian representation from the West Bank.[8] The seating of the PLO, as if a representative of a state, at the Security Council during its January, 1976 session, despite the objection of the United States (its veto was rendered useless because seating was deemed a procedural issue) marked the height of the PLO's recent ascendancy to that of an entity accorded, for all intents and purposes, the status of a government-in-exile.

Today, it is at least doubtful whether the West Bank, given the opportunity to freely decide its political future, would return to Jordan's control. The West Bank's traditional Palestinian establishment of 'notables' and ruling families remain committed to Hussein, but they are no longer as firmly entrenched. The political sympathies of the masses appear to have shifted against Jordan in favor of the PLO, or autonomy generally. This was most clearly witnessed in the elections on the West Bank in April, 1976, when younger PLO-oriented candidates were able to wrest most of the mayoralty seats from the traditional leadership.

In these circumstances, can Jordan be considered the appropriate negotiating power for return of the West Bank? Israel has made it clear it will not withdraw from any portion of the West Bank if control is to be ceded to the PLO. In Israel's view, a Palestinian Arab state already exists under the name of Jordan: it is up to Jordan and Israel to determine its boundaries pursuant to Security Council Resolutions 242 and 338 and up to the Jordanian government and its Palestinian constituency to determine the nature of its internal divisions of control. American foreign policy, so far, is in agreement.[9] And Jordan appears in agreement. Her statements regarding relinquishment of title to the West Bank appear to be rhetorical, their value limited to a display of pan-Arabic unity. By all diplomatic reports, Jordan retains a genuine interest in regaining the West Bank.

### b. *The Idea of a New Independent Palestinian State*

The alternatives to reversion to Jordan that appear to have current political prevalence are either the holding of an immediate plebiscite[10] to determine the political will of the inhabitants or accepting the PLO as Israel's 'negotiating partner.' A free determination by the Palestinian Arabs of their political future is the choice most conducive to an Arab-Israeli peace capable of resolving all outstanding differences, providing the ideal of self-determination is realized in a fashion which is democratic and which does not threaten Israel's vital security. Achievement of these conditions is however fraught with nigh-insurmountable difficulties. Firstly, plebiscites under occupation rule are suspect indicators of popular sentiment.[11] Due to the 'open bridges' policy and the pattern of family residence on both banks of the Jordan, Jordan can effectively threaten recriminations against the property and families of candidates and their supporters who oppose reversion to Jordanian control. On the other hand, the PLO can effectively threaten revenge on their opponents should they ever gain control. Obviation of this obstacle to a free plebiscite by securing the supervision of a neutral international agency or power is no answer. Neither has the power to deter or prevent the implementation of such threats. Thus an immediate plebiscite is too dubious an indicator of the preferences of the population in Israeli-occupied territory, let alone any portion of the Palestinian population in Lebanon, and elsewhere which might be enfranchised, to be acceptable.

It would be even more dubious to treat the PLO as 'the only true representative' of the Palestinian population, on the West Bank and elsewhere, and accept it as the negotiator of a Palestine peace. The Arab population of the West Bank has been notably conservative, capitalist, and peaceful. It has, however, become fashionable to believe that the PLO may, if Israel would but negotiate with it, engineer a West Bank-Gaza Palestinian state as a panacea to the conflict. Yet sight is lost of the fact that the PLO in its present state is itself far from interested in 'a Palestinian state.' It appears intent on gaining control of all of Palestine, not the proposed diminutive mini-state of the West Bank and Gaza.[12]

The Palestinians in Jordan, comprising more than one half of its population, wish to retain Jordan as their national home, albeit perhaps under a leadership that more faithfully reflects the ethnic composition of its population. This is the lesson of the Jordanian Civil War of 1970–71, when the great majority of the Palestinians supported King Hussein against the guerrillas. Similarly, the conservative establishment of ruling families on the West Bank continues to receive money from Jordan and to support her. The masses may well increasingly identify with the PLO, although this has rarely taken an active form, such as harboring of guerrillas. It would seem that, despite the political shifts of the 1976 West Bank elections, the views of the West Bank's traditional leadership continue to prevail and that, like it or not, the realpolitik of the West Bank's position prevents any real break with Hussein and meaningful collaboration with the PLO. Given this present political climate, cession of the West Bank to PLO control would almost inevitably give rise to armed conflict between the PLO, aided perhaps by some of the disadvantaged or disenchanted masses, and the West Bank elite, aided by their counterparts on the East Bank. The resulting imbroglio would be an open invitation to intervention by Israel and Jordan to assure results favorable to them and to police the region against the PLO's more terroristically inclined rivals and splinter groups within. The Soviet Union would continue to supply arms and money to the PLO, hoping to capitalize on the PLO's victory and thus enlarging the degree of its political and military control of the region. Syria, too, under whom the Palestine Liberation Army is presently trained, may try to move in to expand its control in the area.

In sum, without a change in its National Covenant the PLO cannot be termed a *negotiating* partner with Israel for return of the West Bank. Even assuming a change in the PLO's official position, the seeds of a near certain political explosion would be planted by allowing it to freely assume control. Fearful of this, the international community has in the past deemed Jordan to be the legitimate negotiating partner for a return of the West Bank, with Palestinian-Jordanian differences to be worked out under the aegis of Jordanian control. This solution was not ideal. Reversion to Jordan may constitute a denial of self-determination. But allowance of self-determination by requiring Israeli cession of control to the PLO, as presently constituted, would be an unacceptable risk to take for a region that has had its share of catastrophes, each in turn affecting world peace. The PLO's relations with Israel, Jordan and the larger Arab world are fast moving and in constant flux. The future is difficult to foresee but there appears little to warrant much optimism. The change in the Israeli government from Labour to Likud in 1977 made the prospect of talks with the PLO even dimmer. Perhaps Israel will yet negotiate with the PLO at Geneva, but it will then be a different organization than the one of today. It will be dominated by Jordan and perhaps Syria as well. Neither Jordan nor Syria can easily forget the lessons of the 1971 Jordanian civil war and the 1975–76 Lebanese war. Each has reason to fear 'free' Palestinian rule under PLO leadership. The art of future diplomacy affecting the West Bank will, therefore, necessarily be one of symbol manipulation. In form, Palestinian autonomy, perhaps even under PLO leadership, may emerge on the West Bank and Gaza. In fact the area will, in all likelihood, be subject to Jordanian control.

Security Council Resolution 242 of November 22, 1967, proposed terms for solution of the Arab-Israeli conflict that did not address themselves to the issue of Palestinian self-determination. Self-determination was viewed as an internal matter for the Arab states and Israel to work out between themselves and their Palestinian Arab population. Interstate peace between Israel and its Arab neighbors was the central concern of Resolution 242. Resolution of the issue of self-determination was secondary to resolution of the issue of regional and world peace.

## 2. *The Special Problem of Jerusalem*

Unlike the West Bank, Jerusalem was placed under Israeli civilian administration shortly after the 1967 War. On June 27, 1967, Israel's Parliament passed *The Law and Administration Ordinance (Amendment No. 11) Law,* permitting extension of '[t]he law, jurisdiction, and administration of the State of Israel to any area of Eretz Israel (Palestine) designated by the Government by order.'[13] The following day Israel's government passed Administrative and Judicial Order No. 1 extending Israel's law, jurisdiction and administration to East Jerusalem.[14]

Israel's extension of her civil jurisdiction and administration to East Jerusalem was immediately condemned as violative of international law by the United Nations General Assembly which called upon Israel 'to rescind all measures already taken and desist from taking any action which will alter the status of Jerusalem.'[15] Israel's Foreign Minister, Abba Eban, attempted to justify the 'measures' which Israel used to incorporate East Jerusalem on the ground that they did not constitute annexation. Rather, he argued, 'The term annexation used by the supporters of the resolution is out of place. The measures adopted related to the integration of Jerusalem in the administrative spheres, and furnish a legal basis for the protection of the Holy Places in Jerusalem.'[16] Though the distinction made is appealing, it is not legally convincing. Extension of full civilian government to occupied territory may, from the standpoint of municipal law, constitute annexation.[17] For purposes of international law, however, annexation requires at least a claim, unequivocal in nature, to permanent control of a region. The Israel Government refrained in the early years of occupation from explicitly making this claim. Nevertheless, from the outset, Israel continually integrated East Jerusalem into Israel proper, despite consistent United Nations condemnation.[18] From the present vantage point, Israel appears to have rejected the possibility of any reversion of the territory of Jerusalem, although Israel has suggested a willingness, within the framework of a peace treaty, to relinquish control over Jerusalem's non-Jewish holy places and to allow for a semi-autonomous Arab sector.

### a. *Internationalization Proposals*

Jerusalem's future is clouded by problems distinct from those of the West Bank proper. This is apparent upon an examination of the unique diplomatic history of this troubled city. The U.N. Partition Resolution provided that Jerusalem be an international city. A special international regime for Jerusalem was to be established under the administration of the United Nations' Trusteeship Council. The city was to be united and access to the holy places and religious sites of all religions was to be unrestricted. The regime was to last only for an initial period of ten years. It would then have been subject to reexamination with a view to enabling 'the residents of the city . . . to express by means of a referendum their wishes as to possible modifications of the regime of the city.'[19]

Of course, the establishment of Jerusalem as an international city never materialized. Bearing primary responsibility for its abandonment was Arab frustration of the Partition Resolution through military invasion aimed at achieving Arab control over all of Palestine. After the 1948 War, both Jordan and Israel repudiated the concept.[20] As a result, internationalization became an unworkable proposition. For this reason, the United States voted against an Australian resolution before the General Assembly in 1949 seeking to revive the internationalization of Jerusalem feature of the 1947 U.N. Partition Resolution.[21]

In 1950 the U.N. Trusteeship Council approved a Statute for the City of Jerusalem, as it was required to do under the U.N. 1947 Partition Plan, but it soon came to the conclusion that neither Jordan nor Israel was interested in implementing it.[22] No resolutions to this effect have subsequently been passed at the U.N. Thus, since 1950, the international community has essentially abandoned internationalization as a viable solution to the political status of Jerusalem, although calls for its reexamination as a solution do appear from time to time in scholarly journals and elsewhere.[23]

Arguments have been made that internationalization survives as a viable option to the extent that it is of a type termed 'functional,' being limited to international control of the religious shrines and historical sites.[24] This concept too has been effectively abandoned by the international community. In 1950 a Swedish draft resolution proposed functional internationalization. The U.N., through a commissioner, was to be given authority for protecting the Holy Places and guaranteeing free access thereto. Full control over each part of the area was to be exercised by the states concerned.[25] Jordan rejected the proposal as an unacceptable infringement of its sovereignty.[26] Israel supported the proposal as did the United States. It was defeated. A subsequent Belgian draft to the same effect suffered the same fate.[27] The last record of an attempt to reintroduce the concept of functional internationalization occurred in 1952.[28] Since then the concept of international rather than regional religious control of the Holy Places has been abandoned. Today, Israel does not claim any unnegotiable right to exclusive jurisdiction of the Holy Places. Its present policy is that they are the responsibility of those who hold them sacred. Regarding the future, Israel's position is that she is 'willing to discuss the principle (of control) with those traditionally concerned' and that 'there is a versatile range of possibilities for working out the status of the Holy Places in a manner conducive to Middle East peace and ecumenical harmony.'[29]

b. *Unification*

If the concept of Jerusalem's internationalization, functional or otherwise, must be deemed to have been rejected at the United Nations, so too, at the other extreme, must the concept of a redivided Jerusalem. Jerusalem remains a city of great religious significance to the three major faiths. Reunification of the city in 1967 made the Holy Places, for the first time since 1948, accessible to all the faiths.[30] Continued unification is the best guarantee of that right as well as the best insurance against desecration of Holy Sites, such as had occurred under Jordanian control.[31] Equally important is the fact that unification has made possible the first direct contact between Arabs and Israelis. Generally speaking, this has had a positive effect in dispelling mutually held stereotyped prejudices. Moreover, by increasing economic and social contact, it has sown the seeds for possible future cooperation.[32] Today, Jordan and Israel seem in accord with the principle that the city remain united.[33] The United States officially endorses the concept of a continued open city.[34] In this light, Israeli measures taken to unite the city administratively do not merit condemnation. Whether such measures are permissible when viewed as going beyond unification of administrative control to assertion of sovereignty, is the subject of our next inquiry.

c. *Sovereignty*

No valid distinction appears to exist between the legitimacy of Israeli claims to sovereignty over the West Bank and those made in regard to East Jerusalem. Both seem to stand or fall on the same merits. One searches in vain in the academic literature and history of diplomatic debates on the issue for any thesis advancing the claim that Israeli claims to sovereignty over East Jerusalem are doctrinally distinct from those pertaining to the West Bank. Thus, Prof. Blum, writing on the Israeli legal position states:

> It will be recalled that the provisions of the law of June 27, 1967 (The Law and Administration Ordinance – Amendment No. 11) have so far been applied merely to the eastern part of Jerusalem; but as has already been pointed out above, its non-application to other parts of Eretz Israel that came under Israeli control as a result of the Six-Day War is explained by *political* – as distinct from *legal* – considerations.[35] (emphasis in the original)

The above argument is, of course, double-edged. If Israeli sovereignty over East Jerusalem is no less than that of Israeli sovereignty over the West Bank generally, then the reverse is certainly also true. It has been the thesis of this work that Israel's legitimate stake in the West Bank is limited to belligerent or, at best, trustee occupation, until the advent of a peace treaty establishing final recognized borders.

d. *Condominium*

The question therefore arises as to whether the strongly held differing Arab- and Israeli interests in Jerusalem can be reconciled within the framework of a united city wherein freedom of access is guaranteed to all of its citizens. This goal does appear realizable, but not without considerable municipal restructure. The best arrangement appears to be that of a condominium whereby the administration of joint aspects of the city's life might be shared among Israel and either a Palestinian state or Jordan, or a combination of the two, depending on the ultimate disposition of control of the West Bank. Also serving as partners in this condominium might be one or two neutral states designated by both parties. Each of the holy places would be under the control of its own religious community but supervision of fulfillment of the guarantees of free access to and preservation of the holy places and historical sites would lie with the condominium partners as a whole.

The advantage of this scheme is that it makes the prospect of a peace settlement more realizable. Unitary control over all of Jerusalem appears to be unacceptable to all of the parties. Equally unacceptable is the prospect of a redivided city. A balance can be struck by a condominium arrangement or its functional equivalent. Its terms would be agreed upon by negotiation and established in a treaty of peace. Clearly, administration of joint aspects of the city's life may give rise to frequent dispute. But the parties involved may well be less hostile to each other than popularly imagined when their tasks are reduced to administrative matters. A measure of cooperation between East and West Jerusalem and between Israel and Jordan on matters of joint economic concern has already been established through contact since 1967.

The alternatives most frequently suggested to this condominium arrangement are: (1) the status quo post-1967; (2) the status quo ante-1967; (3) complete, partial, or functional internationalization; (4) formation of a U.N. Trust Territory; or (5) the creating of a borough system.

The first alternative is the popular choice in Israel and would, perhaps, be welcomed by many West Bank residents as well. The argument for retention of the status quo post-1967 is illustrated by the following statement:

> The once divided and war-torn city, an arena of Arab-Israeli conflict, is now the model of Arab-Jewish coexistence and cooperation. We believe that the peace and prosperity of Jerusalem and the flourishing of its diverse religions and cultures testify to the desirability – indeed, the necessity – of maintaining Israel's sovereignty over a united city.[36]

Continuation of the status quo post-1967 does have the advantage of autonomous control of the religious shrines and freedom of access thereto. East Jerusalemites can participate in the municipal government through normal election procedures. Yet, it appears clear that the degree of autonomy presently given is insufficient to satisfy legitimate Arab demands.

The second alternative, physical redivision and reinstitution of restricted access to Holy Places, is for reasons already discussed, unacceptable and, indeed, one apparently mutually rejected by the parties. For the same reasons, alternative (3), internationalization in any of its forms, is an unviable option.

Alternative (4), that of establishing either the Holy Places or Jerusalem as a whole as a trust territory, amounts, in practical terms, to little more than a commitment to increased U.N. supervision of fulfillment of the guarantees of preservation of free access to the Holy Places by the state maintaining control. Trusteeship implies the power of effective supervision and control, which the United Nations does not at present possess. Moreover, as Israel's role as trustee for the Holy Places has come under little criticism, little is to be gained by terminating the present arrangement in favor of a U.N. Trust Territory.

Finally, alternative (5), that of a borough system providing for redivision of Jerusalem into an Arab and a Jewish borough with a single municipal government is merely euphemistic for what currently exists. As such, a single municipal government for Arabs and Israelis has proved to be an unsatisfactory arrangement to the Arab minority population.

By contrast, the condominium scheme here favored restricts municipal government to coordination of problems common to two separately run municipalities and to questions of control over the Holy Places. It appears to be the only arrangement guaranteeing the minimum legitimate rights of all parties while, at the same time, being susceptible to mutual agreement.

## B. ANTICIPATING POSTLIMINIUM CLAIMS

### 1. *Recognition and Review of Legislative Acts of the Occupant*

During the course of occupation, the ousted power may legislate in fields affecting the occupied territory providing the legitimate objectives of the occupant are not hampered. Ernst Feilchenfeld, in his respected treatise on the economic law of belligerent occupation, states:

> One would go too far in assuming, as has been done by various authorities, that an absent sovereign is absolutely precluded from legislating for occupied territories. The sovereignty of the

> absent sovereign over the region remains in existence and, from a more practical point of view, the occupant may and should have no objection to timely alterations of existing laws by the old sovereign in those fields which the occupant has not seen fit to subject to his own legislative power.[37]

Moreover, the ousted power may properly threaten to subsequently deem invalid, upon its resumption of control, any rights or obligations accruing under occupation decrees which it considers violative of international law.[38]
Oppenheim states:

> If the occupant has performed acts which, according to International Law, he was not competent to perform, postliminium (reversion of territory to the legitimate sovereign) makes the invalidity of these illegitimate acts apparent. Therefore, if the occupant has sold moveable state property, such property may afterwards be claimed from the purchaser, whoever he is, without compensation. If he has appointed individuals to offices for terms outlasting the occupation, they may afterward be dismissed. If he has appointed and sold such private or public property as may not legitimately be appropriated by a military occupant, it may afterward be claimed from the purchaser without payment or compensation.[39]

Any decree of the occupant outside the scope of his authority may be declared invalid ab initio.[40]

State practice reveals no tendency to abuse this right as, generally, postliminium, states have upheld occupants' measures promulgated within the bounds of their legitimate authority.[41] They have seldom sought to invalidate occupation measures solely on the grounds that the occupation itself was unlawful. Where such allegations have been raised, courts have tended not to rule on the issue directly but to decide on alternative grounds. The case of the *Blue Star Line* v. *Burmeister and Wain (The Adelaide Star)*,[42] is illustrative. The defendants were sued for non-performance of their alleged contractual obligation to build the 'Adelaide Star'. The contract was made prior to World War II and a substantial amount was paid in advance. Upon Germany's invasion, the nearly completed vessel was requisitioned. The plaintiff argued that the requisition was invalid ab initio because, as Germany had waged an unlawful war, the normal rights of occupants to requisition did not apply and that, accordingly, the defendants were still bound to perform. The Court refused to reach a decision on the question of whether an unlawful occupant could be held to a different standard and confined itself to stating that no liability arose because the German occupation was an event which the shipbuilders were incapable of anticipating.[43]

But, whereas the restored sovereign is obligated to recognize the validity of rights and obligations accrued during the occupation period, in so far as they stem from legitimate legislative measures, he is, of course, not obligated to retain legislative acts of the occupant subsequent to the transfer of power. Indeed, almost immediately after resumption of control, the returning sovereign will tend to abrogate all exisiting occupation measures. Relations growing out of the occupation do not continue but usually automatically terminate with occupation, even in the absence of an invalidating decree by the returning power. *Woo Chan Shi and Pak Chuen Woo v. Brown*[44] is illustrative. There the Supreme Court of Hongkong held that, although the appointment in 1943 of the plaintiffs as executors by the Japanese occupation courts was lawful, it became automatically ineffective immediately subsequent to British reoccupation of Hongkong in 1945.[45]

Regarding juridical decisions rather than legislative acts of occupants, states have fairly uniformly annulled or amended occupation judgments reached by either military or civilian courts. Convictions in both criminal and civil cases will often be reopened if the decision was in any way tainted by the political character of the occupation.[46] The returning sovereign's power to annul or amend judgments is not confined to those violations of international law, but can, for the sake of convenience, extend to judgments even if they were in accordance with international law.[47] In the interests of stability and ease of transition, returning sovereigns would, however, be well advised to honor judgments made in conformity with international law and limit invalidation to judgments of a clearly political nature.

*Claims to Restitution and Reparations*

a. *The Private Sector*

Subsequent to termination of occupation and reversion of control, the occupied populace may be expected to press for restitution of property allegedly taken by the occupant unlawfully and now in the possession either of the restored government or of individuals within its jurisdiction. Adjudication of this claim has to be made by the municipal courts of the returning sovereign on the basis of whether the initial requisition or confiscation order was compatible with the relevant international law.

Whether the occupant gained entry into the region by defensive or aggressive means should be of no relevance in determining the validity of the initial requisition or confiscation order. Perhaps the best known case illustrating this proposition is *N. V. de Bataafsche Petroleum Maatschapij and others v. War Damage Commission.*[48] The claimants, three Dutch companies, held oil concessions on the island of Sumatra. During the Japanese occupation, the plaintiffs' installations were used to extract and refine oil stocks. The Dutch companies subsequently sued for restitution, claiming that the Japanese never acquired title to the oil and thus the stocks remained their property. Several grounds served as the basis of this assertion. The predominant one was that Japan, as an aggressor-occupant, could acquire no title to property in occupied territory. Another ground was that crude oil, when 'in the ground', was a 'raw' material and not a 'munition de guerre', and that, as such, its seizure was in violation of Article 53 of the Hague Regulations limiting seizure to war material.

The conclusion of the Board hearing the case was that the oil stocks were 'munitions de guerre' and hence subject to confiscation. It stated that the illegality of the war waged by Japan could not deprive it from acquiring title to property which, under the terms of the Hague Regulations, an occupant is entitled to seize. The Court reasoned:

> It seems at least possible to this Board that if an illegal aggressor acquired no benefits under the rules of warfare, he similarly

> may be deemed to owe no obligations and if this is so, it is clearly in the interest of at least the smaller Powers that even an aggressor should be deemed to be within the provision of the Hague Convention.[49]

In the subsequent appeal hearing, the Singapore Court reversed the Board's decision, holding that oil *in situ* could not be considered as 'munitions de guerre', as it was immovable property 'not susceptible of direct military use'. The Court declined, however, to review the question of whether an aggressor-occupant could acquire title to enemy property under the Hague Regulations. It said the 'uncertainty of the law' prevented it from giving a decisive answer.[50] Justice Whitton dissented:

> The doctrine that the provisions of Hague Convention No. IV and the Regulations attached to it do not apply in 'total war' must be emphatically rejected. In this connection, it is to be borne in mind that Japan, like Germany, was a signatory to the Hague Convention. Akin to this view is the conception that even a state waging illegal war is entitled to the benefit of the Hague Regulations, a conception which appears to have been acted upon by the European Courts dealing with cases arising out of the Second World War and which has now received the authority of Dr. Lauterpacht's acceptance.[51]

b. *The Public Sector*

Soon after reversion of control of the Abu Rhodeis oil fields in Sinai to Egypt in 1975, Egypt announced that she would institute claims for restitution of Israeli profits from operations of the wells while under Israeli control.[52] The claim is typical of the restitution demands that may be expected to be lodged against the former occupant by the returning sovereign.

According to the terms of the Hague Regulations the former occupant will be liable in restitution only for the value of seized private property involving means of communication and transport. Article 53 provides that such property 'must be restored and compensation fixed when peace is made.'[53] Regarding other property, Article 52 permits requisition in kind and services 'for the needs of the army of occupation' and

Article 53 permits seizure of 'all moveable property belonging to the State which may be used for military operations.' No reference is made to any right to restitution by the restored power for the value of such property.

In regard to profits flowing from the use of commandeered immovable state property, a claim for restitution may be validly asserted where the capital of these properties has not been safeguarded in accordance with the rules of usufruct, as stipulated in Article 55 of the Hague Regulations. Although a conflict of laws problem may appear to be present in these instances regarding the applicable domestic law of usufruct, the better view is that an international rule has developed which should control. This rule establishes as the test of abuse of the usufructuary obligation, whether the real property has been systematically and purposefully exploited beyond normal use, so that depletion of the property's resource is the likely result; that is to say, has the occupant been guilty of spoliation as defined by the Nuremberg Tribunal.[54] Thus, the opening of new mines or exploration for new oil sources is not proscribed unless such activity is injurious to the corpus of the property.[55]

The trend of state practice has been to impose, via the peace treaty, penalties on an aggressor-occupant for property practices, regardless of their conformity to the standards of the Geneva and Hague Conventions. For example, the peace treaties terminating the second World War stipulated that restitution be made for appropriated property regardless of the validity of such measures under the terms of the Hague Regulations.[56] Article 26 of the Paris Peace Treaty provided—as did the corresponding articles of the other Peace Treaties of World War II—that Germany

> shall restore *all* the legal rights and interests in Hungary of the United Nations and their nationals as they existed on September 1, 1939, and shall return *all* property in Hungary of the United Nations and their nationals as it now exists.[57]

Subsequently, all German seizures, requisitions and confiscations of occupied state or private property occurring between September 1, 1939 and the coming into force of the Peace Treaty were declared null and void[58] regardless of permissibility under the Hague Regulations.

This disregard of the Hague Regulations in requiring restitution of all property confiscated or requisitioned was, however, justified as the product of post-surrender rather than belligerent occupation. The Allied Peace Treaties were thus legally entitled to contain any type of provisions other than those violative of basic humanitarian principles. By contrast, a party negotiating a peace treaty in a belligerent occupation context may not validly insert a clause requiring the former occupant to pay restitution for all appropriated property, independent of the validity of their seizure under the Hague and Geneva Conventions.[59]

c. *Reparations*

Reparations, the obligation to compensate for war losses, has traditionally been a common feature of peace treaties.[60] The Treaty of Versailles is the most popularly known instance. In the 1947 Treaties of Peace with Hungary, Bulgaria and Rumania, reparations were exacted because of their role as 'an ally of Hitlerite Germany.' In the Treaty with Italy, Italy's role in having 'undertaken a war of aggression and thereby provoked a state of war with the Allied and Associated Powers' was specifically invoked as grounds for reparations.

Provisions for reparations, like those for restitution, are validly and regularly imposed in peace treaties where one party has surrendered. Claims for their imposition in peace treaties seeking to terminate the state of belligerent occupation are, however, difficult to support insofar as both parties to the conflict seek its resolution. Reparations constitute compensatory and punitive penalties for damages incurred in defending against a war of aggression. Authoritative determinations of aggression in belligerent-occupation contexts are however difficult to obtain. In any event, belligerent-occupants will not freely agree to peace treaties containing reparation clauses. Thus if accommodation by treaty is sought, reparation claims will hardly advance that end.

3. *Challenging the Validity of the Peace Treaty: 'Coercion' and Treaty Invalidation*

Exponents of the Arab legal position have advanced the claim that any peace treaty reached with Israel while she remains in control of the territories conquered in 1967 would be subject to invalidation on the grounds of being the product of 'coercion.' Thus, for example, Dr. Ibrahim Shihata, citing Article 52 of the Vienna Convention on The Law of Treaties[61] as authority for this proposition, writes that 'An agreement reached under alien military occupation through which an occupied sovereign state is forced to relinquish part of its territory is likely at any rate to be deemed invalid under international law. . . vitiated by coercion.'[62] Such an approach flies in the face of Security Council Resolutions 96, 242 and 338, all of which require a permanent political solution prior to Israeli withdrawal from occupied territories in exchange for peace guarantees. Moreover, although this position is not without strong support by many writers on international law, and especially by the community of developing nations, its implementation carries dangerous overtones to both regional and international peace and stability.

Article 52 of the Vienna Convention, Coercing a State by the Threat or Use of Force, states:

> A treaty is void if its conclusion has been procured by force in violation of the principles of international law embodied in the Charter of the United Nations.

It does not purport to deem invalid all 'unequal treaties'. If it did, no peace treaty would be secure from repudiation. Only those are deemed void which are imposed 'in violation of the principles of international law embodied in the Charter of the United Nations'. The International Law Commission, which bore principal responsibility for the drafting of the Convention, has gone on record as stating that Article 52 was meant to apply exclusively to situations where a treaty was procured by the threat or use of force in violation of Article 2:4 of the Charter, and that other forms of pressure such as economic and political threats were insufficient.[63]

Many third world states were, however, unsatisfied with the International Law Commission's definition of coercion and sought to amend it to include any 'economic or political pressure.'[64] They maintained, during the course of the deliberations on the final form of the Vienna draft, that Article

2:4 of the Charter inherently prohibits economic as well as military coercion.[65] The Chilean delegate ably responded to this argument stating:

> . . . the Brazilian delegation to the 1945 San Francisco Conference had proposed the inclusion of an express reference to the prohibition of economic pressure, and its proposal had been rejected. Consequently any references to the principles of the Charter in that respect must be a reference to the kind of force which all the Member States had agreed to prohibit, namely, physical or armed force[66]

The issue was best summed up by the Dutch representative:

> In itself, the rule stated in article (52) was perfectly clear and precise. (It) supported the principle underlying the article, namely, the principle that an *aggressor State* should not, in law, benefit from a treaty it had forced its victim to accept. Nervertheless it must be borne in mind that there was a fundamental difference of opinion as to the meaning of the words 'threat or use of force' in Article 2, paragraph 4, of the United Nations Charter. If those words could be interpreted as including all forms of pressure exerted by one state on another, and not just the threat or use of armed force, the scope of article (52) would be so wide as to make it a serious danger to the stability of treaty relations[67] (emphasis added)

But, as Richard Kearney, the American Ambassador to the Conference, has pointed out,[68] those pressing for the above revision of the International Law Commission draft text were clearly in the majority, and a compromise with them had to be reached by the Western states:

> (In) the course of the debate (those pressing for a broad interpretation of 'force') had made it clear that if the amendment were put to the vote it would carry by quite a substantial majority. On the other hand, in private discussions it had been made quite clear to the proponents that adoption would wreck the conference because states concerned with the stability of treaties found the proposed revision intolerable.[69]

The compromise achieved accord at the price of precision of meaning. The definition of 'force' was left sufficiently ambiguous to enable both sides to claim that their interpretation had prevailed. It was agreed that a draft declaration adopting a broad definition of force would be introduced, while Article 52 itself would remain intact. The Draft Declaration, adopted by a vote of 102 to 0 with 4 abstensions, read:

> The United Nations Conference on the Law of Treaties . . . condemns the threat or use of pressure in any form, military, political or economic, by any State to perform any act relating to the conclusion of a treaty in violation of the principles of sovereign equality of States and freedom of consent. . .[70]

Those states that argued for the liberalization of the International Law Commission's Draft looked upon the Draft Declaration as being the legal equivalent of a provision of the Convention. It was urged that the Draft Declaration interpreted the

> . . . word 'force' as employed in The United Nations Charter and in Article 49 (52) of the draft to cover all forms of force starting with threats and including, in addition to bombardment, *military occupation,* invasion or terrorism, and more subtle forms such as technical and financial assistance or economic pressure in the conclusion of treaties.[71] (emphasis added)

The Western states and Japan took an opposite view. To them the Draft Declaration was merely a resolution of the Conference to the Convention and not really a provision of the Convention. It did not broaden the definition of coercion to permit invalidation of treaties other than in the instance of *unlawful* use of *armed* force.[72] Notwithstanding arguments to the contrary by many developing states, Article 52 was not viewed as directed against the operation of 'unequal treaties'.

In the intervening years since promulgation of the Vienna Convention on Treaties, the Third World states, now the majority in the United Nations General Assembly, have reshaped much of international law to reflect their views. This is dramatically illustrated in the direction taken by the U.N. Special Committee on the Question of Defining Aggression.[73] In reaching its definition by consensus in March 1974, the Special Committee recommended and the General Asembly later adopted a definition whereby the following acts, among others, would qualify as aggression:

> 3 (a) The invasion or attack by the armed forces of a State of the territory of another State, or *any* military occupation, however temporary, resulting from such invasion or attack, or *any* annexation by the use of force of the territory of another State or part thereof; (emphasis added)

Britain made explicit at the time of the Resolution's adoption that only such occupation resulting from unlawful invasion, itself aggression, fell within this provision. Nevertheless, interpreted literally, the Resolution condemns any occupation as 'aggression'. Commenting on this turn of events, Benjamin Ferencz has written that 'The final text is a further indication of the political nature of the consensus definition.'[74]

The drafters of Article 52 sought to make contemporary international law's primary distinction between the lawful and unlawful use of force[75] more meaningful by invalidating peace treaties imposed on the victims of clear aggression, *viz.*, through the use of military force in violation of Article 2(4) of the Charter.[76] The 'Third World' bloc, now joined by the Soviet Union and its allies would, in the interests of promoting their national interests as well as in exploiting an opportunity to condemn Israeli occupation, destroy the lawful-unlawful use of force dichotomy as a basis for treaty invalidation in favor of the unequal treaties test. Were the lawful-unlawful dichotomy applied to the Arab-Israeli conflict, Israel would be deemed a lawful occupant, having been deemed 'the' aggressor in neither the 1967 nor 1973 War. Accordingly any peace settlement entered into between Israel and her neighbors would not be subject to subsequent vitiation on the grounds of coercion. If, on the other hand, 'inequality' rather than unlawfulness be adopted as the basis for treaty invalidation, any Israel-Arab treaty, or any other for that matter, would be short -lived. The security of every armistice agreement and peace settlement would be endangered. Termination of conflict by these modes would thus become more difficult. Moreover, by making breaches of the peace treaty easier to justify, the proclivity to resume war is increased. The interests of peaceful dispute settlement demand that the Vienna Convention on the Law of Treaties be interpreted as vitiating only such treaties as are procured by the unlawful, non-defensive use of military power. To permit invalidation of treaties because they are 'unequal' is to undermine the stability of all international arrangements.

NOTES

1. D. Horowitz, *Political Adaptation Under Military Occupation: The Cause of the West Bank, June 1967–October 1973,* Paper No. 9, International Political Science Ass'n. Conference, Jerusalem, Sept. 9–13, 1971. 12, n. 45.
2. *See,* for example, reaction of former Nablus mayor, Hamdi Canaan, to a statement made by King Hussein in an interview appearing in the December 6 issue of the *Sunday Times* of London. Hussein had stated: 'The future of the West Bank and the Palestinians can only transpire after and not before a general settlement along the lines of the 1967 U.N. Security Council Resolution.' In the Dec. 8 issue of East Jerusalem's *El Quds,* Canaan took issue with Hussein's stand saying: 'Why after liberation? Why shouldn't Hussein right now, in advance of the end of occupation, amend the constitution of Jordan, adding a clause giving Palestine the right to autonomy, with the West Bank and the east bank in a federation, not a mere annexation? ... (West Bankers) are very concerned with what will happen after Israeli withdrawal. They don't want the catastrophic rule they endured before the six day war . . . West Bankers are not begging for autonomy but insist upon it. We will accept no other solution'. Reprinted in 1970 *Facts on File* 908.
3. *See* Nimrod, 'Military Government in the Occupied Territories: An Israeli View.' *Middle East Journal,* 177–90 (1969).
4. *See* regarding the 'open bridges' policy, Gazit, 'The Administered Territories—Policy and Action', 204 *Ma'arachot* (Journal of Israel Defense Forces) (In Hebrew) 20 (1970).
5. *El Ahram,* July 19, 1971, as reported in the *Jerusalem Post,* July 20, 1971.
6. *Newsweek,* December 17, 1973 at 47.
7. *See Time,* November 11, 1974 at 27.
8. *See New York Times,* November 10, 1974. *See* also interview with King Hussein in *New York Times,* Nov. 4, 1974, where the monarch explained that as a result of the Rabat conference 'the situation has altered very basically. A new reality exists and Jordan must adjust to it. The West Bank is no longer Jordan, and we have no place in the negotiations for its future.'
9. *See Id.,* December 30, 1975, testimony by Sect'y of State Kissinger before Senate Foreign Relations Comm. 11/19/75. *See* note, p. 234.
10. This is to be distinguished from the nature of the plebiscite envisioned in Gerson, 'Trustee-Occupant: The Legal Status of Israel's Presence in the West Bank', 14 *Harv. Int'l L. J.* (1973) wherein a plebiscite was to be conducted after a span of several years and after representative political institutions had been allowed to develop.
11. *See* for comprehensive bibliography and discussion of plebiscites in contemporary international affairs, Reisman and Chen, *supra* note I, 40 at 660–9.
12. *See* NBC Meet the Press Interview with Yasir Arafat, February, 1976.

See also report in the New York Times, February 17, 1976 of announcement by the PLO that under no circumstances would it recognize the state of Israel because 'This is something we cannot bargain about.' See, also, 'Document: The Revised National Covenant (1968)' and Commentary thereon by Y. Harkabi, 3 *N.Y.U. J. of Int'l. L. & Politics* 209 (1970). *See* however reports by U.N. Sect'y General Kurt Waldheim in January 1977 that the PLO is ready to recognize and live in peace with Israel in exchange for control of the West Bank and Gaza. There is however little evidence that the PLO has altered the opposition it voiced to proposals made by West Bankers in 1970 for an independent West Bank state as a solution to the conflict. In response to this proposal the PLO officially declared: 'Our final aim is very clear: the liberation of all of Palestine and the establishment of a democratic non-Zionist, non-Israeli Palestinian state. We will continue the armed struggle until we reach this final aim, and any idea of a scarred, puppet entity that might be discussed or thought about will be resisted and rejected by the resistance movement.' 1970 *Facts on File* 908. This aim has remained unaltered. For latest confirmation of this fact see statement by Libya's Kaddafi at the December 5 meeting in Tripoli of Arab leaders opposed to the Sadat peace initiative: All Palestinian leaders regard such a state (the West Bank and Gaza) only as 'space for them to continue their struggle for the liberation of their homeland'. *New York Times,* Dec. 5, 1977.

13. 21 *LSI* 75 (1967). Note that extension of civilian control over Jerusalem could have been accomplished under existing Israeli legislation. *See supra* note III, 6.
14. K.T. 2690 (1967).
15. G. A. Res. 2253, 22 U.N. GAOR, 5th emergency special sess., Supp. I, U.N. Doc. A/6798 (1967). Other 'measures' referred to passed on the same day as the Law and Administration Ordinance were an amendment to the *Municipal Corporations Ordinance (Amendment) Law, 1967,* empowering the Minister of Interior to enlarge the area of any municipality by the inclusion of an area designated under the first measure, and the *Protection of Holy Places Law, 1967.*
16. U.N. Docs. A/6753; S/8052 (1967).
17. *See,* e.g., Statement of Minister of Justice Shapiro who, during the Knesset debate over passage of the Administrative and Judicial Order No. 1, termed such passage an 'act of sovereignty.' 49 *Knesset Proceedings* 2420 (1967). *See also Rijuni and Others v. Military Court in Hebron,* 24 (20) (hereinafter P.D.) 419 (Israel Supreme Court sitting as the High Court of Justice, October 1970) (in Hebrew), where two of the three sitting judges ruled that East Jerusalem had been annexed. Justice Cohn, concurring, ruled that the question of East Jerusalem's annexation had been decided only for the purpose of the instant case in which the defendant had agreed, without argument, to several legal assumptions. This and similar cases are discussed in Dinstein, 'Zion Shall Be Redeemed in International Law,' 27 *HaPraklit* (in Hebrew) 5, (1971).

18. Israel's integrationist policy regarding East Jerusalem has subjected her to continued U.N. condemnation. *See* G. A. Res. 2254, 22 U.N. GAOR, 5th emergency special sess., Supp. 1, U.N. Doc. A/6798 (1967); U.N. Docs. S/RES/252 (1968), 267 (1969), 271 (1969). *See* Dinstein, 'The Legal Issues of Para-War and Peace in the Middle East,' 44 *St. John's L. Rev*. 466, 478–81 (1970).
19. G. A. Res. 181 (II), Part III (D).
20. Jordan opposed any international supervision of the care and access to the Holy Places, while Israel expressed agreement to such supervision. *See* GAOR, Dec. 6, 1949 at 351; GAOR, Ad Hoc Political Committee, Annexes, Vol. II, p. 5 (1949), 223–234. Report of the Conciliation Commission for Palestine, Sept. 2, 1950, U.N. Coc. A/1367/Rev.1 at 10–11. *See* Blum: 'The Juridical Status of Jerusalem,' 2 *Jerusalem Papers on Peace Problems* 25–32 (1974).
21. See R. Stebbins, *The United States in World Affairs,* 1949 (Published for the Council of Foreign Relations) 410 (1950).
22. See Spec. Rept. of the Trusteeship Council, U.N. Doc. A/1286.
23. *See* Wilson, 'The Internationalization of Jerusalem,' 23 *Middle East Journal* 1 (1969); Ward, 'Economics of an Internationalized Jerusalem,' 2 *Int'l. Journal of Middle East Studies* 311 (1971). Cf. 'Statement by Christian Leaders Opposing Internationalization,' *Congressional Record,* June 16, 1974.
24. *See* Mark, The Status of Jerusalem, memorandum prepared for the House Committee on Foreign Affairs, Subcommittee on Near East for Hearings of July 28, 1971. *See,* however, Blum, *supra* note 20 at 24–32, who, in using the term 'functional internationalization,' refers to autonomous control of religious shrines by their religious affiliations.
25. A/Ac. 38/L.63.
26. The U.S. Representative, John C. Ross, stated to the Ad Hoc Committee that he was considerably disappointed 'by Jordan's reaction.' *See* World Peace Foundation, VII *Documents on Foreign Relations* 667 (1950).
27. A/Ac. 38/L.71.
28. On December 11, 1952 the Ad Hoc Political Committee adopted a resolution urging 'the governments concerned to enter at an early date . . . into direct negotiations for the establishment of . . . a settlement, bearing in mind the resolutions as well as the principal objectives of the U.N. on the Palestine Question, including the religious interests of the third parties.' *Yr' bk. of the U.N., 1951* at 308. When this resolution was considered at the plenary session of the General Assembly, the Philippines representative proposed to amend the resolution by inserting at the end the phrase 'and, in particular, the principle of the internationalization of Jerusalem.' The amendment was defeated. *See* for discussion of the voting patterns *Israel and the United Nations* (Carnegie Endowment of International Peace publication) 138 (1956).
29. Address of Israeli Foreign Minister, Abba Eban, to the U.N. General Assembly on Sept. 19, 1969. U.N. GAOR 24th Session, 1757th Plenary Meeting, p. 20.

30. Jordan has denied Israeli Jews free access to the Western Wall in Jerusalem – Judaism's holiest shrine – and the Tomb of Rachel on the outskirts of Jerusalem. Jordan claims to have barred Israeli Jews from the Western Wall in retaliation for Israeli restrictions against Israeli Moslems crossing to the Dome of the Rock and the al-Aqsa Mosque. *See* Institute for Palestine Studies, *The Rights and Claims of Moslems and Jews in Connection with the Wailing Wall at Jerusalem* (1968).
31. It was only in 1967, upon Israel's entry into East Jerusalem that the desecration of the Jewish cemetery at the Mount of Olives was discovered.
32. *See* M. Benvenisti, *Jerusalem: The Torn City* (1976). 'Jews and Arabs strove for opposing goals, but life proved stronger than ideology . . . both sides became fully aware of the existence of the other, an existence which one had tried to ignore and the other had seen merely as something to be overcome. They progressed a bit on the road to peace . . . it was clear, however, that the two nations living in Jerusalem had no desire to return to the point at which they had started.' (at 36). *See also* U. Benziman, *Jerusalem, City Without Walls* (Hebrew) (1973).
33. *See* Mark, *supra* note 24, at 30.
34. *Ibid.*
35. Blum, *supra* note 20, at 23.
36. Statement by American-Israel Public Affairs Committee, *Hearings before the Subcommittee on the Near East of the Committee on Foreign Affairs,* House of Representatives, 92d Congress, July 28, 1971 at 171.
37. H. Feilchenfeld, *The International Economic Law of Belligerent Occupation* 135 (1942).
38. *See* Schwelb, 'Legislation for Enemy Occupied Territory in the British Empire', 30 *Tr. Grotius Soc.* 239 (1944); Schwelb, 'Legislation in Exile: Czechslovakia', 24, *J. Comp. Leg. Int'l L.* 120 (1942); Oppenheimer, 'Governments and Authorities in Exile' 36 *AM. J. Int'l L.* 568 (1942); Stein 'Application of the Law of Absent Sovereign in Territory Under Belligerent Occupation: The Schio Massacre' 46 *Mich. L. Rev.* 341 (1948). Perhaps the best known example of an assertion during war time of competence to review,upon reversion,all acts of the occupant is the Allied Declaration of January 5, 1943 relating to acts of dispossession committed in Axis-occupied countries. It provided that the parties to it:

    reserve all their rights to declare invalid any transfers of, or dealings with, property, rights and interests of any description whatsoever which are, or have been, situated in the territories which have come under the occupation or control, direct or indirect, of the governments with which they are at war or which belong, or have belonged, to persons, including juridical persons resident in such territories. This warning applies whether such transfers or dealings have taken the form of open looting or plunder, or of transactions apparently legal in form, even when they purport to be voluntarily effected.

    *U.S. Dept of State Bull.,* Jan. 9, 1943, p. 21. Note that the Declaration did not mention whether the methods of dispossession which it would invalidate were to be those deemed unlawful by The Hague Regulations.

39. II *Lauterpacht-Oppenheim* (7th ed., 1955) 619.

40. *See* Morgenstern 'Validity of the Acts of the Belligerent Occupant' 38 *Brit. Y. B. of Int'l. L.* 291 (1952). Of course the returning sovereign may, if he wishes, give continuing effect to statutes and ordinances of the occupant promulgated in violation of international law. Easing the transition from war to postwar conditions can be accomplished by stabilizing expectations in this manner. The Netherlands government found this reasoning persuasive when it passed Decree No. 93 on Occupation Measures, September 17, 1944 permitting the continuation of certain invalidly enacted occupation decrees. *See* Jansma, 'The Dutch Government's Treatment of Decrees Made by the German Authorities during the Occupation of the Netherlands' 29 *J. Comp. Leg. Int'l. L.* 52 (1947); *Bedriffsgroep Bouw en Aardewer Kambackten. The Hague v. Vonk, Annual Digest* 1947, Case No. 114.

41. For illustration of state practice in recognizing rights established pursuant to lawful decrees of occupants, *see* Ordinance issued on October 9, 1945 by the new De Gaulle Government in France, recognizing as having continuing effect laws enacted by the Vichy government in reference to marriage and marital rights. See Delaune, 'Enemy Legislation and Judgments in France' 30 *J. Comp. Leg. Int'l. L.* 32 (1948); Constitutional Art. No. 58 of 1945, passed by the restored Greek government in 1945, authorized the Greek cabinet to declare which decrees promulgated by Germany were valid. Most laws compatible with the Hague Regulations were not invalidated. *See* Zepos, 'Enemy Legislation and Judgments in Liberated Greece' 30 *Id.* 27 (1948). The Greek courts held validly enacted occupation measures to be not only productive of legal effects emanating from the time of occupation but to have continuing legal effect after occupation, until such time as they may be repealed. Generally, the termination of any prospective operation of occupation measures will be among the first order of business of the restored sovereign. *See*, for example, Proclamation No. 1, August 1, 1945 by the Supreme Allied Commander, South East Asia upon re-occupation of Malaysia and adjacent areas in Donnson, *British Military Administration in the Far East, 1943–46* 451 (1956); Proclamation issued October 23, 1944, by the Commander of the United States Forces upon reoccupying the Philippines in 41 Official Gazette 784 (Comm. of the Philippines, 1945).

42. Supreme Court of Denmark, October 22, 1948, 15 *Annual Digest* 421 (1948).

43. See for further discussion of this issue in a prominent case wherein the court ruled negatively on the merits of the argument that a different standard be applied to unlawful occupants, *N. V. de Bataafsche Petroleum Maatschapij and others v. War Damage Commission, infra* note 48.

44. 13 *Annual Digest* 368 (1946).

45. *See,* in accord, *Banaag v. Encarnacion* 83 Philippines 825 (1949) where a fishing lease, validly granted during Japanese occupation, became automatically ineffective.
46. Stabell, 'Enemy Legislation and Judgments in Norway' 31 *J. Comp. Leg. Int'l. L.* 3 (1949); Zepos, *supra* note 41 at 27; Note 'Powers and Duties of Enemy Occupant' 12 *Malayan L. J.* (1946). *See* generally, McDougal & Feliciano, supra note I, 10 at 789–90 for excellent comparative analysis of the restored governments in Burma, Indonesia and the Philippines juxtaposed with those of France, Greece, Norway and Singapore. The authors conclude that the former grouping paid more deference to judgments of the occupation regimes.
47. Wolff, 'Municipal Courts of Justice in Enemy Occupied Territory' 29 *Tr. Grotius Soc.* 99, 115 (1943).
48. 23 *Annual Digest* 810 (1956). *See* 22 *Malayan L. J.* 155 (1956);51 *Am. J. Int'l. L.* 802 (1957); 71 *Harv. L. Rev.* 568 (1958); 'B' *The Case of the Singapore Oil Stocks* 5 *Int'l. & Comp. L. Q.* 84 (1956). *See also* E. Lauterpacht, 'The Hague Regulations and the Seizure of Munitions de Guerre' 32 *Brit. Y. B. Int'l. L.* 218 (1955).
49. 22 *Malaya L. J.* 155. 158 (1956).
50. 23 *Annual Digest* 810, 826 (1956).
51. *Id.* 845.
52. *New York Times* December 4, 1975.
53. *See* generally, Jessup 'A Belligerent Occupant's Power over Property' 38 *Am. J. Int'l. L.* (1944); I Vasarhelyi, *Restitution in International Law* (Budapest) 51–66 (1964).
54. *See* the *I. G. Farben Trial.* supra note III, 186 and the *Krupp Trial supra* note III, 191 and text thereof.
55. *See* Gerson, 'Offshore Oil Exploration by a Belligerent Occupant', *Am. J. Int'l. L.* (1976). For a differing view, *see* Cummings 'Oil Resources in Occupied Territories' 9 *J. of Int'l L. & Economics* 533, 563–6 (1974) relying on Roman, French & Italian law and some Anglo-American decisions to reach his conclusions, while ignoring the import of the relevant international law on the subject as developed by the Nuremberg Tribunal.
56. *See* Treaty of Peace with Hungary T.I.A.S. No. 1651 (effective September 15, 1947); Treaty of Peace with Bulgaria T.I.A.S. No. 1650 (same date as above); Treaty of Peace with Rumania.
57. Treaty of Peace with Hungary, *Id.*
58. Paragraph 3 of Article 26 of the Peace Treaty with Hungary contained what might be considered a qualifying term. It stipulated that property transfers shall be required to be invalidated only where they were product of fraud or duress. As the context in which appropriations were made was coercive by nature irrespective of 'voluntary' consent and as the burden of disproving the presumption of invalidity vested with the Axis powers, the proviso limiting invalidation of transfers to instances of coercion was of little qualification.
59. *See* Martin, 'Private Property, Rights, and Interests in the Paris Peace Treaties' 24 *Brit. Y. B. Int'l. L.* 273, 276, 282 (1947).

60. II *Lauterpacht-Oppenheim,* 7th ed. (1955) at 594.
61. U.N. Doc. A/Conf. 39/27 (1969); 8 *Int'l Legal Materials* 679, 698 (1969). *See* generally S. Rosenne, *Law of Treaties: Guide to the Legislative History of the Vienna Convention* (1970).
62. Shihata, 'Destination Embargo of Arab Oil: Its Legality Under International Law,' 68 *Am. J. Int'l.* 591, 606 (1974). *See* also, making the same argument more forcefully, H. Cattan, *Palestine and International Law* (2nd ed., 1976) at 205–7. Cattan maintains that even a treaty whereby Israel relinquished all territories gained in 1967 in exchange for guarantees of peace would not be binding on the Arab side as 'whichever State of Israel is intended (1947, 1949, 1967 or beyond), its continued *existence* violates the rights of the Palestinians, the principles of justice and international law' at 215. The only lawful solution in his view is the 'dismantling of the State of Israel,' at 220. *See also* Hargrove, 'Abating the Middle East Crisis Through the United Nations' *Kansas Law Review* 369 (1971).
63. See II *Yrbk of the Int'l Law Commiss.* 1966, 246–7; 61 *Am. J. Int'l L.* 407 (1967). The Commission further stated that a treaty procured by a threat or use of force in violation of the principles of the Charter must be characterized as void, rather than as voidable at the instance of the injured party, *Id.* The Commission was making reference to Article 49 of its 1966 draft of the Vienna Convention, which essentially remained identical in effect as Article 52 of the final treaty.
64. U.N. Doc. A/Conf. 39/C.l/L,67/Rev.l/Corr.7 (1968). The initiative for the amendment came from Afghanistan, Algeria, Bolivia, Congo (Brazzaville), Sierra Leone, Syria, U.A.R., United Republic of Tanzania, Yugoslavia and Zambia. Eventually the revision they urged became referred to as the 'Nineteen State Amendment'. See generally regarding the confrontation, at the convention between the developed and less developed nations, Kearney & Dalton, 'The Treaty on Treaties' 64 *Am. J. Int'l. L.* 495, 532–8 (1970) and the excellent discussion in Malawer 'A New Concept of Consent and World Public Order: 'Coerced Treaties' and the Convention on the Law of Treaties,' 4 *Vanderbilt Int'l L. J.* 1 (1970).
65. *See* statements by Mr. Ed. Dessouki, Delegate from Egypt U.N. Doc. A/Conf. 39/11 (1968) at 274 and Mr. Nachake, Delegate from Syria *Id* at 274. Other delegations from Afro-Asian, Soviet bloc and Latin American states alleged that the prohibition against the use of economic and political pressure had already become a rule of customary international law. *See* statement by Mr. Tahibi, Delegate from Afghanistan, citing the OAS Charter, the Declaration of Non-Aligned Countries (Belgrade, 1961) and a similar declaration made in Cairo in 1964, *Id.* at 3.
66. Doc. *Id.* at 276.
67. *Id.* at 275.
68. See *supra* note 64 at 534–5.
69. *Id.*
70. U.N. Doc. A/Conf. 39/26 (1969).

71. Statement by Mr. Mutale, Delegate from Democratic Republic of the Congo. *supra* note 65, at 110.
72. *See* as representative of this view, statement by Mr. Tesutuoka, Delegate from Japan, *supra* note 65, at 101.
73. *See* Ferencz *supra* note I, (Vol. II) 5 at 1 ff.
74. *Id.* at 34.
75. H. Lauterpacht states in *Recognition in International Law* 426 (1947):

    Thus a treaty imposed by the victor upon the vanquished as a consequence of a war undertaken by the former is devoid of legal force in all cases in which he resorted to war *contrary to the obligations under the Charter of the United Nations* (emphasis added).

    It follows that a peace imposed by the victorious aggressor has no legal validity, notwithstanding the rule that international law disregards the vitiating effect of duress. For the latter rule applies only to wars which are not prohibited by international law *(Lauterpacht-Oppenheim* (7th ed.) at 219–20).
76. *See* statement by Sir Humphrey Waldock, Special Rapporteur to International Law Commission on its preparation of a draft convention on the law of treaties.

    (I)f 'coercion' were to be regarded as extending to other forms of pressure upon a state, to political or economic pressure, the door to evasion of treaty obligations might be opened very wide; for these forms of 'coercion' are much less capable of definition and much more liable to subjective appreciations. Moreover, the operation of political and economic pressures is part of the normal working of the relations between States, and international law does not yet seem to contain the criteria necessary for making distinctions between the legitimate and illegitimate uses of such forms of pressure as a means of securing consent to treaties. Accordingly. . . the Special Rapporteur feels that it would be unsafe in the present state of international law to extend the notion of 'coercion' beyond the illegal use or threat of force. . . .

    II *Yrbk. of the Int'l Law Commiss.* 1963 at 52.

    (*See supra,* note 9, p. 227) Although the Carter Administration has gone beyond previous Administrations in its advocacy of the need for 'a Palestinian homeland', it has urged that this be achieved under the aegis of a West Bank-Jordan confederation.

# Summation

Although recent developments in the Middle East have given new cause for hope, the danger that the Arab-Israeli conflict will engulf the world in its web of tragedy has not ebbed. The conflict of Soviet and American interests in this part of the world has widened, rather than narrowed. The economies of the industralized nations remain hostage to Arab petro-dollar power. More sophisticated weaponry is increasingly being introduced into the conflict and the spectre of nuclear alternatives looms ahead. Certainly, now more than ever, the entire order of international stability appears to have as its pivot peace in the Middle East.

At the heart of the dispute lies the controversy over the management and disposition of the West Bank. After conclusion of the Armistice Agreements between Jordan and Israel in 1949, and after some initial hostility by the Arab League in the early 1950s to Jordan's incorporation of the West Bank, the world at large appeared generally content to treat the issue of the West Bank as an internal concern of Jordan. Matters changed when Israel gained control of the region as a consequence of the 1967 war. Israel claimed that the status of the region had never become clearly defined in international law. And indeed it had not. Jordan itself acknowledged in 1950, upon absorption of the West Bank, that its administration of the area was without prejudice to the ultimate settlement of the Palestinian problem. Sovereignty over the West Bank was never unequivocally proclaimed by Jordan, nor recognized by the international community.

The unresolved legal status of the West Bank caused Israel to encounter immediate difficulty in its choice of appropriate management policies. Ostensibly, the relevant matrix of international rules and regulations governing Israel's administration was the body of law collectively known as the law of belligerent occupation. Its aim is the conclusion of a peace treaty, whereby all or much of the territory presently occupied would be exchanged for guarantees of peaceful relations. As a means toward this end, the occupying power is required to preserve the *status quo ante*. Changes in the fundamental social, economic and political institutions of the ousted power are viewed as counter-productive to peace-making, creating vested interests in the occupying power for indefinite retention of control and a hardening of the ousted power's resolve against accommodation.

Israel, however, questioned the applicability of the law of belligerent occupation to its military administration. It cited as its reason for concern the tenuousness of Jordan's legal claim to reversion of that territory. Israel feared that its acknowledgment of the *de jure* applicability of the Fourth Geneva Convention, the primary codification of this law, would be interpreted as an acknowledgment or recognition of Jordan as the West Bank's legitimate sovereign. Instead, Israel chose to 'leave open' the question of the *de jure* applicability of the Geneva Convention while continuing to apply it, *de facto*.

The solution was only partially successful. Ultimately, and perhaps inevitably, Israel's questioning of the relative superiority of Jordan's claim to the West Bank affected its administration of the territory, particularly on the sensitive issue of the acquisition and settlement of land by Israeli nationals. While the institutional structures of the governmental and educational systems were left basically intact, Israel's land purchase and settlement policies altered the status quo of the property system and caused much controversy, at home and abroad. Having implicitly laid claim to best title to the region, Israel experienced increasing domestic pressure for land purchase and settlement activity. Passage of the Galili Paper in April 1973 marked the zenith of this momentum. In providing for increased civilian settlement on a wide scale, the Galili Paper marked the abandonment of Israel's commitment to *de facto* compliance with the Geneva Convention insofar as civilian settlement was concerned. However, the setbacks in the 1973 War caused a re-examination of this policy before it had an opportunity to be implemented. It was decided to curtail settlement activity at its current level, and, at the least, to postpone the land purchase and settlement activity envisaged by the Galili Plan. Internal pressures for settlement continued however to grow, prompting the Government in May of 1976 to declare its commitment to a policy of continued limited settlement.

Israeli land practices, though perhaps diplomatically and otherwise unsound, never reached unlawful proportions.

Under the existing international law of belligerent occupation, settlement and purchase are deemed impermissible only where systematic in nature, involving displacement of the occupied population, and generally evidencing a clear intent to annex the territory. Israeli policy fell short. Nevertheless, it went against the grain of the Geneva Convention, assuming its applicability. It has complicated, if not diminished, the prospects for peaceful accommodation. In its wake, other more positive aspects of Israeli rule have been overlooked and the goodwill they engendered, eroded.

Turning from management to disposition problems, widespread optimism appears to prevail that creation of a new Palestinian state on the West Bank might prove a panacea to the conflict. As matters now stand it is only an invitation to increased turmoil. Should the PLO assume control, as is likely, it is highly improbable that the effect would be sufficiently sobering to transform its leaders into statesmen willing to abide by recognized criteria and restraints. So far the PLO has rejected as contrary to its principles the peaceful professions many would ascribe to it.

Yet self-determination for the West Bank is a necessary condition for a just resolution of the Arab-Israeli conflict. The difficulty lies in achieving this goal without running the risk of either a PLO-controlled state, or a Palestinian West Bank canton which is 'autonomous' in name only.

Genuine West Bank autonomy will require vast legal and institutional change in the region. Outmoded and unpopular laws will have to be revised or replaced. New economic institutions will have to be developed to channel foreign investment into the area and reduce its dependence on Israel. This cannot, however, be accomplished under the regime of belligerent-occupation at present deemed applicable to Israel's administration. The strict rule of *status quo ante* no longer has anything to recommend it in the present circumstances where neither Jordan, nor any other party on its behalf, presses its unqualified right to reversion of the West Bank.

As it is highly unlikely, and unreasonable to ask, that Israel agree to an immediate withdrawal from the West Bank rather than at some further point in time when responsible self-government might replace Israel's rule, a new international status of occupation, legally sound and politically acceptable, must be devised. The concept formulated by the author is that of 'trustee-occupancy' whereby the occupying power would, insofar as not directly injurious to his security, permit and further the development of autonomous institutions. It would be appropriate for Israel, unilaterally or by agreement, to assume this role. Israel, however, has not done so and has instead repeatedly expressed its intent to comply *de facto* with the Geneva Convention, and other codes applicable to belligerent-occupants, while continuing to 'leave open' the question of their applicability, *de jure*.

Applying the standard of a lawful belligerent-occupant, Israel may continue occupation until such time as a peace treaty is concluded or until such time as peace treaty terms are offered whereby the legitimate rights of all parties to the conflict may be secured. These rights would not encompass Israeli sovereignty over the West Bank, although Israel may legitimately negotiate for cession of non-populated areas whose retention is vital to its defense capability, and for demilitarization and other special arrangements for the area as a whole. East Jerusalem presents special problems. Clearly, it must remain an undivided city with equal access to all. A condominium system of municipal government encompassing separate sovereign spheres was suggested as the most favorable arrangement.

Of course formidable risks are inherent in the pursuit of peace, as well as in inaction. The occupying power will need to yield tangible security for largely intangible declarations of peaceful intent. The task of international law is to mitigate these risks. Statements by the Soviet bloc, Arab states and others that peace treaties signed while territory is under occupation are subject to invalidation on grounds of coercion are not helpful. Rather, only treaties that have been procured by 'aggression' are properly subject to invalidation. Israel's occupation cannot be faulted on this ground.

But while international law can help safeguard against distrust, it cannot dispel it. This is the province of creative diplomacy. Once there is the will for peace, as there now appears to be, international law can be most fruitfully exploited, no longer to define the perimeters of belligerent rights but to provide principles upon which the foundations of enduring peace can and must be established.

# APPENDICES

## A. Documents

## B. Maps

*Gratitude is expressed to the distinguished historian Dr Martin Gilbert for permission to use maps 1 to 5 from his 'The Arab-Israeli Conflict: Its History in Maps', and to 'Foreign Affairs' for map 6.*

# Documents

## 1. THE SYKES-PICOT AGREEMENT, MAY 16, 1916

*Sir Edward Grey to M. Cambon*
'(Secret.)
'Your Excellency, 'FOREIGN OFFICE, *May 15, 1916*

'I shall have the honour to reply fully in a further note to your Excellency's note of the 9th instant, relative to the creation of an Arab State, but I should meanwhile be grateful if your Excellency could assure me that in those regions which, under the conditions recorded in that communication, become entirely French, or in which French interests are recognised as predominant, any existing British concessions, rights of navigation or development, and the rights and privileges of any British religious, scholastic, or medical institutions will be maintained.

'His Majesty's Government are, of course, ready to give a reciprocal assurance in regard to the British area.

'I have, &c.
E. GREY'

*Sir Edward Grey to M. Cambon*
'(Secret.)
'Your Excellency, 'FOREIGN OFFICE. *May 16, 1916*

'I have the honour to acknowledge the receipt of your Excellency's note of the 9th instant, stating that the French Government accepts the limits of a future Arab State, or Confederation of States, and of those parts of Syria where French interests predominate, together with certain conditions attached thereto, such as they result from recent discussions in London and Petrograd on the subject.

'I have the honour to inform your Excellency in reply that the acceptance of the whole project, as it now stands, will involve the abdication of considerable British interests, but, since His Majesty's Government recognise the advantage to the general cause of the Allies entailed in producing a more favourable internal political situation in Turkey, they are ready to accept the arrangement now arrived at, provided that the co-operation of the Arabs is secured, and that the Arabs fulfil the conditions and obtain the towns of Homs, Hama, Damascus, and Aleppo.

'It is accordingly understood between the French and British Governments—

'1. That France and Great Britain are prepared to recognise and protect an independent Arab State or a Confederation of Arab States in the areas (A) and (B) marked on the annexed map [not here reproduced], under the suzerainty of an Arab chief. That in area (A) France, and in area (B) Great Britain, shall have priority of right of enterprise and local loans. That in area (A) France, and in area (B) Great Britain, shall alone supply advisers or foreign functionaries at the request of the Arab State or Confederation of Arab States.

'2. That in the blue area France, and in the red area Great Britain, shall be allowed to establish such direct or indirect administration or control as they desire and as they may think fit to arrange with the Arab State or Confederation of Arab States.

'3. That in the brown area there shall be established an international administration, the form of which is to be decided upon after consultation with Russia, and subsequently in consultation with other Allies, and the representatives of the Shereef of Mecca.

'4. That Great Britain be accorded (1) the ports of Haifa and Acre, (2) guarantee of a given supply of water from the Tigris and Euphrates in area (A) for area (B). His Majesty's Government, on their part, undertake that they will at no time enter into negotiations for the cession of Cyprus to any third Power without the previous consent of the French Government.

'5. That Alexandretta shall be a free port as regards the trade of the British Empire, and that there shall be no discrimination in port charges or facilities as regards British shipping and British goods; that there shall be freedom of transit for British goods through Alexandretta and by railway through the blue area, whether those goods are intended for or originate in the red area, or (B) area, or area (A); and there shall be no discrimination, direct or indirect, against British goods on any railway or against British goods or ships at any port serving the areas mentioned.

'That Haifa shall be a free port as regards the trade of France, her dominions and protectorates, and there shall be no discrimination in port charges or facilities as regards French shipping and French goods. There shall be freedom of transit for French goods through Haifa and by the British railway through the brown area, whether those goods are intended for or originate in the blue area, area (A), or area (B), and there shall be no discimination, direct or indirect, against French goods on any railway, or against French goods or ships at any port serving the areas mentioned.

'6. That in area (A) the Bagdad Railway shall not be extended southwards beyond Mosul, and in area (B) northwards beyond

Samarra, until a railway connecting Bagdad with Aleppo via the Euphrates Valley has been completed, and then only with the concurrence of the two Governments.

'7. That Great Britain has the right to build, administer, and be sole owner of a railway connecting Haifa with area (B), and shall have a perpetual right to transport troops along such a line at all times.

'It is to be understood by both Governments that this railway is to facilitate the connexion of Bagdad with Haifa by rail, and it is further understood that, if the engineering difficulties and expense entailed by keeping this connecting line in the brown area only make the project unfeasible, that the French Government shall be prepared to consider that the line in question may also traverse the polygon Banias-Keis Marib—Salkhad Tell Otsda—Mesmie before reaching area (B).

'8. For a period of twenty years the existing Turkish customs tariff shall remain in force throughout the whole of the blue and red areas, as well as in areas (A) and (B), and no increase in the rates of duty or conversion from *ad valorem* to specific rates shall be made except by agreement between the two powers.

'There shall be no interior customs barriers between any of the above-mentioned areas. The customs duties leviable on goods destined for the interior shall be collected at the port of entry and handed over to the administration of the area of destination.

'9. It shall be agreed that the French Government will at no time enter into any negotiations for the cession of their rights and will not cede such rights in the blue area to any third Power, except the Arab State or Confederation of Arab States, without the previous agreement of His Majesty's Government, who, on their part, will give a similar undertaking to the French Government regarding the red area.

'10. The British and French Governments, as the protectors of the Arab State, shall agree that they will not themselves acquire and will not consent to a third Power acquiring territorial possessions in the Arabian peninsula, nor consent to a third Power installing a naval base either on the east coast, or on the islands, of the Red Sea. This, however, shall not prevent such adjustment of the Aden frontier as may be necessary in consequence of recent Turkish aggression.

'11. The negotiations with the Arabs as to the boundaries of the Arab State or Confederation of Arab States shall be continued through the same channel as heretofore on behalf of the two Powers.

'12. It is agreed that measures to control the importation of arms into the Arab territories will be considered by the two Governments.

'I have further the honour to state that, in order to make the agreement complete, His Majesty's Government are proposing to the

Russian Government to exchange notes analogous to those exchanged by the latter and your Excellency's Government on the 26th April last. Copies of these notes will be communicated to your Excellency as soon as exchanged.

'I would also venture to remind your Excellency that the conclusion of the present agreement raises, for practical consideration, the question of the claims of Italy to a share in any partition or rearrangement of Turkey in Asia, as formulated in article 9 of the agreement of the 26th April, 1915, between Italy and the Allies.

'His Majesty's Government further consider that the Japanese Government should be informed of the arrangements now concluded.

'I have, &c.
E. GREY'

## 2. THE BALFOUR DECLARATION, NOVEMBER 2, 1917

Foreign Office,
November 2nd, 1917.

Dear Lord Rothschild,

I have much pleasure in conveying to you, on behalf of His Majesty's Government, the following declaration of sympathy with Jewish Zionist aspirations which has been submitted to, and approved by, the Cabinet

> 'His Majesty's Government view with favour the establishment in Palestine of a national home for the Jewish people, and will use their best endeavours to facilitate the achievement of this object, it being clearly understood that nothing shall be done which may prejudice the civil and religious rights of existing non-Jewish communities in Palestine, or the rights and political status enjoyed by Jews in any other country'.

I should be grateful if you would bring this declaration to the knowledge of the Zionist Federation.

Yours
Arthur James Balfour

## 3. ARTICLE 22 OF THE COVENANT OF THE LEAGUE OF NATIONS, JUNE 28 1919

1. To those colonies and territories which as a consequence of the late war have ceased to be under the sovereignty of the States which formerly governed them and which are inhabited by people not yet able to stand by themselves under the strenuous conditions of the modern world, there should be applied the principle that the well-being and development of such peoples form a sacred trust of civilization and that securities for the performance of this trust should be embodied in this Covenant.

2. The best method of giving practical effect to this principle is that the tutelage of such peoples should be entrusted to advanced nations who by reason of their resources, their experience or their geographical position can best undertake this responsibility, and who are willing to accept it, and that this tutelage should be exercised by them as Mandatories on behalf of the League.

3. The character of the mandate must differ according to the stage of the development of the people, the geographical situation of the territory, its economic conditions and other similar circumstances.

4. Certain communities formerly belonging to the Turkish Empire have reached a stage of development where their existence as independent nations can be provisionally recognized subject to the rendering of administrative advice and assistance by a Mandatory until such time as they are able to stand alone. The wishes of these communities must be a principal consideration in the selection of the Mandatory.

5. Other peoples, especially those of Central Africa, are at such a stage that the Mandatory must be responsible for the administration of the territory under conditions which will guarantee freedom of conscience and religion, subject only to the maintenance of public order and morals, the prohibition of abuses such as the slave trade, the arms traffic and the liquor traffic, and the prevention of the establishment of fortifications or military and naval bases and of military training of the natives for other than police purposes and the defence of territory, and will also secure equal opportunities for the trade and commerce of other Members of the League.

6. There are territories, such as South West Africa and certain of the South Pacific Islands, which, owing to the sparseness of their population, or their small size, or their remoteness from the centres of civilization, or their geographical contiguity to the territory of the Mandatory, and other circumstances, can be best administered under the laws of the Mandatory as integral portions of its territory, subject

to the safeguards above mentioned in the interest of the indigenous population.

7. In every case of mandate, the Mandatory shall render to the Council an annual report in reference to the territory committed to its charge.

8. The degree of authority, control, or administration to be exercised by the Mandatory shall, if not previously agreed upon by the Members of the League, be explicitly defined in each case by the Council.

9. A permanent Commission shall be constituted to receive and examine the annual reports of the Mandatories and to advise the Council on all matters relating to the observance of the mandates.

## 4. EXTRACTS, U.N. GENERAL ASSEMBLY RESOLUTION ON THE FUTURE GOVERNMENT OF PALESTINE (PARTITION RESOLUTION)

November 29, 1947

*The General Assembly,*

*Having met* in special session at the request of the mandatory Power to constitute and instruct a special committee to prepare for the consideration of the question of the future government of Palestine at the second regular session;

*Having constituted* a Special Committee and instructed it to investigate all questions and issues relevant to the problem of Palestine, and to prepare proposals for the solution of the problem, and

*Having received and examined* the report of the Special Committee (document A/364) including a number of unanimous recommendations and a plan of partition with economic union approved by the majority of the Special Committee,

*Considers* that the present situation in Palestine is one which is likely to impair the general welfare and friendly relations among nations;

*Takes note* of the declaration by the mandatory Power that it plans to complete its evacuation of Palestine by 1 August 1948;

*Recommends* to the United Kingdom, as the mandatory Power for Palestine, and to all other Members of the United Nations the adoption and implementation, with regard to the future government of Palestine, of the Plan of Partition with Economic Union set out below;

*Requests that*

(a) The Security Council take the necessary measures as provided for in the plan for its implementation;

(b) The Security Council consider, if circumstances during the transitional period require such consideration, whether the situation in Palestine constitutes a threat to the peace. If it decides that such a threat exists, and in order to maintain international peace and security, the Security Council should supplement the authorization of the General Assembly by taking measures, under Article 39 and 41 of the Charter, to empower the United Nations Commission, as provided in this resolution, to exercise in Palestine the functions which are assigned to it by this resolution;

(c) The Security Council determine as a threat to the peace, breach of the peace or act of aggression, in accordance with Article 39 of the Charter, any attempt to alter by force the settlement envisaged by this resolution;

(d) The Trusteeship Council be informed of the responsibilities envisaged for it in this plan;

*Calls upon* the inhabitants of Palestine to take such steps as may be necessary on their part to put this plan into effect;

*Appeals* to all Governments and all peoples to refrain from taking any action which might hamper or delay the carrying out of these recommendations, and

*Authorizes* the Secretary-General to reimburse travel and subsistence expenses of the members of the commission referred to in Part I, Section B, paragraph 1 below, on such basis and in such form as he may determine most appropriate in the circumstances, and to provide the Commission with the necessary staff to assist in carrying out the functions assigned to the Commission by the General Assembly.

## *Plan of Partition with Economic Union*
## *Part I—Future Constitution and Government of Palestine*

### *A. Termination of Mandate Partition and Independence*

1. The Mandate for Palestine shall terminate as soon as possible but in any case not later than 1 August 1948.

2. The armed forces of the mandatory Power shall be progressively withdrawn from Palestine, the withdrawal to be completed as soon as possible but in any case not later than 1 August 1948.

The mandatory Power shall advise the Commission, as far in

advance as possible, of its intention to terminate the Mandate and to evacuate each area.

The mandatory Power shall use its best endeavours to ensure that an area situated in the territory of the Jewish State, including a seaport and hinterland adequate to provide facilities for a substantial immigration, shall be evacuated at the earliest possible date and in any event not later than 1 February 1948.

3. Independent Arab and Jewish States and the Special International Regime for the City of Jerusalem, set forth in part III of this plan, shall come into existence in Palestine two months after the evacuation of the armed forces of the mandatory Power has been completed but in any case not later than 1 October 1948. The boundaries of the Arab State, the Jewish State, and the City of Jerusalem shall be described in parts II and II below.

4. The period between the adoption by the General Assembly of its recommendation on the question of Palestine and the establishment of the independence of the Arab and Jewish States shall be a transitional period . . .

*Steps Preparatory to Independence*

1. A commission shall be set up consisting of one representative of each of five Member States. The Members represented on the Commission shall be elected by the General Assembly on as broad a basis, geographically and otherwise, as possible.

2. The administration of Palestine shall, as the mandatory Power withdraws its armed forces, be progressively turned over to the Commission; which shall act in conformity with the recommendations of the General Assembly, under the guidance of the Security Council. The mandatory Power shall to the fullest possible extent co-ordinate its plans for withdrawal with the plans of the Commission to take over and administer areas which have been evacuated.

In the discharge of this administrative responsibility the Commission shall have authority to issue necessary regulations and take other measures as required.

The mandatory Power shall not take any action to prevent, obstruct or delay the implementation by the Commission of the measures recommended by the General Assembly.

3. On its arrival in Palestine the Commission shall proceed to carry out measures for the establishment of the frontiers of the Arab and Jewish States and the City of Jerusalem in accordance with the general lines of the recommendations of the General Assembly on the partition of Palestine. Nevertheless, the boundaries as described in part II of this plan are to be modified in such a way that village areas

as a rule will not be divided by state boundaries unless pressing reasons make that necessary.

4. The Commission, after consultation with the democratic parties and other public organizations of the Arab and Jewish States, shall select and establish in each State as rapidly as possible a Provisional Council of Government. The activities of both the Arab and Jewish Provisional Councils of Government shall be carried out under the general direction of the Commission.

If by 1 April 1948 a Provisional Council of Government cannot be selected for either of the States, or, if selected, cannot carry out its functions, the Commission shall communicate that fact to the Security Council for such action with respect to that State as the Security Council may deem proper, and to the Secretary-General for communication to the Members of the United Nations.

5. Subject to the provisions of these recommendations, during the transitional period the Provisional Councils of Government, acting under the Commission, shall have full authority in the areas under their control, including authority over matters of immigration and land regulation.

6. The Provisional Council of Government of each State, acting under the Commission, shall progressively receive from the Commission full responsibility for the administration of that State in the period between the termination of the Mandate and the establishment of the State's independence.

7. The Commission shall instruct the Provisional Councils of Government of both the Arab and Jewish States, after their formation, to proceed to the establishment of administrative organs of government, central and local.

8. The Provisional Council of Government of each State shall, within the shortest time possible, recruit an armed militia from the residents of that State, sufficient in number to maintain internal order and to prevent frontier clashes.

This armed militia in each State shall, for operational purposes, be under the command of Jewish or Arab officers resident in that State, but general political and military control, including the choice of the militia's High Command, shall be exercised by the Commission.

9. The Provisional Council of Government of each State shall, not later than two months after the withdrawal of the armed forces of the mandatory Power, hold elections to the Constituent Assembly which shall be conducted on democratic lines.

The election regulations in each State shall be drawn up by the Provisional Council of Government and approved by the Commission. Qualified voters for each State for this election shall be persons over eighteen years of age who are: (a) Palestinian citizens residing in that State and (b) Arabs and Jews residing in the State, although not Palestinian citizens, who, before voting, have signed a notice of intention to become citizens of such State.

Arabs and Jews residing in the City of Jerusalem who have signed a notice of the Jewish State, shall be entitled to vote in the Arab and Jewish States respectively.

Women may vote and be elected to the Constituent Assemblies.

During the transitional period no Jew shall be permitted to establish residence in the area of the proposed Arab State, and no Arab shall be permitted to establish residence in the area of the proposed Jewish State, except by special leave of the Commission.

10. The Constituent Assembly of each State shall draft a democratic constitution for its State and choose a provisional government to succeed the Provisional Council of Government appointed by the Commission. The constitutions of the States shall embody chapters 1 and 2 of the Declaration provided for in section C below and include inter alia provisions for:

(a) Establishing in each State a legislative body elected by universal suffrage and by secret ballot on the basis of proportional representation, and an executive body responsible to the legislature;

(b) Settling all international disputes in which the State may be involved by peaceful means in such a manner that international peace and security, and justice, are not endangered;

(c) Accepting the obligation of the State to refrain in its international relations from the threat or use of force against the territorial integrity or political independence of any State, or in any other manner inconsistent with the purposes of the United Nations;

(d) Guaranteeing to all persons equal and non-discriminatory rights in civil, political, economic and religious matters and the enjoyment of human rights and fundamental freedoms, including freedom of religion, language, speech and publication, education, assembly and association;

(e) Preserving freedom of transit and visit for all residents and citizens of the other State in Palestine and the City of Jerusalem, subject to considerations of national security, provided that each State shall control residence within its borders.

11. The Commission shall appoint a preparatory economic commission of three members to make whatever arrangements are possible for economic co-operation, with a view to establishing, as soon as practicable, the Economic Union and the Joint Economic Board, as provided in section D below.

12. During the period between the adoption of the recommendations on the question of Palestine by the General Assembly and the termination of the Mandate, the mandatory Power in

Palestine shall maintain full responsibility for administration in areas from which it has not withdrawn its armed forces. The Commission shall assist the mandatory Power in the carrying out of these functions. Similarly the mandatory Power shall co-operate with the Commission in the execution of its functions.

13. With a view to ensuring that there shall be continuity in the functioning of administrative services and that, on the withdrawal of the armed forces of the mandatory Power, the whole administration shall be in the charge of the Provisional Councils and the Joint Economic Board, respectively, acting under the Commission, there shall be a progressive transfer, from the mandatory Power to the Commission, of responsibility for all the functions of government, including that of maintaining law and order in the areas from which the forces of the mandatory Power have been withdrawn.

14. The Commission shall be guided in its activities by the recommendations of the General Assembly and by such instructions as the Security Council may consider necessary to issue.

The measures taken by the Commission, within the recommendations of the General Assembly, shall become immediately effective unless the Commission has previously received contrary instructions from the Security Council.

The Commission shall render periodic monthly progress reports, or more frequently if desirable, to the Security Council.

15. The Commission shall make its final report to the next regular session of the General Assembly and to the Security Council simultaneously.

[The Resolution continues with a stipulation as to the nature of the declarations to be made to the United Nations by the provisional governments of each proposed state prior to independence. They pertain to protection of rights to the Holy Places, protection of religious and minority rights and citizenship, international conventions and obligations. Other provisions of the Resolution pertain to economic union and transit, admission to membership in the United Nations, boundaries and the statute for the proposed special regime of Jerusalem].

## 5. U.N. SECURITY COUNCIL RESOLUTION 50 OF MAY 29, 1948

*The Security Council,*

*Desiring* to bring about a cessation of hostilities in Palestine without prejudice to the rights, claims and position of either Arabs or Jews:

1. *Calls upon* all Governments and authorities concerned to order a cessation of all acts of armed force for a period of four weeks;

2. *Calls upon* all Governments and authorities concerned to undertake that they will not introduce fighting personnel into Palestine, Egypt, Iraq, Lebanon, Saudi Arabia, Syria, Transjordan, and Yemen during the ceasefire;

3. *Calls upon* all Governments and authorities concerned, should men of military age be introduced into countries or territories under their control, to undertake not to mobilize or submit them to military training during the cease-fire;

4. *Calls upon* all Governments and authorities concerned to refrain from importing or exporting war material into or to Palestine, Egypt, Iraq, Lebanon, Saudi Arabia, Syria, Transjordan or Yemen during the cease-fire;

5. *Urges* all Governments and authorities concerned to take every possible precaution for the protection of the Holy Places and of the City of Jerusalem, including access to all shrines and sanctuaries for the purpose of worship by those who have an established right to visit and worship at them;

6. *Instructs* the United Nations Mediator in Palestine, in concert with the Truce Commission, to supervise the observance of the above provisions, and decides that they shall be provided with a sufficient number of military observers;

7. *Instructs* the United Nations Mediator to make contact with all parties as soon as the cease-fire is in force with a view to carrying out his functions as determined by the General Assembly;

8. *Calls upon* all concerned to give the greatest possible assistance to the United Nations Mediator;

9. *Instructs* the United Nations Mediator to make a weekly report to the Security Council during the cease-fire;

10. *Invites* the States members of the Arab League and the Jewish and Arab authorities in Palestine to communicate their acceptance of this resolution to the Security Council not later than 6 p.m. New York standard time on 1 June 1948;

11. *Decides* that if the present resolution is rejected by either party or by both, or if, having been accepted, it is subsequently repudiated or violated, the situation in Palestine will be reconsidered with a view to action under Chapter VII of the Charter of the United Nations;

12. *Calls upon* all Governments to take all possible steps to assist in the implementation of this resolution.

## 6. U.N. SECURITY COUNCIL RESOLUTION 54 OF 15 JULY 1948

*The Security Council,*

*Taking into consideration* that the Provisional Government of Israel has indicated its acceptance in principle of a prolongation of the truce in Palestine; that the States members of the Arab League have rejected successive appeals of the United Nations Mediator and of the Security Council in its resolution 53(1948) of 7 July 1948 for the prolongation of the truce in Palestine; and that there has consequently developed a renewal of hostilities in Palestine:

1. *Determines* that the situation in Palestine constitutes a threat to the peace within the meaning of Article 39 of the Charter of the United Nations;
2. *Orders* the Governments and authorities concerned, pursuant to Article 40 of the Charter, to desist from further military action and to this end to issue cease-fire orders to their military and paramilitary forces, to take effect at a time to be determined by the Mediator, but in any event not later than three days from the date of the adoption of this resolution;
3. *Declares* that failure by any of the Governments or authorities concerned to comply with the preceding paragraph of this resolution would demonstrate the existence of a breach of the peace within the meaning of Article 39 of the Charter requiring immediate consideration by the Security Council with a view to such further action under Chapter VII of the Charter as may be decided upon by the Council;
4. *Calls upon* all Governments and authorities concerned to continue to co-operate with the Mediator with a view to the maintenance of peace in Palestine in conformity with resolution 50(1948) adopted by the Security Council on 29 May 1948;
5. *Orders* as a matter of special and urgent necessity an immediate and unconditional cease-fire in the City of Jerusalem to take effect twenty-four hours from the time of the adoption of this resolution, and instructs the Truce Commission to take any necessary steps to make this cease-fire effective;
6. *Instructs* the Mediator to continue his efforts to bring about the demilitarization of the City of Jerusalem without prejudice to the future political status of Jerusalem, and to assure the protection of and access to the Holy Places, religious buildings and sites in Palestine;
7. *Instructs* the Mediator to supervise the observance of the truce and to establish procedures for examining alleged breaches of the

truce since 11 June 1948 authorizes him to deal with breaches so far as it is within his capacity to do so by appropriate local action, and requests him to keep the Security Council currently informed concerning the operation of the truce and when necessary to take appropriate action;

8. *Decides* that, subject to further decision by the Security Council or the General Assembly, the truce shall remain in force, in accordance with the present resolution and with resolution 50(1948) of 29 May 1948, until a peaceful adjustment of the future situation of Palestine is reached;

9. *Reiterates* the appeal to the parties contained in the last paragraph of its resolution 49(1948) of 22 May 1948 and urges upon the parties that they continued conversations with the Mediator in a spirit of conciliation and mutual concession in order that all points under dispute may be settled peacefully;

10. *Requests* the Secretary-General to provide the Mediator with the necessary staff and facilities to assist in carrying out the functions assigned to him under General Assembly resolution 186 (S–2) of 14 May 1948 and under this resolution;

11. *Requests* that the Secretary-General make appropriate arrangements to provide necessary funds to meet the obligations arising from this resolution.

## 7. U.N. SECURITY COUNCIL RESOLUTION 61 OF 4 NOVEMBER 1948

*The Security Council,*

*Having decided* on 15 July 1948 that, subject to further decision by the Security Council or the General Assembly, the truce shall remain in force in accordance with resolution 54(1948) of that date and with resolution 50(1948) of 29 May 1948 until a peaceful adjustment of the future situation of Palestine is reached,

*Having decided* on 19 August that no party is permitted to violate the truce on the ground that it is undertaking reprisals or retaliations against the other party, and that no party is entitled to gain military or political advantage through violation of the truce,

*Having decided* on 29 May that, if the truce was subsequently repudiated or violated by either party or by both, the situation in

Palestine could be reconsidered with a view to action under Chapter VII of the Charter of the United Nations,

*Takes note* of the request communicated to the Government of Egypt and the Provisional Government of Israel by the Acting Mediator on 26 October following upon the decisions adopted by the Security Council on 19 October 1948,

*Calls upon* the interested Governments, without prejudice to their rights, claims or positions with regard to a peaceful adjustment of the future situation of Palestine or to the position which the members of the United Nations may wish to take in the General Assembly on such peaceful adjustment:

1. To withdraw those of their forces which have advanced beyond the positions held on 14 October, the Acting Mediator being authorized to establish provisional lines beyond which no movement of troops shall take place;
2. To establish, through negotiations conducted directly between the parties, or failing that, through the intermediaries in the service of the United Nations, permanent truce lines and such neutral or demilitarized zones as may appear advantageous, in order to ensure henceforth the full observance of the truce in that area. Failing an agreement, the permanent lines and neutral zones shall be established by decision of the Acting Mediator;

*Appoints* a committee of the Council, consisting of the five permanent members together with Belgium and Colombia to give such advice as the Acting Mediator may require with regard to his responsibilities under this resolution and in the event that either party or both should fail to comply with sub-paragraphs (1) and (2) of the preceding paragraph of this resolution within whatever time limits the Acting Mediator may think it desirable to fix, to study as a matter of urgency and to report to the Council on further measures it would be appropriate to take under Chapter VII of the Charter.

## 8. U.N. SECURITY COUNCIL RESOLUTION OF 16 NOVEMBER 1948

*The Security Council,*

*Reaffirming* its previous resolutions concerning the establishment and implementation of the truce in Palestine, and recalling particularly its resolution 54 (1948) of 15 July 1948 which determined that the situation in Palestine constitutes a threat to the peace within the meaning of Article 39 of the Charter of the United Nations.

*Taking note* that the General Assembly is continuing its consideration of the future government of Palestine in response to the request of the Security Council in its resolution 44(1948) of 1 April 1948,

*Without prejudice* to the actions of the Acting Mediator regarding the implementation of Security Council resolution 61 (1948) of 4 November 1948,

1. *Decides* that, in order to eliminate the threat to the peace in Palestine and to facilitate the transition from the present truce to permanent peace in Palestine, an armistice shall be established in all sectors of Palestine;

2. *Calls upon* the parties directly involved in the conflict in Palestine, as a further provisional measure under Article 40 of the Charter, to seek agreement forthwith, by negotiations conducted either directly or through the Acting Mediator, with a view to the immediate establishment of the armistice, including:

(a) The delineation of permanent armistice demarcation lines beyond which the armed forces of the respective parties shall not move;

(b) Such withdrawal and reduction of their armed forces as will ensure the maintenance of the armistice during the transition to permanent peace in Palestine.

## 9. EXTRACTS, ISRAEL-JORDAN ARMISTICE AGREEMENT, 1949

[*The following extracts from the Israel-Jordan Armistice Agreement, signed under United Nations auspices at Rhodes, April 13, 1949, are identical with the Armistice Agreements signed by Israel and Egypt, Israel and Syria, and Israel and Lebanon.*]

### Security Council Document S/1302/Rev.1

Cablegram dated 3 April 1949 from the United Nations Acting Mediator to the Secretary-General transmitting the text of the General Agreement between the Hashemite Jordan Kingdom and Israel.

[Original text: English]
*Rhodes, 3 April 1949*

*For the President of the Security Council*

I have the honour to inform you that an armistice agreement between the Hashemite Jordan Kingdom and Israel has been signed this evening, 3 April 1949, at Rhodes. The text of the agreement follows.

RALPH J. BUNCHE
Acting Mediator

## Hashemite Jordan Kingdom—Israel General Armistice Agreement Rhodes, 3 April 1949

### PREAMBLE

The Parties to the present Agreement,

Responding to the Security Council resolution of 16 November 1948, calling upon them, as a further provisional measure under Article 40 of the Charter of the United Nations and in order to facilitate the translation from the present truce to permanent peace in Palestine, to negotiate an Armistice;

Having decided to enter into negotiations under United Nations chairmanship concerning the implementation of the Security Council resolution of 16 November 1948; and having appointed representatives empowered to negotiate and conclude an Armistice Agreement,

The undersigned representatives of their respective Governments, having exchanged their full powers found to be in good and proper form, have agreed upon the following provisions:

### ARTICLE I

With a view to promoting the return of permanent peace in Palestine and in recognition of the importance in this regard of mutual assurances concerning the future military operations of the Parties, the following principles, which shall be fully observed by both Parties during the armistice, are hereby affirmed:

1. The injunction of the Security Council against resort to military force in the settlement of the Palestine question shall henceforth be scrupulously respected by both Parties;

2. No aggressive action by the armed forces—land, sea or air—of either Party shall be undertaken, planned, or threatened against the people or the armed forces of the other; it being understood that the

use of the term 'planned' in this context has no bearing on normal staff planning as generally practiced in military organization;

3. The right of each Party to its security and freedom from fear of attack by the armed forces of the other shall be fully respected;

4. The establishment of an armistice between the armed forces of the two Parties is accepted as an indispensable step toward the liquidation of armed conflict and the restoration of peace in Palestine.

ARTICLE III

1. In pursuance of the foregoing principles and of the resolution of the Security Council of 16 November 1948, a general armistice between the armed forces of the two Parties—land, sea and air—is hereby established.

2. No element of the land, sea or air, military or para-military forces of either Party, including non-regular forces, shall commit any warlike or hostile act against the military or para-military forces of the other party, or against civilians in territory under the control of that Party; or shall advance beyond or pass over for any purpose whatsoever the Armistice Demarcation Lines set forth in articles V and VI of this Agreement; or enter into or pass through the air space of the other Party.

3. No warlike act or act of hostility shall be conducted from territory controlled by one of the Parties to this Agreement against the other Party.

[*The following article is specific to the Israel-Jordan Armistice Agreement, as it deals with the agreement between the two countries providing for free access to Mount Scopus, holy places and cultural institutions, use of the cemetery on the Mount of Olives, and other matters connected with the Jerusalem area.*]

ARTICLE VIII

1. A Special Committee, composed of two representatives of each Party designated by the respective Governments, shall be established for the purpose of formulating agreed plans and arrangements designed to enlarge the scope of this Agreement and to effect improvements in its application.

2. The Special Committee shall be organized immediately following the coming into effect of this Agreement and shall direct its attention to the formulation of agreed plans and arrangements for such matters as either Party may submit to it, which, in any case, shall include the following on which agreement in principle already exists: free movement of traffic on vital roads, including the Bethlehem and

Latrun-Jerusalem roads; resumption of the normal functioning of the cultural and humanitarian institutions on Mount Scopus and free access thereto: free access to the Holy Places and cultural institutions and use of the cemetery on the Mount of Olives; resumption of operation of the Latrun pumping station; provision of electricity for the Old City; and resumption of operation of the railroad to Jerusalem.

3. The Special Committee shall have exclusive competence over such matters as may be referred to it. Agreed plans and arrangements formulated by it may provide for the exercise of supervisory functions by the Mixed Armistice Commission established in article XI.

### ARTICLE XI

1. The execution of the provisions of this Agreement, with the exception of such matters as fall within the exclusive competence of the Special Committee established in article VIII, shall be supervised by a Mixed Armistice Commission composed of five members, of whom each Party to this Agreement shall designate two, and whose chairman shall be the United Nations Chief of Staff of the Truce Supervision Organization or a senior officer from the observer personnel of that organization designated by him following consultation with both Parties to this Agreement.

2. The Mixed Armistice Commission shall maintain its headquarters at Jerusalem and shall hold its meetings at such places and at such times as it may deem necessary for the effective conduct of its work.

3. The Mixed Armistice Commission shall be convened in its first meeting by the United Nations Chief of Staff of the Truce Supervision Organization and not later than one week following the signing of this Agreement.

4. Decisions of the Mixed Armistice Commission, to the extent possible, shall be based on the principle of unanimity. In the absence of unanimity, decisions shall be taken by a majority vote of the members of the Commission present and voting.

5. The Mixed Armistice Commission shall formulate its own rules of procedures. Meetings shall be held only after due notice to the members by the Chairman. The quorum for its meetings shall be a majority of its members.

6. The Commission shall be empowered to employ observers, who may be from among the military organizations of the Parties or from the military personnel of the United Nations Truce Supervision Organization, or from both, in such numbers as may be considered essential to the performance of its functions. In the event United Nations observers should be so employed, they shall remain under

the command of the United Nations Chief of Staff of the Truce Supervision Organization. Assignments of a general or special nature given to United Nations observers attached to the Mixed Armistice Commission shall be subject to approval by the United Nations Chief of Staff or his designated representative on the Commission, whichever is serving as Chairman.

7. Claims or complaints presented by either Party relating to the application of this Agreement shall be referred immediately to the Mixed Armistice Commission through its Chairman. The Commission shall take such action on all such claims or complaints by means of its observation and investigation machinery as it may deem appropriate, with a view to equitable and mutually satisfactory settlement.

8. Where interpretation of the meaning of a particular provision of this Agreement, other than the preamble and articles I and II, is at issue, the Commission's interpretation shall prevail. The Commission, in its discretion and as the need arises, may from time to time recommend to the Parties modifications in the provisions of this Agreement.

9. The Mixed Armistice Commission shall submit to both Parties reports on its activities as frequently as it may consider necessary. A copy of such report shall be presented to the Secretary-General of the United Nations for transmission to the appropriate organ or agency of the United Nations.

10. Members of the Commission and its observers shall be accorded such freedom of movement and access in the area covered by this Agreement as the Commission may determine to be necessary, provided that when such decisions of the Commission are reached by a majority vote United Nations observers only shall be employed.

11. The expenses of the Commission, other than those relating to United Nations observers, shall be apportioned in equal shares between the two Parties to this Agreement.

[*Article XII of this Agreement stipulates that the Parties may call upon the U.N. Secretary-General to convoke a conference of the representatives for the purpose of reviewing, revising, or suspending any of its provisions other than articles I and III.*]

ARTICLE XII

1. The present Agreement is not subject to ratification and shall come into force immediately upon being signed.

2. This Agreement, having been negotiated and concluded in pursuance of the resolution of the Security Council of 16 November 1948 calling for the establishment of an armistice in order to eliminate

the threat to peace in Palestine and to facilitate the transition from the present truce to permanent peace in Palestine, shall remain in force until a peaceful settlement between the Parties is achieved, except as provided in paragraph 3 of this article.

3. The Parties to this Agreement may, by mutual consent, revise this Agreement or any of its provisions, or may suspend its application, other than articles I and III, at any time. In the absence of mutual agreement and after this Agreement has been in effect for one year from the date of its signing, either of the Parties may call upon the Secretary-General of the United Nations to convoke a conference of representatives of the two Parties for the purpose of reviewing, revising, or suspending any of the provisions of this Agreement other than articles I and III. Participation in such conference shall be obligatory upon the Parties.

4. If the conference provided for in paragraph 3 of this article does not result in an agreed solution of a point in dispute, either Party may bring the matter before the Security Council of the United Nations for the relief sought on the grounds that this Agreement has been concluded in pursuance of Security Council actions toward the end of achieving peace in Palestine.

5. This Agreement is signed in quintuplicate, of which one copy shall be retained by each Party, two copies communicated to the Secretary-General of the United Nations for transmission to the Security Council and to the United Nations Conciliation Commission on Palestine, and one copy to the United Nations Acting Mediator on Palestine.

DONE at Rhodes, Island of Rhodes, Greece, on the third of April one thousand nine hundred and forty-nine in the presence of the United Nations Acting Mediator on Palestine and the United Nations Chief of Staff of the Truce Supervision Organization.

For and on behalf of the Government of the Hashemite Jordan Kingdom
*(signed)*
COLONEL AHMED SUDKI EL-JUNDI
LIEUTENANT-COLONEL MOHAMED MAAYTE

For and on behalf of the Government of Israel
*(signed)*
REUVEN SHILOAH
LIEUTENANT-COLONEL MOSHE DAYAN

## 10. EXTRACTS, THE PALESTINIAN NATIONAL CHARTER OF 1968 (Palestine Liberation Organization)*

*Article 1:* Palestine is the homeland of the Arab Palestinian people; it is an indivisible part of the Arab homeland, and the Palestinian people are an integral part of the Arab nation.

*Article 2:* Palestine, with the boundaries it had during the British mandate, is an indivisible territorial unit.

*Article 3:* The Palestinian Arab people possess the legal right to their homeland and have the right to determine their destiny after achieving the liberation of their country in accordance with their wishes and entirely of their own accord and will.

*Article 4:* The Palestinian identity is a genuine, essential and inherent characteristic; it is transmitted from parents to children. The Zionist occupation and the dispersal of the Palestinian Arab people, through the disasters which befell them, do not make them lose their Palestinian identity and their membership of the Palestinian community, nor do they negate them.

*Article 5:* The Palestinians are those Arab nationals who, until 1947, normally resided in Palestine regardless of whether they were evicted from it or have stayed there. Anyone born, after that date, of a Palestinian father—whether inside Palestine or outside it—is also a Palestinian.

*Article 6:* The Jews who had normally resided in Palestine until the beginning of the Zionist invasion will be considered Palestinians.

*Article 7:* That there is a Palestinian community and that it has material, spiritual and historical connection with Palestine are indisputable facts. It is a national duty to bring up individual Palestinians in an Arab revolutionary manner. All means of information and education must be adopted in order to acquaint the Palestinian with his country in the most profound manner, both spiritual and material, that is possible. He must be prepared for the armed struggle and ready to sacrifice his wealth and his life in order to win back his homeland and bring about its liberation.

*Article 8:* The phase in their history, through which the Palestinian people are now living, is that of national struggle for the

---

*Decisions of the National Congress of the Palestine Liberation Organization held in Cairo from 1–17 July 1968. *See* S. Kadi, *Basic Political Documents of the Armed Palestinian Resistance Movement* (Palestine Books No. 27, Palestine Liberation Organization Research Center, 1969).

liberation of Palestine. Thus the conflicts among the Palestinian national forces are secondary, and should be ended for the sake of the basic conflict that exists between the forces of Zionism and of imperialism on the one hand, and the Palestinian Arab people on the other. On this basis the Palestinian masses, regardless of whether they are residing in the national homeland or in diaspora, constitute—both their organizations and the individuals—one national front working for the retrieval of Palestine and its liberation through armed struggle.

*Article 9:* Armed struggle is the only way to liberate Palestine. Thus it is the overall strategy, not merely a tactical phase. The Palestinian Arab people assert their absolute determination and firm resolution to continue their armed struggle and to work for an armed popular revolution for the liberation of their country and their return to it. They also assert their right to normal life in Palestine and to exercise their right to self-determination and sovereignty over it.

*Article 10:* Commando action constitutes the nucleus of the Palestinian popular liberation war. This requires its escalation, comprehensiveness and the mobilization of all the Palestinian popular and educational efforts and their organization and involvement in the armed Palestinian revolution. It also requires the achieving of unity for the national struggle among the different groupings of the Palestinian people, and between the Palestinian people and the Arab masses so as to secure the continuation of the revolution, its escalation and victory.

*Article 11:* The Palestinians will have three mottoes: national unity, national mobilization and liberation.

* * * *

*Article 15:* The liberation of Palestine, from an Arab viewpoint, is a national duty and it attempts to repel the Zionist and imperialist aggression against the Arab homeland, and aims at the elimination of Zionism in Palestine. Absolute responsibility for this falls upon the Arab nation—peoples and governments—with the Arab people of Palestine in the vanguard. Accordingly the Arab nation must mobilize all its military, human, moral and spiritual capabilities to participate actively with the Palestinian people in the liberation of Palestine. It must, particularly in the phase of the armed Palestinian revolution, offer and furnish the Palestinian people with all possible help, and material and human support, and make available to them the means and opportunities that will enable them to continue to carry out their leading role in the armed revolution, until they liberate their homeland.

*Article 16:* The liberation of Palestine, from a spiritual point of view, will provide the Holy Land with an atmosphere of safety and tranquillity, which in turn will safeguard the country's religious sanctuaries and guarantee freedom of worship and of visit to all, without discrimination of race, color, language, or religion. Accordingly, the people of Palestine look to all spiritual forces in the world for support.

*Article 17:* The liberation of Palestine, from a human point of view, will restore to the Palestinian individual his dignity, pride and freedom. Accordingly the Palestinian Arab people look forward to the support of all those who believe in the dignity of man and his freedom in the world.

*Article 18:* The liberation of Palestine, from an international point of view, is a defensive action necessitated by the demands of self-defence. Accordingly, the Palestinian people, desirous as they are of the friendship of all people, look to freedom-loving, justice-loving and peace-loving states for support in order to restore their legitimate rights in Palestine, to re-establish peace and security in the country, and to enable its people to exercise national sovereignty and freedom.

*Article 19:* The partition of Palestine in 1947 and the establishment of the state of Israel are entirely illegal, regardless of the passage of time, because they were contrary to the will of the Palestinian people and to their natural right in their homeland, and inconsistent with the principles embodied in the Charter of the United Nations, particularly the right to self-determination.

*Article 20:* The Balfour Declaration, the mandate for Palestine and everything that has been based upon them, are deemed null and void. Claims of historical or religious ties of Jews with Palestine are incompatible with the facts of history and the true conception of what constitutes statehood. Judaism, being a religion, is not an independent nationality. Nor do Jews constitute a single nation with an identity of its own; they are citizens of the states to which they belong.

*Article 21:* The Arab Palestinian people, expressing themselves by the armed Palestinian revolution, reject all solutions which are substitutes for the total liberation of Palestine and reject all proposals aiming at the liquidation of the Palestinian problem, or its internationalization.

*Article 22:* Zionism is a political movement organically associated with international imperialism and antagonistic to all action for liberation and to progressive movements in the world. It is

racist and fanatic in its nature, aggressive, expansionist and colonial in its aims, and fascist in its methods. Israel is the instrument of the Zionist movement, and a geographical base for world imperialism placed strategically in the midst of the Arab homeland to combat the hopes of the Arab nation for liberation, unity and progress. Israel is a constant source of threat *vis-à-vis* peace in the Middle East and the whole world. Since the liberation of Palestine will destroy the Zionist and imperialist presence and will contribute to the establishment of peace in the Middle East, the Palestinian people look for the support of all the progressive and peaceful forces and urge them all, irrespective of their affiliations and beliefs, to offer the Palestinian people all aid and support in their just struggle for the liberation of their homeland.
[Articles 23–33 omitted].

## 11. U.N. SECURITY COUNCIL RESOLUTION 242 OF NOVEMBER 22, 1967

*The Security Council,*
*Expressing* its continuing concern with the grave situation in the Middle East,
*Emphasizing* the inadmissibility of the acquisition of territory by war and the need to work for a just and lasting peace in which every state in the area can live in security,
*Emphasizing* further that all member states in their acceptance of the Charter of the United Nations have undertaken a commitment to act in accordance with Article 2 of the Charter.

1. *Affirms* that the fulfillment of Charter principles requires the establishment of a just and lasting peace in the Middle East which should include the application of both the following principles:
   (i) Withdrawal of Israeli armed forces from territories occupied in the recent conflict;
   (ii) Termination of all claims or states of belligerency and respect for and acknowledgment of the sovereignty, territorial integrity and political independence of every state in the area and their right to live in peace within secure and recognized boundaries free from threats or acts of force;

2. *Affirms further* the necessity

(a) For guaranteeing freedom of navigation through international waterways in the area;

(b) For achieving a just settlement of the refugee problem;

(c) For guaranteeing the territorial inviolability and political independence of every state in the area, through measures including the establishment of demilitarized zones;

3. *Requests* the Secretary General to designate a Special Representative to proceed to the Middle East to establish and maintain contacts with the states concerned in order to promote agreement and assist efforts to achieve a peaceful and accepted settlement in accordance with the provisions and principles in this resolution.

4. *Requests* the Secretary General to report to the Security Council on the progress of the efforts of the Special Representative as soon as possible.

## 12. U.N. GENERAL ASSEMBLY RESOLUTION 2949 OF DECEMBER 8, 1972

*The General Assembly,*

*Having considered* the item entitled 'The Situation in the Middle East',

*Having received* the report of the Secretary-General of 15 September 1972 on the activities of his Special Representative to the Middle East,[1]

*Reaffirming* that Security Council resolution 242 (1967) of 22 November 1967 must be implemented in all its parts,

*Deeply perturbed* that Security Council resolution 242 (1967) and General Assembly resolution 2799 (XXVI) of 13 December 1971 have not been implemented and, consequently, the envisaged just and lasting peace in the Middle East has not been achieved,

*Reiterating its grave concern* at the continuation of the Israeli occupation of Arab territories since 5 June 1967,

*Reaffirming* that the territory of a State shall not be the object of

---

[1] A/8815–S/10792.

occupation or acquisition by another State resulting from the threat or use of force.
*Affirming* that changes in the physical character or demographic composition of occupied territories are contrary to the purposes and principles of the Charter of the United Nations, as well as to the provisions of the relevant applicable international conventions,
*Convinced* that the grave situation prevailing in the Middle East constitutes a serious threat to international peace and security,
*Reaffirming* the responsibility of the United Nations to restore peace and security in the Middle East in the immediate future,

1. *Reaffirms* its resolution 2799 (XXVI);

2. *Deplores* the non-compliance by Israel with General Assembly resolution 2799 (XXVI), which in particular called upon Israel to respond favorably to the peace initiative of the Special Representative of the Secretary-General to the Middle East;

3. *Expresses its full support* for the efforts of the Secretary-General and his Special Representative;

4. *Declares once more* that the acquisition of territories by force is inadmissible and that, consequently, territories thus occupied must be restored;

5. *Reaffirms* that the establishment of a just and lasting peace in the Middle East should include the application of both the following principles:

(*a*) Withdrawal of Israeli armed forces from territories occupied in the recent conflict;

(*b*) Termination of all claims or states of belligerency and respect for and acknowledgement of the sovereignty, territorial integrity and political independence of every State in the area and its right to live in peace within secure and recognized boundaries free from threats or acts of force;

6. *Invites* Israel to declare publicly its adherence to the principle of non-annexation of territories through the use of force;

7. *Declares* that changes carried out by Israel in the occupied Arab territories in contravention of the Geneva Conventions of 1949[2] are null and void, and calls upon Israel to rescind forthwith all such measures and to desist from all policies and practices affecting the physical character or demographic composition of the occupied Arab territories;

8. *Calls upon* all States not to recognize any such changes and measures carried out by Israel in the occupied Arab territories and invites them to avoid actions, including actions in the field of aid, that could constitute recognition of that occupation;

---

[2]United Nations, *Treaty Series,* vol. 75, Nos. 970–973.

9. *Recognizes* that respect for the rights of the Palestinians is an indispensable element in the establishment of a just and lasting peace in the Middle East;

10. *Requests* the Security Council, in consultation with the Secretary-General and his Special Representative, to take all appropriate steps with a view to the full and speedy implementation of Security Council resolution 242 (1967), taking into account all the relevant resolutions and documents of the United Nations in this connexion;

11. *Requests* the Secretary-General to report to the Security Council and the General Assembly on the progress made by him and his Special Representative in the implementation of Security Council resolution 242 (1967) and of the present resolution;

12. *Decides* to transmit the present resolution to the Security Council for its appropriate action and requests the Council to keep the General Assembly informed.

## 13. U.N. SECURITY COUNCIL RESOLUTION 338 OF OCTOBER 22, 1973

*The Security Council*

1. *Calls upon* all parties to the present fighting to cease all firing and terminate all military activity immediately, no later than 12 hours after the moment of the adoption of this decision, in the positions they now occupy;

2. *Calls upon* the parties concerned to start immediately after the cease-fire the implementation of Security Council resolution 242 (1967) in all of its parts;

3. *Decides* that, immediately and concurrently with the cease-fire, negotiations start between the parties concerned under appropriate auspices aimed at establishing a just and durable peace in the Middle East.

# Maps

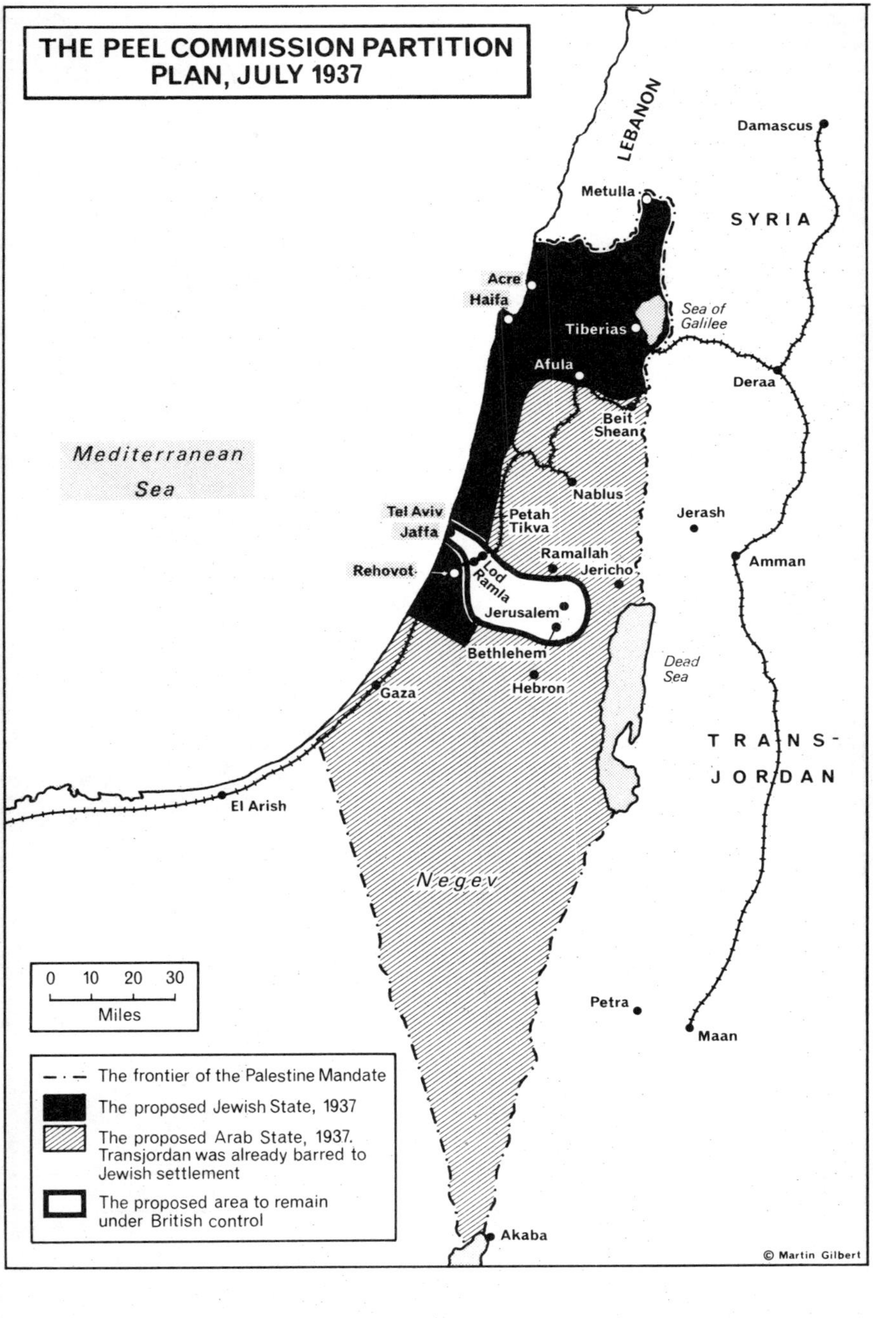

THE PEEL COMMISSION PARTITION PLAN, JULY 1937
LEBANON
Damascus
Metulla
SYRIA
Acre
Haifa
Tiberias
Sea of Galilee
Afula
Deraa
Beit Shean
Mediterranean Sea
Nablus
Jerash
Tel Aviv
Jaffa
Petah Tikva
Ramallah
Amman
Rehovot
Lod
Ramla
Jericho
Jerusalem
Bethlehem
Dead Sea
Hebron
Gaza
TRANS-JORDAN
El Arish
Negev
0 10 20 30
Miles
Petra
Maan
The frontier of the Palestine Mandate
The proposed Jewish State, 1937
The proposed Arab State, 1937. Transjordan was already barred to Jewish settlement
The proposed area to remain under British control
Akaba
© Martin Gilbert

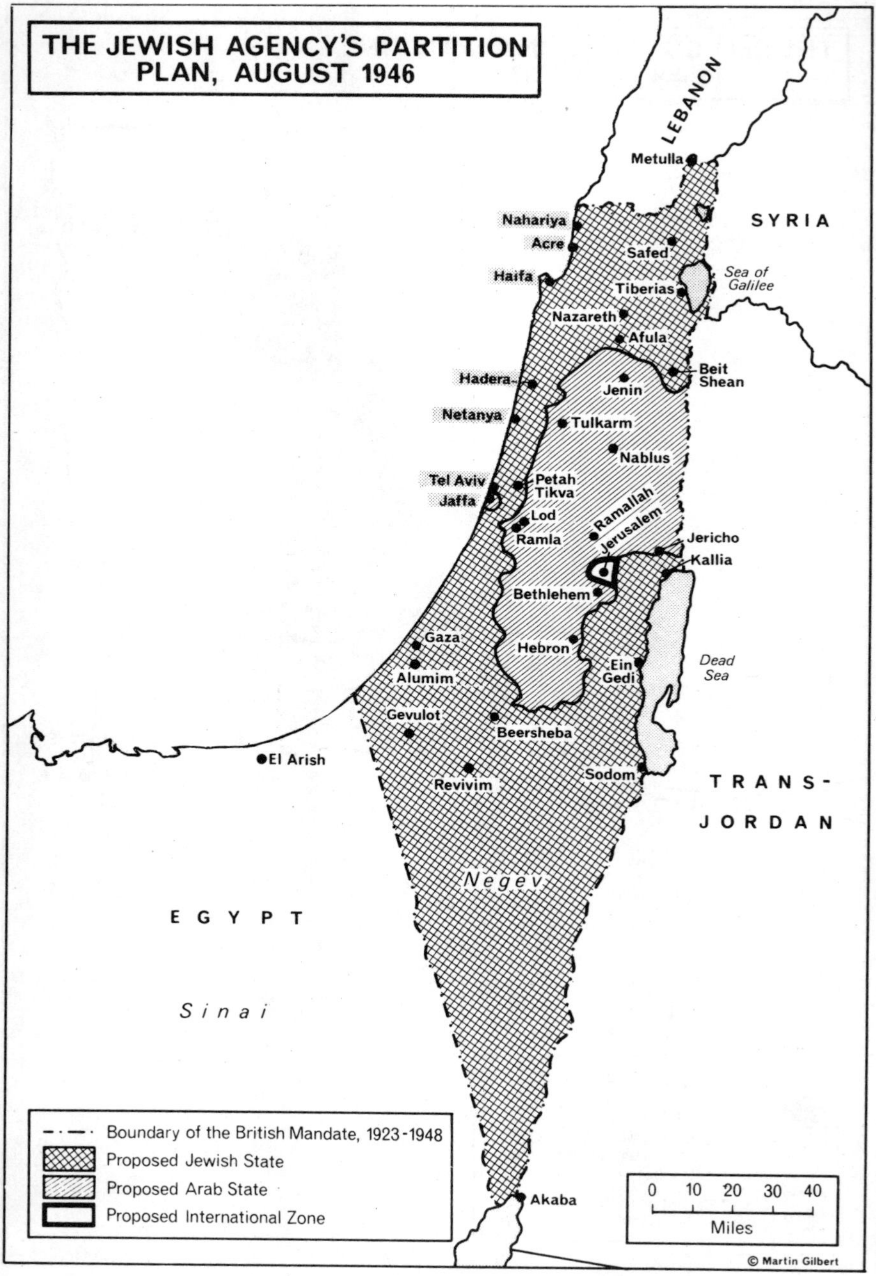

THE JEWISH AGENCY'S PARTITION PLAN, AUGUST 1946
LEBANON
SYRIA
Metulla
Nahariya
Acre
Safed
Haifa
Sea of Galilee
Tiberias
Nazareth
Afula
Beit Shean
Hadera
Jenin
Netanya
Tulkarm
Nablus
Tel Aviv
Jaffa
Petah Tikva
Lod
Ramla
Ramallah
Jerusalem
Jericho
Kallia
Bethlehem
Hebron
Gaza
Alumim
Ein Gedi
Dead Sea
Gevulot
Beersheba
El Arish
Sodom
Revivim
TRANS-JORDAN
Negev
EGYPT
Sinai
Boundary of the British Mandate, 1923-1948
Proposed Jewish State
Proposed Arab State
Proposed International Zone
Akaba
0 10 20 30 40
Miles
© Martin Gilbert

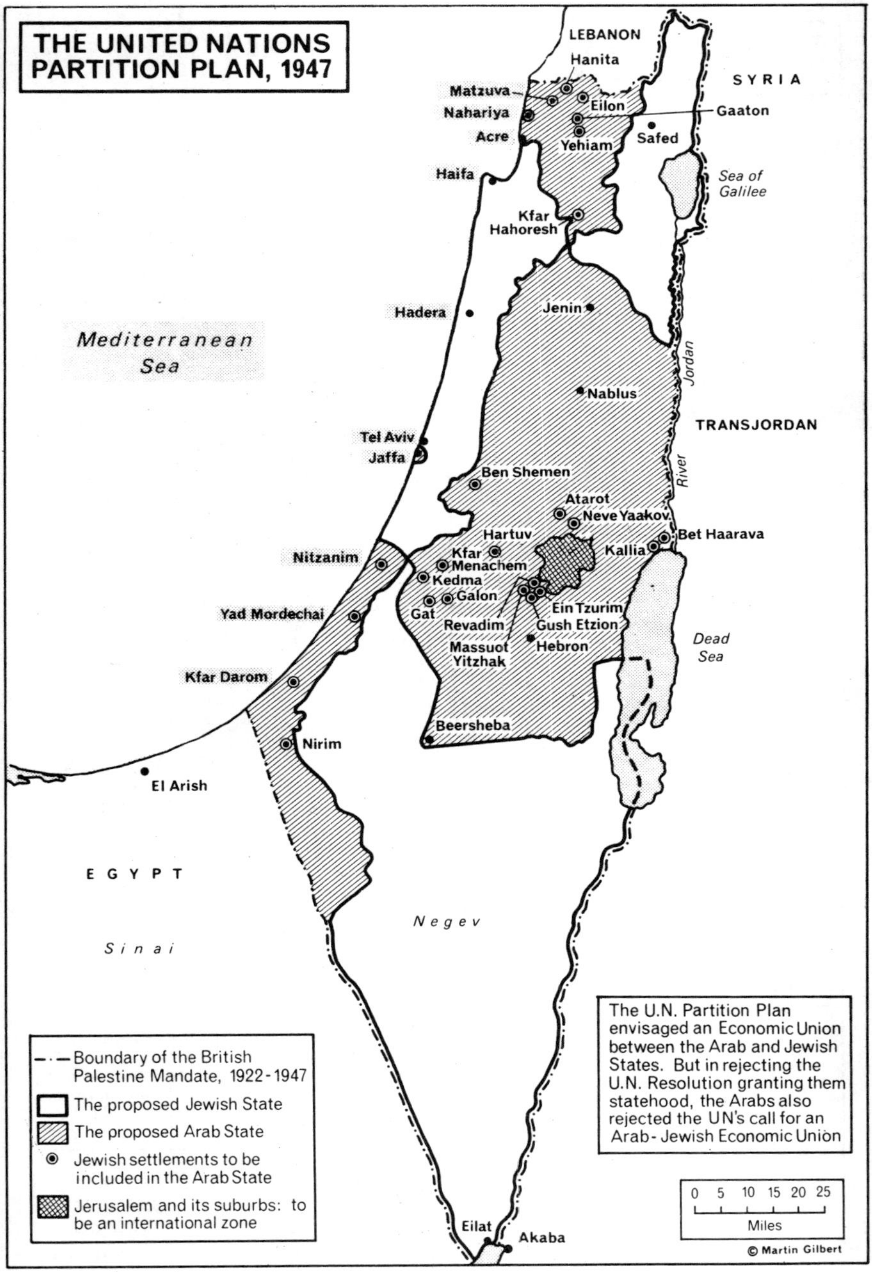
THE UNITED NATIONS PARTITION PLAN, 1947
LEBANON
SYRIA
Hanita
Matzuva
Eilon
Nahariya
Gaaton
Acre
Safed
Yehiam
Haifa
Sea of Galilee
Kfar Hahoresh
Hadera
Jenin
Mediterranean Sea
Jordan
Nablus
TRANSJORDAN
Tel Aviv
Jaffa
River
Ben Shemen
Atarot
Neve Yaakov
Hartuv
Bet Haarava
Kallia
Nitzanim
Kfar Menachem
Kedma
Galon
Yad Mordechai
Gat
Ein Tzurim
Revadim
Gush Etzion
Dead Sea
Massuot Yitzhak
Hebron
Kfar Darom
Beersheba
Nirim
El Arish
EGYPT
Negev
Sinai
Boundary of the British Palestine Mandate, 1922-1947
The proposed Jewish State
The proposed Arab State
Jewish settlements to be included in the Arab State
Jerusalem and its suburbs: to be an international zone
The U.N. Partition Plan envisaged an Economic Union between the Arab and Jewish States. But in rejecting the U.N. Resolution granting them statehood, the Arabs also rejected the UN's call for an Arab-Jewish Economic Union
0 5 10 15 20 25
Miles
Eilat
Akaba
© Martin Gilbert

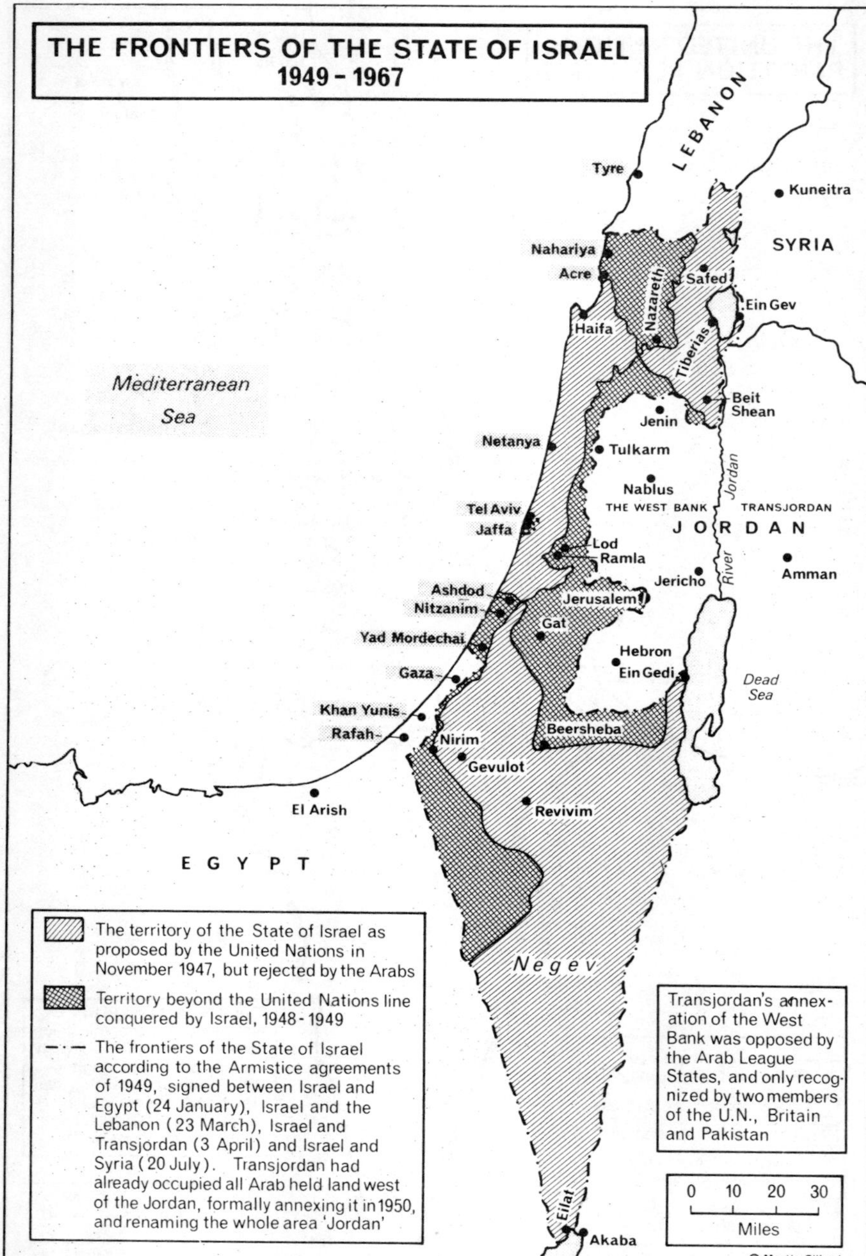
THE FRONTIERS OF THE STATE OF ISRAEL
1949 - 1967
LEBANON
Tyre
Kuneitra
SYRIA
Nahariya
Acre
Safed
Nazareth
Ein Gev
Haifa
Tiberias
Mediterranean Sea
Beit Shean
Jenin
Netanya
Tulkarm
Jordan
Nablus
THE WEST BANK
TRANSJORDAN
JORDAN
Tel Aviv
Jaffa
Lod
Ramla
Amman
Jericho
River
Ashdod
Nitzanim
Jerusalem
Gat
Yad Mordechai
Hebron
Gaza
Ein Gedi
Dead Sea
Khan Yunis
Rafah
Beersheba
Nirim
Gevulot
El Arish
Revivim
EGYPT
Negev
The territory of the State of Israel as proposed by the United Nations in November 1947, but rejected by the Arabs
Territory beyond the United Nations line conquered by Israel, 1948-1949
The frontiers of the State of Israel according to the Armistice agreements of 1949, signed between Israel and Egypt (24 January), Israel and the Lebanon (23 March), Israel and Transjordan (3 April) and Israel and Syria (20 July). Transjordan had already occupied all Arab held land west of the Jordan, formally annexing it in 1950, and renaming the whole area 'Jordan'
Transjordan's annexation of the West Bank was opposed by the Arab League States, and only recognized by two members of the U.N., Britain and Pakistan
0 10 20 30
Miles
Eilat
Akaba
© Martin Gilbert

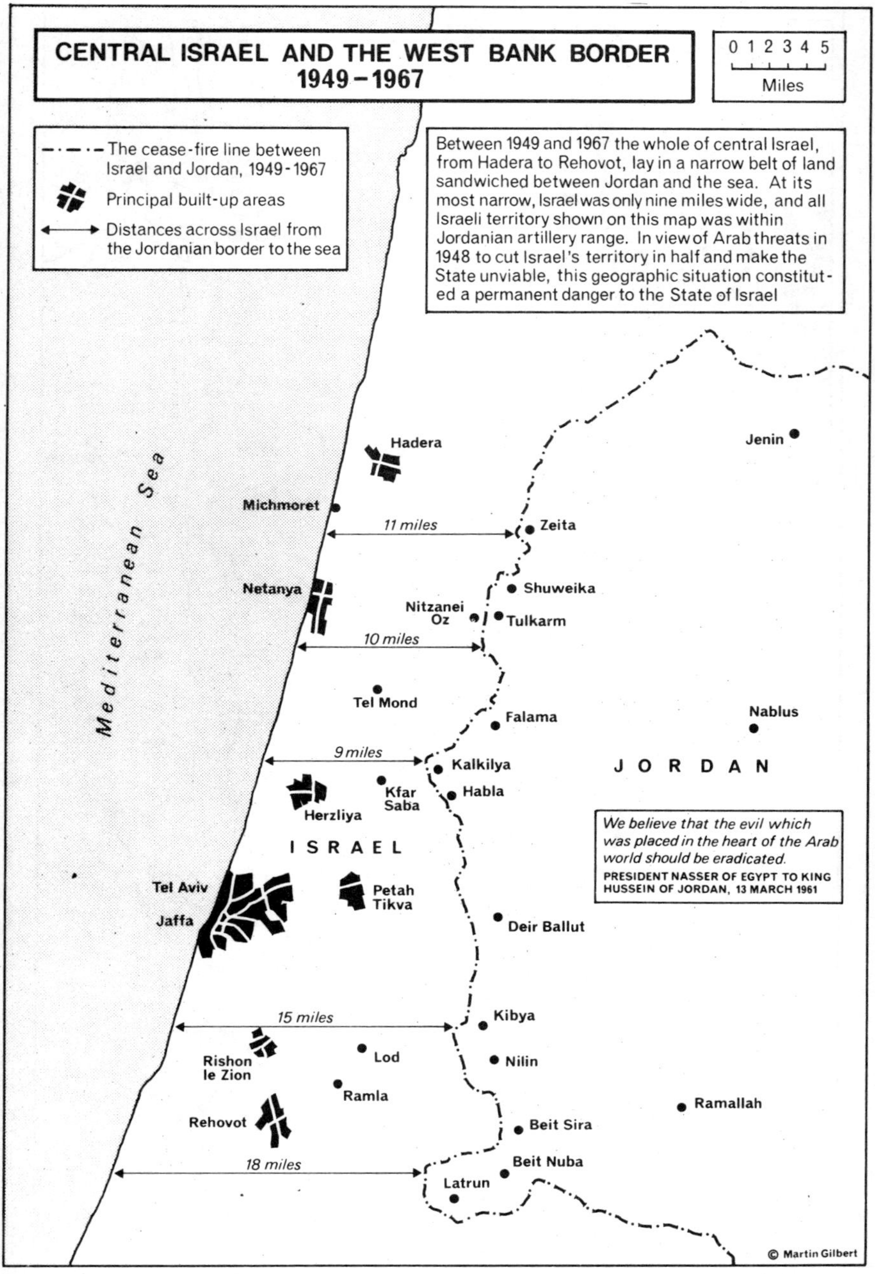
CENTRAL ISRAEL AND THE WEST BANK BORDER 1949 – 1967
0 1 2 3 4 5
Miles
The cease-fire line between Israel and Jordan, 1949 - 1967
Principal built-up areas
Distances across Israel from the Jordanian border to the sea
Between 1949 and 1967 the whole of central Israel, from Hadera to Rehovot, lay in a narrow belt of land sandwiched between Jordan and the sea. At its most narrow, Israel was only nine miles wide, and all Israeli territory shown on this map was within Jordanian artillery range. In view of Arab threats in 1948 to cut Israel's territory in half and make the State unviable, this geographic situation constituted a permanent danger to the State of Israel
Mediterranean Sea
Hadera
Jenin
Michmoret
11 miles
Zeita
Netanya
Shuweika
Nitzanei Oz
Tulkarm
10 miles
Tel Mond
Falama
Nablus
9 miles
Kalkilya
JORDAN
Habla
Kfar Saba
Herzliya
ISRAEL
We believe that the evil which was placed in the heart of the Arab world should be eradicated.
PRESIDENT NASSER OF EGYPT TO KING HUSSEIN OF JORDAN, 13 MARCH 1961
Tel Aviv
Jaffa
Petah Tikva
Deir Ballut
15 miles
Kibya
Rishon le Zion
Lod
Nilin
Ramla
Ramallah
Rehovot
Beit Sira
18 miles
Beit Nuba
Latrun
© Martin Gilbert

# PROPOSED ALLON PLAN 1976

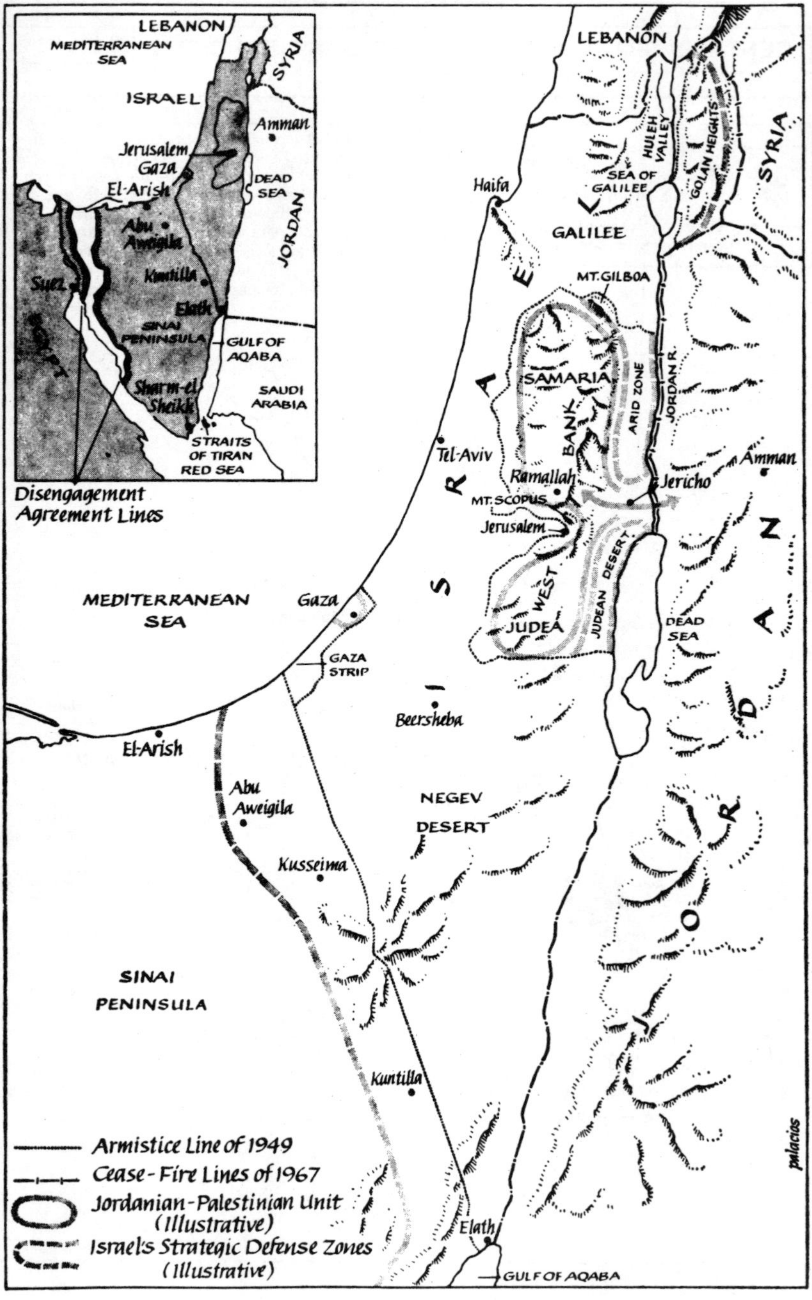

# Index of Law Cases

# Index